# Managing Information Systems

# *PARADIGM BOOKS*

## ACADEMIC

Dhillon
Enterprise Cyber Security. Principles and Practice

Hunter and Dhanda
Information Systems: The Challenges of Theory and Practice

Hunter and Dhanda
Information Systems: Exploring applications in business and government

Wenn and Dhanda
Engaging Executive IS Practice

Hunter and Wenn
Information Systems in an E-World

Dhillon
Security Challenges in the New Millennium

Wenn and Dhanda
Enabling Executive Information Technology Competencies

Kamel and Irani
Information Technologies for Organizational Enhancement

Irani and Kamel
Improving Business Performance through Knowledge Management

Dhillon and Sa-Soares
Issues in protecting intangible organizational assets

Dhillon and Sarin
Facing the Information Society

Hunter and Burgess
Grand Challenges in Business and Information Management Processes

Dhanda and Hackney
Engaging Academia and Enterprise Agendas

Sa-Soares
Social and Ethical Impact of Technology

Dhanda and Hunter
Grand Challenges in Technology Management

Dhillon
Strategic Information Systems Planning

**General Interest**
Sharma
Maverick of success

Dhillon
The Inner Truth

Nand
Partition

Bhullar
The Enquiring Guru. Questions by the Sikh Gurus and their answers

# Managing Information Systems

**Gurpreet Dhillon, PhD**
*Virginia Commonwealth University, PhD*

Paradigm books

Published by Paradigm Books an imprint of Aldwych Associates
2020 Pennsylvania Avenue NW, Ste 904
Washington DC 20006, USA
books@aldwychassociates.com



Made and printed in USA
Typeset in Garamond

ISBN-13: 978-0692748404 (Paradigm Books)
ISBN-10: 0692748407

This book is dedicated to all my students, who over the years have contributed to my learning, challenged me, worked with me and have forged life long friendships.

# Table of Contents

# 1. MANAGING INFORMATION SYSTEMS IN MODERN ORGANIZATIONS

There was a time when computers were used solely for the purpose of research in government agencies. At that time, the data was inserted into the system using punch cards. Businesses, let alone common man had no access, no idea of how to use computers for their benefit. Over the years, technology has changed and computers have become more accessible and user friendly.

Businesses were run on paper; there were no databases to store data or reports generated to compare results as everything was done by hand. Today, the business world is a different picture. Businesses have become more electronic; even small coffee shops have some kind of computer system in place to assist them in doing business.

In order to sketch the nature and scope of information technology related changes and how it evolved and has helped business in improving quality of work, let us consider a company, International Heavy Machines (IHM) and see how the involvement of information technology in its business processes has changed its working structure.

IHM traces its roots back to a modest start from a garage in 1960. The company has grown over the years, becoming a leading global provider of industrial solutions and infrastructure development products. Revenues by geographic region in 2003 were as follows: North America 62%; Europe 25%; Asia Pacific 10% and Latin America 3%.

The Industrial Solutions segment comprises a diverse group of businesses that focus on providing solutions to enhance customer industrial efficiency. The segment includes two divisions: Air and Productivity Solutions and Power Solutions. Air and Productivity makes air compressors, fluid products, micro-turbines, and industrial tools. Power Solutions makes gas compressors, gas and steam turbines, and engines.

The Infrastructure Development segment primarily makes skid steer loaders, mini-excavators, electric and gasoline powered golf and utility vehicles, portable compressors and light towers, road construction and repair equipment, and a broad line of drills and drill accessories.

IHM is head headquartered in Richmond, Virginia. The company has Sales and Service offices in Germany, Japan, Australia and Brazil. The company also has five manufacturing sites: Richmond, Munich, Melbourne, Austin and Beijing.

IHM grew not only by organic growth but also by acquiring three other smaller players. IHM gained the technical skills, manufacturing facilities and customers of the companies it acquired but it also inherited the different management structures, accounting practices and IT systems.

In order to minimize the impact to the businesses that IHM acquired it left the systems it inherited in place. Each site has its management structure with site head reporting to division head at Richmond. The Sales and Service team was largely left untouched to make the transition seamless to the customer with the exception of merging the teams where there was geographical overlap. The Sales and Service team was given some cross training to sell and support the whole portfolio worldwide.

The IT systems are available and functional at each site. For global communication, IHM uses Microsoft Outlook. Richmond, Austin and Munich use SAP as their inventory management system, production management system, sales and financial IT system, while Beijing and Melbourne use custom solutions. Each site posts a detailed weekly report in standardized format using a proprietary system on to the Cloud. These reports are also available to other sites through Richmond.

Manufacturing for industrial solutions segments is at Richmond, Munich and Beijing and for infrastructure segment is at Austin, Melbourne, Beijing and Richmond. Each site has a fully operational product design, research and development, manufacturing and quality department.

Recently the demand for mini-excavators increased due to infrastructure development taking place in China and India. IHM did not have enough capacity to fulfill all orders and decided to source sub-assemblies and put them together in-house to meet the demand. Being a very mature product for IHM, the transition from manufacturing the complete mini-excavator to assembling sub-assemblies went very smooth.

IHM realized multiple benefits from this strategy. They were able to increase the capacity without much capital investment. This also provided them with better flexibility for future demand fluctuation. They were able to reduce the number for vendors for this machine. The biggest benefit was they were able to reduce cost by 15% and free up resources to develop newer products.

IHM saw that they had to make changes in their business processes in order to be profitable. There were several factors that were driving the company to make changes. Recently, the company had seen some price competition from their competitors. The other companies were getting a portion of production done in cheaper labor markets and saving on production costs, and thus able to sell their products at a lower price than IHM. This was cutting into the market share of IHM.

Another factor was that IHM wanted to increase their efficiency. Their production sites were located all over the globe. Each site had its own R&D, own management, own finance handling. Since the takeovers of smaller companies, IHM had not consolidated its processes. Instead of having an R&D department at each site, the company thought of collapsing all the R&D work at one site. This would save costs in terms of infrastructure and materials. This would also bring together all the scientists and experts under one roof and make them more productive.

IHM also wanted to focus on improving customer satisfaction. Lately, there had been some complaints about the steam engines - the quality of the product was not to the liking of the customer. IHM prided itself on the quality of its work, and the company could not afford to lose its reputation, otherwise they would lose their customers to rival companies.

One of the big factors driving the company to make changes was rapidly changing technology. New technology was available to help design and test new equipment. For the company to be competitive, they have to introduce new and better versions of their equipment. Advanced technology would also assist in building the products, further automating production and thus reducing labor, resulting in cost savings and increases in capacity.

For the company to be more efficient and productive, a project team was set up to analyze the current business processes and their deficiencies, as well as to find ways of improving them. According to Leavitt [6], there are five elements that should be considered when making changes in organizations. It may not be necessary to make amendments to all five segments, but they all must be taken into account to culminate in a successful project. Generally, companies make hasty decisions while making important changes in their organization; some reasons are cost, rapidly changing technology and business environment. It's important to note that just by changing technology a company can rarely become more productive. The impact of the changed technology has to be analyzed from every angle: how it fits into the existing organizational structure and business strategy, the skills of the workforce, among other things. The five elements to be considered are:

- Structure: The existing organizational structure. How the company is organized, whether it is centralized, decentralized or hybrid. Does the new business processes fit well into the existing structure or does the structure of the organization need to be modified in order to incorporate the changes? Does the company have a separate IT department or outsource its information technology to vendors?
- Strategy: This is to analyze whether the new business applications are high potential, strategic, key operational or support. How would the company benefit from investing into these applications?
- Business and Operational process: The way work is done currently in the organization. Would the business and operational processes be changed to incorporate the new processes? Would this benefit the company or make it more complicated?
- Roles and skills: What are the skills of employees? Would they need extra training or new staff would have to be hired?
- Technology: The existing information technology in place. What kind of computer systems the company is using, what kind of software? Would the new processes require new technology to be implemented?

## ROLES, RESPONSIBILITIES AND SKILLS

The days of static job descriptions are over for most organizations as companies realize that in order to survive, adaptation is the key. Buzzwords today include "change management," "strategic planning," "business process re-engineering" and the like. Rapidly changing technology is only one driver for change; company consolidations and acquisitions as well as market and economy issues may also factor into the impetus for organizational adaptation. At IHM, competitive disadvantage and the desire to increase efficiency and customer satisfaction as well as technological advances were the driving forces.

It would seem obvious that as organizations include people, major considerations in change management are the job roles, responsibilities and skills of personnel who work within the company, however it has been an afterthought in many failed projects. IHM was no exception, even until the last decade – considering how 'necessary changes' would affect users and customers was not a large part of the thought process. As people in general dislike and/or fear change, changing job roles and responsibilities can be a significant undertaking. If managed correctly, change can be productive on the organizational as well as the individual employee level.

Changing employee roles and responsibilities can be managed successfully with a few key elements:

- Organizational risk assessment
- Upper-level management champion/support of the project/ change
- A positive outlook for change
- Communication with the stakeholders
- Tested and final implementation procedures, tools, documentation and standards

## ORGANIZATIONAL RISK ASSESSMENT

A starting point when considering a large-scale change is to conduct an assessment of risks that the company faces related to personnel. Some things that should raise red flags are [4]:

- Work force not equipped with right job skills for the new operating environment
- Poor or insufficient communications
- Confusion regarding roles, responsibilities and goals
- Perception of leadership as not in touch, not effective
- Conflict resolution plan unclear

These problems can undercut even the best organizational change effort and have been attributed as reasons for a significant number of change failures. The risk assessment should be conducted throughout the life cycle of the project in order to effectively monitor if the changes are being initiated successfully, otherwise employee morale and retention may be affected adversely. IHM has made this a part of every change initiative after several initiatives have failed.

## Upper-level Management Support

As with any project, a key ingredient for success is the support of upper-level management. Middle and lower-level management that perceives a unified upper-level foundation for a change will pass on a similar view to employees, who will view the change as beneficial and necessary. IHM's upper-level management now realize that serving as champions for change is an important part of their daily work.

## Positive Outlook for Change

As stated previously, people generally dislike, distrust, experience anxiety and/or fear about change to varying degrees, and for good reason – one of the worst being that the employee loses his/her job.

Other fears may be a result of the employee's lack of confidence in the newly defined position ("Will I be able to do the job?), their conception of the change ("Will I like it?" or "This is just another stupid and unnecessary thing the management is making us do."), and so forth. It is vital to the success of change management to present the case for change as positive in order to overcome this natural urge.

## Communication with Stakeholders

An organization with a poor track record of communication to the workforce would not likely be able to easily or successfully implement change. In a change environment, having the employee's cooperation also entails engaging the employee in a discussion of the changes that will affect them. This will help alleviate fears, anxieties and concerns the employee may have.

Direct and honest communication with the workforce that is affected by the change (as well as other stakeholders) is a must, and the message must be repeated until it is clear that it is understood. Feedback is a crucial component of this communication path; it is almost an afterthought for some companies who are used to a one-way communications stream (top-to-bottom), and this omission can be fatal to a project. Enlisting the assistance of the employee and middle management in the success of the change is one part of ensuring that the change is successful, and feedback can be a helpful tool.

Other stakeholders in a change initiative may include customers, dealers, partners and vendors; it is important to include them in communicating any changes that would directly or indirectly affect these individuals/entities. IHM now includes these individuals/entities by engaging in discussions, conducting surveys, and most importantly, being honest about how the change will work.

## Tested and final implementation procedures

Enlisting the cooperation of the workforce in a change includes providing them with the procedures they will need to perform tasks that are different from their previous tasks. In addition, they will need to be equipped with the tools to do the job, the documentation to support the task and standards by which their work will be judged must be communicated. In many cases involving IT applications, training must be provided.

Crucial to the success of change implementation is the status of the new 'system' (IT or operational process) – has it been fully tested and all the bugs worked out? If the employee is training on a beta system, has that information been communicated? If the employee perceives they are working in/on a system that is incomplete or full of bugs without being solicited for improvement ideas, it can contribute to a morale problem and quite possibly to lower motivation and workforce retention.

Techniques for providing the workforce with the skills they need in the new environment:

- Cross-training: Employees learn new skills in different departments/functions to become more useful in the organization
- Specific application training: New systems require that employees receive training in their new function.
- Skills development: Continuing education and training provide employees with more skills that can be utilized.

Organizations aren't the only benefactors of a successful change initiative. Despite the initial pangs of anxiety and fear that an employee can experience, successful change can provide employees with new, marketable skills, increased motivation at work and increased job satisfaction. For IHM, examining the roles, responsibilities and skills of their workforce when considering change has resulted in happier, motivated employees who feel like an important part of the organization, and this is vital for successful change management.

## STRATEGY AND STRUCTURE

The role of an information technology project in terms of an organization's structure and strategy varies from firm to firm, but is marked by the same set of concerns, regardless of the organization. Whereas monolithic industry leaders like IBM were at one point afforded the luxury of forcing a market to acquiesce to its desires, the modern market requires that projects reflect a new strategy on a corporate level rather than as a subdivision of said corporation. Further, any project must be made to adhere to structural guidelines, both in the structure of the project design and in that of the management team itself.

Historically, organizations tended to view new IT projects as panaceas that would create brand new income streams on their own, regardless of how the rest of the organization was configured or how the market was aligned. This method of thinking during the "dot-com" era resulted in half of the Fortune 500 turning over during the 1990s, and as such should be avoided in the modern marketplace [7]. Current thinking regards any IT project, be it involving support functions or new products, to reflect a larger strategy encompassing the organization as a whole.

Corporate strategy relates to the moves and positions that an organization takes to place itself in the most advantageous situation in the marketplace, including how the company is willing to position itself and which products the company is willing to introduce and when. These aspects of the firm are those which are considered critical to its future as a profit-making organization. The role of IT in corporate strategy is usually considered as one involving the rollout of new products or realignment into new ventures.

The rollout of these new products or services has in the past been an enormous component of the cause of giant IT projects and their subsequent failures associated therewith. The history of IT projects is riddled with examples like that of Bank of America's trust management system attempt. In trying to develop a system that would allow its customers to manage their trust funds online and automatically, the bank ended up spending five years and eighty million dollars on a project that was intended to take two years and twenty five million dollars before finally jettisoning the trust business altogether. If the opportunity of the market was there for another player to exploit, why did it take another firm rather than Bank of America to seize it? The reasoning is that Bank of America incurred great development costs due to a failure to plan their system development properly with the needs of the customer in mind, a scenario that repeats itself through the history of IT project development [1].

New ventures also prompt for rearrangement of corporate strategy when large-scale IT development is required. Often companies find it less traumatic on the corporate level to deploy satellite companies to undertake the launch of a new venture, as in the cases of American Airlines SABRE system or Barnes and Noble's online bookstore, Barnesandnoble.com. In each case the organization has profitable operations in one arena and a desire to move into a different product or service line. While the temptation may exists to assert that it is simpler to launch these new facets of the firm under the current banner, doing so runs a high possibility of detrimentally affecting the existing success of a profitable company. Thus, it is often advisable to make a new offshoot of the company to run these new ventures. While it seems inherent that this business model will involve significant redundancy of business processes, it appears that the benefits gained more than outweigh the penalties.

In either case, a new direction in corporate strategy means that there is an increased requirement for cohesion within the organization. IT projects of this magnitude, requiring large scale planning and long term management, must be conceived as a business process of their own accord and not as support processes for the firm as a whole. These projects must be integrated into the strategic management direction of the whole if they are to avoid becoming overlooked and mismanaged business areas. However, achieving this state is not easy. It usually requires that the organization undertake an audit of their own internal culture, political structures, and capabilities, and affect changes on these aspects in order to achieve a new functionality [1]. Furthermore, it is critical that this strategic change be a fundamental, not superficial, change at that. Oftentimes it requires that the organization reengineer not only how jobs are done, but why they are done and for whom. This transition can be costly at best if not carefully managed, and failure to do so usually results in scope creep and rapidly increasing costs to fix problems that arise from poor planning.

Structural conflicts must also be taken into account when considering IT and the design of an organization's processes. In this instance, the term structure relates both to the organization of the project team and that of the organization as a whole. The structure of a project should involve new construction methodologies and development cycles, involving iterative, adaptive development and design.

However, a more critical aspect of structure regards the corporate governances of a project. Organizational change inherent with large-scale projects necessitates that communication between customers and management, both within the project and throughout disparate divisions of the organization as a whole, be increased. This action serves not only to clarify the specifics of requirements, but also to assist in the direction of the goals and milestones of the project. Also, this communication can be critical in the application of a system of checks and balances, designed to monitor increasing costs and decreasing focus by management or developers [1]. Project management teams can benefit from new management altogether if the new management can offer some creative thinking "outside the box", allowing new perspectives to enter into discussion. The goal is to achieve a state of an "open corporation", where communication is free in both directions and the product isn't a segmented deployment of discrete items but a constant stream of new enterprises [8]. The new structure must combine all hierarchical levels of the company and call for cooperation therein.

For one of the best examples of the failure to restructure to adapt to a modern market, and the subsequent corrective action, is the situation of IBM. Long an innovator in the technology and services field, IBM became a follower of market trends during the 1980s and early 90s rather than the leader they had once been as their profits shrank and costs remained level. The primary cause of their change in position has to be that they failed to notice that their market was moving away from the mainframe-based model that IBM had excelled at and moved into microcomputers and distributed systems. Thus, as Microsoft and Intel capitalized upon large market segments, IBM chose to remain resigned to their market share. Where they failed was that they broke the commitment to their customers to provide high-quality service and the commitment to their employees to provide job security. They attempted to rectify their situation by hastily constructing factories and increasing funds for development, only to find that these rushed constructs failed to provide the required processes and needed to be disassembled and re-designed. Furthermore, they were requiring more and more employees to maintain their existing commitments to the legacy systems that they had implemented, and therefore incurred increasing costs as profits fell. The situation began to be righted when new management was hired to divest IBM from its past and to increase their focus on business processes and support. The new IBM is prospering because it has removed itself from the pride and ego aspects of being a large company and become one that rapidly accommodates changes in the market rather than attempts to remove them.

## BUSINESS AND OPERATIONAL PROCESSES

Since the beginning of time there was work to be completed and along with work there was a process. Looking back when Henry Ford began producing his automobiles on an assembly line to the present day, those same processes are constantly being reengineered to complete the task better and faster, but for less money. For a company to achieve these goals, business processes are an excellent tool to utilize. Davenport & Short [2] define business process as a "set of logically related tasks performed to achieve a defined business outcome."

A process is usually characterized in terms of having beginning and ending points with organization units involved. With more and more daily functions changing in various departments, a reengineering of business processes has taken place. The recognition and breaking away from the outdated rules and assumed operational processes provided a means to reorganize the way of doing business in any organization. According to Hammer [5] "The rules of work design are based on assumptions about technology, people, and organizational goals that no longer hold." Thus the principles of reengineering can be put into effect by a team of business analysts (to maximize the effectiveness of a process) and IT systems analysts (redesign the way business is done):

- Organize around outcomes and not tasks
  - Inventory must be taken to assess what an organization wants out of each process. When a company changes to say centralized system, desired outcomes are altered. This causes many processes to be updated accordingly. These updates are not founded on the tasks in the process (since they can change), but based on the outcome.
- Have those who use the output of the process, perform the process?
  - In order for an organization to properly understand and reengineer a business or operational process, they must gather the current methods from those that utilize the process on a day to day basis. This will help to gain the most knowledge of a process in the redesign stage.
- Include information processing work into the real work that produces the information
- Treat geographically dispersed resources as though they were centralized
- Link parallel activities instead of integrating their results
  - Linking activities will help prevent a mesh of processes. When results are integrated they can cause confusion. When companies update technology and rapidly change daily functions, a link to each process will allow easier transition when process overlap.
- Put the decision point where the work is performed, and build control into the process
  - Various processes hold major decision points. With the reorganization and redesign in companies business and systems analysts place point of control where the decision is performed. This allows smooth process flows as well as less complicated managerial decisions.
- Capture information once and at the source.

By companies assessing the changes in their business and operational processes, they are required to take a broader view of information technology and business activity, as well as the relationships between them.

Once the business processes are complete and in order, the operational processes can be aligned. Irrespective of the nature of the business a company might be in, operational processes are key – they have a significant impact on the performance of a business, and process improvement can improve competitiveness in an industry. With rapid technological advances throughout the company their design of work is also highly affected. From these changes, processes of operations also need reengineering. For companies to properly and successfully evaluate operational processes a few steps must be taken.

- Define the process boundaries that make the entry points of the process inputs and the exit points of the process outputs
- Construct a process flow diagram that illustrates the various process activities and their interrelationships
- Determine the capacity of each step in the process.
- Identify the bottleneck
- Evaluate further limitations in order to quantify the impact of the bottleneck
- Use the analysis to make operating decisions and to improve the process

The successful future of companies in part depends on their use of business and operational processes. From historical data, technology constantly changes. Newly discovered techniques and tools have a high degree of obsolesce. With this in mind, companies have to reengineer business and operational processes to prepare for the future. For reference, 70% of Business Process Reengineering projects fail. The greatest challenges that companies may face when completing projects are:

- Lack of sustained management commitment and leadership
- Unrealistic scope and expectations
- Resistance to change

To prevent these challenges from becoming large obstacles, firms must keep all lines of communication open between management, business and systems analysts, as well as the end users, and most of all not to compromise strategic dimensions or overemphasize tactical aspects.

## TECHNOLOGY

The technology needs to be able to support the ways business is conducted in today's environment. As companies grow the technology grows with it. It is important that such technologies are picked that would increase productivity and decrease cost. There was a time when technology was not as apparent as it is today. Much of it was behind the scenes in the form of mainframes that ran the payroll system and other data processing programs. Most of the company employees were not even aware of the technology and never interacted with it. Usually a specific department dealt with the technological needs.

However with time, the use of technology in firms has grown. This has happened not only because of increased global presence and competitive needs, but also because of increased reliance of businesses on technology to transact their business. IT facilitates communication between geographically detached locations, thus facilitating coordination.

Once some of these systems were implemented it becomes difficult to replace them. Not only is such replacement costly, retraining and resistance to change are issues that pose challenges to organizations. In many organizations a given technology may be used for years before realizing that it was too expensive and required too many resources. Other more economical solutions although available, may not be acceptable to employees because of resistance and other human behavioral issues. This is perhaps one reason why management's decide to eat the cost of maintaining a given technology instead of making the obvious choice to switch systems.

Politics therefore can become a major issue in IT management. It is sometimes difficult for systems to be replaced if upper management doesn't recognize the need for change. To help with technological change new management positions can be created in order to oversee the increasingly important IT department. The Chief Information Officer may oversee the information systems department in a company and may work closely with the CEO to communicate the needs of the department as well as relay the needs of the rest of the company to the IT department. It is prudent to recognize that the IT department needs to support the goals of the company as a whole and must work closely with other departments in order to understand the system requirement of applications they are developing.

CEO supported for any change initiative is also central to realize success.

In recent years, internal systems have been consolidated through the use of Enterprise Resource Planning (ERP) systems. ERPs combine many different business applications into one centrally managed system. Each of the individual departments in a company can access this system, but the IT department is responsible for the upkeep and maintenance of the system. ERP systems can manage the finance, inventory, sales, manufacturing, order tracking, and human resources.

ERP is often referred to as back office software, which may facilitate order fulfillment (e.g. taking a customer order and processing it into an invoice and revenue). Traditionally ERP does not deal with front end selling activities. However, in recent years, customer relationship management applications have been developed. When a typical customer service representative enters the customer order information into an ERP system there usually is complete information to process the order. As the order mover from one department to the other, information in the systems keeps getting updated. The inherent logic of an ERP system can be applied to other business processes as well, *viz.*, financial reporting, employee benefits management.

A large number of businesses use one form of an ERP system or the other. The various reasons for ERP adoption can be summarized as follows:

- Integrate financial information
- Integrate customer order information
- Standardize and speed up manufacturing processes
- Reduce inventory
- Standardize Human Resource information

## CONCLUSION

Adequate leveraging of IT can help businesses grow and sustain advantage. What may seem like loss of market share can soon turn around to become profitable if proper conceptualization of technology needs has been undertaken. Dhillon and Lambert [3] describe an interesting case of John Brown Engineering, which was in the business of engineering and construction. Compared with the competition, John Brown was not in a good position to win big contracts. Flour Daniels and Bechtel generated sales close to double that of John Brown. The CEO proposed a strategic vision that was concerned with developing a global capability to leverage expertise. IT would be at the heart of building project teams of people with unique skills from John Brown offices around the world without them having to leave their desks. Eventually John Brown Engineering emerged as a great success story by leveraging expertise in diverse regions and providing rather competitive bids.

Careful consideration of the strategy, structures, management and operation processes, technology and roles and skills sets the stage for managing IT challenges. Planning and implementation of new technologies needs to focus on the future and how technology can completely change the way a business is conducted. If other business processes change then the IT systems could be forced to change as well. The success of a system change can depend on the support of rest of the company.

For companies today, it is critical that projects undertaken reflect an organization that values the expertise of disparate divisions of the company. The skills and experiences of the firm are the best asset when planning new projects if they can be prevented from overtaking the sight of a goal. Furthermore, the development of new systems must be integrated with a commensurate change in organizational strategy is they are to affect a long-term, fundamental change within the firm rather than a superficial one.

To prevent these challenges from becoming large obstacles, organizations must keep all lines of communication open between management, business and systems analysts, as well as the end users, and most of all not to compromise strategic dimensions or overemphasize tactical aspects.

## REFERENCES

1. Ahituv, N., M. Zviran, and C. Glezer, *Top management toolbox for managing corporate IT.* Communications of the ACM, 1999. **42**(4): p. 93-99.

2. Davenport, T.H. and J.E. Short, *The new industrial engineering: information technology and business process redesign.* Sloan Management Review, 1990(Summer): p. 11-27.

3. Dhillon, G. and R. Lambert. *Organisational competence for harnessing IT: the case of a major business transformation to leverage expertise.* in *First UK Academy for Information Systems Conference.* 1996. Cranfield School of Management, Cranfield, Bedford, April 10-12.

4. Griffin, J., *Information Strategy: Change Management: It Shouldn't be Just an Afterthought*, in *DM Review Magazine.* 2003.

5. Hammer, M., *Reengineering work: don't automate, obliterate.* Harvard Business Review, 1990(July-August): p. 119-131.

6. Leavitt, H.J., *Applied organisation change in industry: structural, technical and human approaches*, in *New perspectives in organisation research*, W.W. Cooper, H.J. Leavitt, and M.W. Shelly, Editors. 1964, John Wiley: New York.

7. Peters, T., *Get innovative or get dead.* California Management Review, 1991. **33**(2): p. 9-15.

8. Wagner, H.E., *The open corporation.* California Management Review, 1991. **33**(4): p. 46-61.

## DISCUSSION QUESTIONS

1. You have just taken over as a Project Manager for developing state of the art applications for the State Department of Motor Vehicles. The current systems are archaic and user support from the vendors is about to expire. Your feasibility study suggests that any new technology implementation is bound to impact a range of organizational functions. Sketch out a plan that would help you to conceptualize about the range of technology and organizational issues at hand.

2. Below is an excerpts from a speech given by Dr. John Powell, chairman of the British Medical Association's IT committee at a eHealth Conference in London:

> "Large-scale public IT projects do not have a good track record in the U.K.,

> and so it is paramount that the National Health Services learns the lessons of history and engages with the frontline staff who will be using the new systems."
>
> "So far, the level of engagement and consultation with the medical profession has been wholly inadequate."
>
> "The National Health Services IT program should support health care workers in delivering a better service to their patients. We hope that improvements to IT systems will reduce the administrative burden on doctors so they can spend more time treating patients. But this goal will only be realized if the NHS National Programme for IT can provide systems that are at least as effective as those currently in use."
>
> "Clinical staff must be consulted. There is no point investing billions of pounds in systems that do not have the confidence of users."

Comment on the challenges in introducing new technology into an organization. Identify the range of challenges that there might be. Suggest how such challenges may be dealt with.

# 2. INFORMATION SYSTEMS AND NEW ORGANIZATIONAL FORMS

A Forrester survey of manufacturing firms found that supply chain management investments were being scaled back. New supply chain investments will focus on extending supply chain processes across departmental and partner boundaries. Nearly all respondents said that the primary goal of supply chain management is to improve operational efficiency. Customer service improvements were considered to be important by about half the respondents.

**New Organizational Forms in Action**

Within Asea Brown Boveri (ABB) the major breakthrough was the formation of a new organizational form through its merger with a Swedish electrical engineering company (ASEA). Asea Brown Boveri currently employs more than 200,000 people and is spread geographically across the world. In one of the Financial Times/Price Waterhouse surveys, ABB has been cited as a model multinational industrial enterprise. In theory it follows a matrix structure entailing complex interconnections. The corporate center of ABB is located in Zurich where the executive committee determines the company strategy, identifies key competitive strengths and sets the geographical priorities. Although the central executive committee advocates a strong centralized reporting structure, the transformations over the years have resulted in nearly 1200 units. These are spread across various countries, each further being sub-divided into profit centers employing approximately 45 people. Following the merger with ASEA, the development of ABB took place in two phases, first, dominated by acquisitions and reducing excessive capacities, and the second, a consolidation phase. ABB also eliminated intermediate layers of control, thereby transferring additional responsibility to the operating units. The first level of networking at ABB resulted in the clustering of identical businesses of the company around the world. This resulted in the formation of business areas and management groups. While the groups were responsible for taking a global view in their particular markets this facilitated development of a global strategy for companies within that particular business area. Besides setting worldwide standards for cost, quality and performances, managers also determined the allocation of export markets for each unit and the optimal allocation of research resource and expertise. Activities of purchasing and supply management were also allocated to the Business Area leaders. The actual location of the Business Areas is dependent on the geographical area in which they operate.

The second level of networking resulted in national level clusters. These clusters are headed by a Chief Executive Officer (CEO) for that country. The main responsibility of that CEO was to manage ABB resources with a strong country focus. This country-based focus balanced the specialist emphasis of the Business Area leaders, thus helping to synergize the efforts. Since every country CEO was required to concentrate on national level issues, it helped in harmonizing company's objectives with national interests. This is an important issue especially for countries with emerging economies. In India, for instance, ABB is striving for joint ventures and take-overs in the energy sector. Currently the sector is in the control of the central and state governments where the operations are by no means run efficiently. Hence and redundancies following a take-over becomes a serious national issue. Consequently the CEO had to plan ways and means to handle the situation which calls for a close co-ordination with the governmental agencies. Abetted by the new structure, ABB has been very successful in managing its business.

ABB's style of working involved the formation of multinational teams to look at problems and solutions. People drawn from different nationalities built the teams at the business area levels. The teams had to travel widely, gain first hand knowledge of national issues and were required to interact with people at local level. At times when there was a risk of the teams reverting back to national groupings, the CEO interfered in the hiring decisions, thus acting as a controlling agent. In addition, members of the same function from across the national boundaries were allowed to meet once or twice a year to exchange their experiences. The meetings were often considered a means for creating personnel contacts and networks. During such meetings, the performance data of each unit was widely publicized. This was an integral part of the information exchange program at ABB. The inherent purpose of all these activities was to maintain good communication among employees so that coherent working patterns could be established. Communication channel redundancy is an accepted practice at ABB to ensure that messages do get communicated. It has been reported that there are, however, doubts about the intentions to share such information. The CEO feels that there is a "strong tendency amongst European managers to be selective in this respect" [8]. Within ABB the important potential of information technology became evident through the development of a corporate-wide database of experience and expertise of people. This greatly helped in matching the group themes or issues with the available skills that could contribute to a theme. However, the success of the database depended on how often it is being updated.

---

Information technology (IT) is changing at blinding speeds. As IT changes, so does the role that IT plays within organizations. Moreover, as new information technologies emerge, new organizational forms of business emerge as well in order to exploit these new technological advances and become not only more efficient, but also more flexible in hopes of gaining a competitive advantage. IT substantially changes the relationship between customers and suppliers, allowing it to become much more intimate because it enables the transfer of important information across organizational boundaries.

In conjunction with the rapidly changing world of IT, organizations seem to be in a constant state of "schizoid incoherence," [3] or constant state of change. In fact, advances in information and communication technologies have created a borderless world. Consequently, firms have had to learn to be extremely responsive to this borderless world around them and furthermore, IT has altered the way in which businesses manage their supply chain and has become an incentive to come up with new approaches for managing logistics across organizations. In order to take advantage of this state, businesses have become much more open to the formation of different types of cooperative networks or other types of organizational forms that can quickly and securely exchange important information. In many cases, sharing information through these organizational connections can increase competitive advantage.

In forming these cohesive organizational networks, the relationships of the supplier/customer changes drastically. New types of environments are created in which there is interdependency between the organizations. The agreements that bind these organizations are based on real actions related to success of the partner. Success is also a function of how well information is communicated and managed by the other partner or partners as well as how interrelated the connections are with other organizations. This creates an incentive to not only work effectively together, but also motivates companies to be extremely efficient in maximizing the strengths of each firm within the network.

This chapter explores several of these new organizational forms and discusses the impact that IT has had on these relationships as well as the possibility of strengthening or weakening the relationship. Overall, all these new organizational forms between different independent companies will lead to a higher level of competitive performance, only if they enable higher levels of operational benefits in the relationships between the parties involved. Furthermore, the "success of these emergent organizational forms seems to be based, on a great extent, on an effective co-ordination by means of the use of advanced information systems, which are based on the

Information Technologies (IT)" [9]. In other words, the success that these new networks enjoy can be partially attributed to the role that IT plays in these new organizational forms. To further illustrate this point, Michael Hammer [4] stated, "the power of technology should be used for radically redesigning the business processes and achieving important improvements of the results."

## NETWORKS

A network, according to Knoke and Kuklinski [5], is a "specific kind of relationship joining a particular group of people, objects, or events" and has two factors: "first, a network is formed by a group of elements; second, these elements establish specific relationships among them." There are distinct names for different types of networks as well. There are loosely coupled networks and co-operative networks, which must be a dynamic structures allowing consolidation of competitive positions of members. The competitive nature of such networks allows organizations to concentrate on their core competency, or focus on whatever they do best as a business. These core competencies are crucial to their existence and competitive advantage in the market. However, their competitiveness is reinforced and even enhanced by the connections that they form with other companies who can then help them in the areas in which they are less competitive or simply do not have the time or budget to focus on a particular area that is less critical to them. As other companies also focus on their core competency, the network grows and, more importantly, gains value as they obtain economies of scope.

IT plays an important role to create the network structure, and creating the framework or foundation enables a company the opportunity to expand their cooperative behaviors among them. Although IT can produce the framework or infrastructure for all parties involved, by itself, it does not guarantee the success of the network. Members in the network have to create incentives or a reason for other members to share knowledge and expertise with each other. Evolution of networks from hierarchical structures is shown in figure 2.1.

Figure 2.1 illustrates how the structure of organizations has evolved over a period of time from having strong internal and weak external coalitions to weak internal and strong external coalitions. Such changing relationships are illustrative when organizations have rather strong relationships with vendors and partners. Strong external and weak internal relationships are typically facilitated by IT, making it physically possible to create such organizational arrangements.

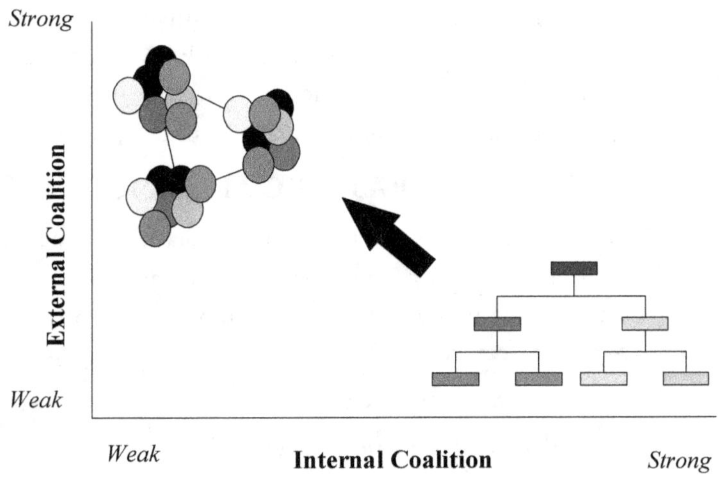


*Figure 2.1, From Hierarchical to loosely coupled networks*

Another issue pointed out by Mani R. Subramani from the University of Minnesota [7], is that often the benefits gained from using IT in the network are often unevenly distributed. In many instances, network leaders (often the buyer firm) retain the largest benefits. For example, the buyer to supplier network, in which Chrysler is linked up with all it suppliers, enables them to better compare prices and supplier offers and then chose the one which best fits their needs. That also may enable Chrysler to pressure its suppliers for lower prices. The supplier, other than the opportunity of being a part of the business, does not gain any real advantages from this network.

Taking this example a step further, in implementing just-in-time (JIT) delivery of products to automobile assemblers, suppliers in the network make significant changes to their own materials, procurement, manufacturing scheduling, and logistics processes. These changes are designed to provide them the capability to deliver to precise lot sizes (determined by the assembler's production plan) at very short and precise intervals before the components are required in auto assembly lines. These specialized investments generate significant benefits by streamlining a range of processes. As the JIT function increases, so does the dependency of the supplier on the buyer, as their supplied parts become more customized and the switchover costs to change to another buyer increase significantly. Therefore, these investments create incentives to maintain the supplier relationship for the auto assembler network, as they would have to forego the benefits (if they ceased the relationship) created by these hard to imitate, specialized investments made over time by the supplier.

## STRATEGIC ALLIANCES

Another type of network is a strategic alliance. Strategic alliances can be defined as the pooling of specific resources and skills by the cooperating organizations in order to achieve common goals. Strategic alliances have three common features:

- They are strategic rather than tactical
- They focus on long-range goals
- They suggest tight linkages among partners and thus emphasize cooperation and collaboration.

Strategic alliances can be non-equity or equity based. In non-equity alliances both parties maintain an independent ownership, such as distribution alliances, manufacturing alliances and R & D alliances. Equity alliances are characterized by partners having a joint venture with each other. One of the major concerns in strategic alliances is that of limited trust, problems of opportunism and social control. Our emphasis in this chapter is on non-equity strategic alliances and the role played by IT.

It is well understood that strategic alliances allow each partner to focus on their core competencies while extending its products and services to new markets. Partnerships provide a lower-risk approach to quickly reacting to the rapidly changing marketplace while minimizing capital investments. IS plays an important role for the success of strategic alliances, especially in the area of information sharing. Strategic partnerships are the most mature, valuable, and difficult type of these relationships. In this case, the partners have a broad understanding of each other's needs and visions, and share important values. Partners involved in a strategic partnership chose to develop a close, long-term relationship. There is also a high level of trust and mutuality, with open information sharing, gain sharing, and concern for mutual well-being. Because the partnership shares so much, it is adaptable to change and transcends tactical difficulties.

In this new organizational form structure, often companies start out with one form and transform to another. For example, in 1994 Air Canada outsourced their IT operation to IBM as a first step. In 2001, having implemented a successful outsource relationship with IBM, Air Canada then went a step further and announced a strategy partnership with IBM. This partnership between Air Canada and IBM was a seven-year, $1.4 billion strategic partnership to e-enable the airline, enhance customer service and develop future solutions. Air Canada expected to save approximately $200 million in IT costs over the term of the contract. As strategic business partners, IBM and Air Canada will work together pursuing new business opportunities in the areas of customer service and leading edge travel industry solutions. These jointly developed solutions will be offered to other companies through a marketing alliance created between Air Canada and IBM. "We are entering into a strategic partnership with IBM which will go far beyond managing our computer systems and which, we expect, will set a new standard in the airline industry," claims Air Canada's Calin Rovinescu, Executive VP, Corporate Development & Strategy. Besides the IT operations, IBM will also manage Air Canada's IT infrastructure, including application development and maintenance, 20,000 workstations, employee help desk services and network and server operations.[1]

## OUTSOURCING

Another new organizational form, whose popularity seems to have increased in the last couple of years, is outsourcing. This is where an organization starts purchasing a service that was previously internally provided. This definition can be expanded to; simply hiring another company to take over and run a service it can perform better and more

---

[1] http://www.attis.com/aviainfo/Newsletter%20Folder/attisnewsjuly2701.pdf.

efficiently than your company can. In general, companies outsource those activities that do not necessarily give them competitive advantage or various activities that lie within their parity zone, which include key operational and support systems.

The top two areas for outsourcing in an organization are IT and HR services, due to the fact that at first glance, the cost savings seem to be substantial. Herb Kelleher co-founder of Southwest Airlines simply puts it, "people who are in the business full-time can do it better and cheaper." Essentially, outsourcing has helped corporations become more efficient, flexible and nimble. The logical perception is that companies that provide outsourcing should be the experts in the area for the service that they provide and should be able to offer better and more efficient services than an average company, which has their core-competence in other areas. Focusing on the outsourcing of IT more specifically, it can be defined as commissioning of a third party to manage a client organization's IT assets, people and/or activities required.

In April 2002, CIO Magazine surveyed 179 IT professionals whose companies outsourced their IT services. The results of this survey showed that the key factors for companies to outsource their IT services were lack of internal staff and the need to reduce IT costs. In 2004, the issues remain unchanged. One such company, which is a good example of having a lack of internal staff, was Palm Inc, which was spin off in 1999 from its parent company 3Com. Palm's Vice President and CIO Marina Levinson said in 1999, "we were a three billion dollar company growing at 100% a year and we needed to build internal capabilities fast." As a result, Palm outsourced 90% of its IT infrastructure. The survey also offered more detailed reasons for an organization to outsource IT, which includes: 32% of organizations have lack of internal staff, 29% of the companies were looking for costs savings, while 20% of organization wanted that quality of the IT services to improve.

Interestingly, the results were a little different for companies who already implemented the outsource process than they were before the implementation process began. For example, before implementation, 29% of the organization outsourced for lower prices. When the organizations were asked about the benefits of implementing the outsourcing of IT, only 25% of the organizations mentioned low cost. Already from these simple results of the survey, we can assume that not all organizational expectations were fulfilled by outsourcing their IT services. The overall results are displayed in the table 2.1.

One issue of enormous importance, in order to create a successful outsourcing effort, is to create a good relationship between the organizations and outsource provider. The scope of the relationship between the service provider and the customer needs to reflect the fact that in business, like other aspects of life, nothing remains static. The service requirements laid out on the first day may be vastly different to those prescribed after three years of being in this partnership.

*Table 2.1, Organizational expectations*

| Why does your organizations outsource? | | What did outsourcing result in? | |
|---|---|---|---|
| Lack of Internal Staff | 32% | Improve quality | 29% |
| Lower cost | 29% | Lower cost | 25% |
| Improve Quality | 20% | Faster Time to market | 21% |

Survey: by CIO Magazine April 2002

Furthermore, a long-term outsourcing contract is, by its very nature, uncertain. This is because a lengthy relationship will inevitably develop and change in response to the service requirements of the customer. The contract needs to address this uncertainty, but before this can happen, both the customer and supplier must ensure that they understand the shared aims and objectives involved. This shared understanding relies on forging a real partnership, supported by a good balance of risks and rewards. Many of the problems associated with long-term outsourcing relationships are caused during the process of reaching the agreement. The motivations of a person seeking to sell an outsourcing service differ vastly from those seeking to deliver it, and a long-term relationship between the provider and receiver will only prosper if the chemistry is right. There is little hope of achieving this healthy relationship if the people who agree to the contract terms have no direct personal responsibility for its successful delivery.

Drafting a contract with those issues in mind can be time-consuming and expensive, but it often proves to be an extremely worthwhile investment. Still, groundwork and planning can help to reassure both sides that all the important issues have been covered. In addition, it is not unusual for a long-term outsourcing project to take three to six months to finalize. Moreover, for an outsourcing partnership to succeed, IT professionals stressed the need for a partnership that is equitable to both parties and one that is based on trust and mutual dependence.

There are various issues to address regarding the risk associated with outsourcing of the IT department of an organization. The most common contributing factors to the failure of outsourcing relationships include:

1) Often, pricing and service levels for outsourcing are established at the start of the contract; which usually contain no meaningful mechanisms for continuous improvement.

2) Differences in buyer and supplier cultures often cause misunderstanding and distrust.

Even if the cultures are compatible, the two parties still have fundamentally different goals and objectives that are frequently difficult to harmonize. One example where cultural differences lead to the failure of an outsourcing relationship is Kodak. Although the company is seen as a pioneer of outsourcing, and was one of the first major U.S. firms to successfully outsource part of its information service department to IBM in 1989, its outsourcing relationship with Digital Equipment Corporation (DEC) was not so glorious. In the same year, Kodak outsourced its voice networks to DEC. The computer maker's high-flying entrepreneurial culture and less-than-formal management style clashed with Kodak's buttoned-downed culture and management style, according to sources familiar with the engagement, and the outsourcing partnership ended.

Other issues to be addressed include outsourcing contracts, which are based on key assumptions regarding technologies, business conditions, personnel, and other relevant issues. As soon as the contract is signed, these assumptions begin to change, and may lead to very different results than expected. However detailed the contract or favorable the terms, most contracts cannot anticipate the changes in an evolving environment. This phenomenon tends to ensure that at least one (if not both) of the parties will become disenchanted with the relationship. Longer-term contracts that lack flexibility tend to increase the likelihood of dissatisfaction.

Likewise, many buyers do not believe they have to spend any time at their outsourced operation, which is a mistake. Buyers frequently underestimate the time and attention required to manage an outsourcing relationship, or worse, they hand over the management responsibility to the vendor. The outsourcer begins to operate in a priority vacuum, and service levels tend to deteriorate because the outsourcer's agenda is not in sync with the buyer's business objectives. Another problem is a lack of management oversight, which normally is the result of two factors: first, the team that negotiated the contract often does not stay engaged in contract management and secondly, the new team, that may or may not understand the contract's intentions, is given responsibility for managing the relationship. Employees that understood the pre-outsourced environment have been transferred to the outsourcer's team. This disruption in continuity can have significant adverse effects on the outsourcing relationship. All these issues can enormously and negatively affect the outsourcing process. A 1993 study from the International Facility Management Association asked organizations what they regarded to be the biggest disadvantages of outsourcing after implementation. And 51% of the organizations said they felt that contract employees were less company oriented. Furthermore, 44% of organizations said they disliked the lengthy bid process and 35% of the organizations stated that the outsourced units resulted in longer response times to problems. Also, 31% of the organizations were concerned about the loss of control of their outsourced services. A decade later the statistics is not too dissimilar.

Other than planning and choosing the outsource partner carefully, there are two other pieces of advice to companies considering outsourcing that could help to partially overcome some of the disadvantages experienced, especially due to false expectations. First, before getting into an outsourcing program, a company should consider where and why others have failed. Secondly, outsourcers are prone to sell more than they can achieve. There seems to be a case for both sides of the argument that points to the need for the organization seeking to outsource, to choose their partners carefully. A close examination of their methods and installation programs, to ensure it is as deliverable as they say it is, is suggested as a must. Penalty and get out clauses have also been suggested as an area also to be explored. It appears as though the outsourcing strategy is one that is here to stay; outsourcing is clearly a plus for those companies seeking a competitive advantage.

## ELECTRONIC DATA INTERCHANGE

One of the ways that networks can communicate using information technology is through electronic data exchange (EDI). EDI actually is an idea taken from Morse code and the telegraph industry of the 19th Century. Present day EDI started in the 1980s and can be defined as "the electronic transmission of information or documents between the computer systems in different organizations based on a standard, structured, and machine-retrievable format" [2].

With EDI, "buyers exchange data with suppliers in a form directly readable by a computer either by exchanging magnetic tapes or discs (primarily in Japan) or by sending data from one computer to another by modem or telecommunication links (primary in the U.S.)" [1]. Basically, it establishes a broadband communication channel to exchange detailed (and sometimes strategic) information on a continuous basis across multiple functional areas: purchasing, engineering, and quality and production control. This type of information sharing requires a great deal of mutual trust and interaction and therefore can cause tension between the parties involved, especially when the EDI system is drawn into an unequal relationship where there is not the same reciprocity on both sides. In recent years, however EDI has migrated to the Internet allowing for use of secure and private networking between suppliers and buyers. Such inter-relationships have even evolved into networks of communities. Networking of this kinds and participation in a range of business to business exchanges has helped achieve the purpose of becoming less involved and dependent on the other company so that the relationship is not forcibly permanent.

There are other forms of exchanging data electronically (such as the electronic funds transfer, or EFT, and the automated clearinghouse, or ACH), but any form of electronic data interchange can provide a significant advantage for a company because it "has been widely accepted as an essential business tool used to facilitate inter-organizational transactions and sometimes to enhance internal operations by integrating internal and external systems. It is also claimed to achieve quick response and just-in-time stock handling in order to gain competitive advantage" [2]. In fact, many JIT programs utilize EDI to handle the frequent processing of information between trading companies. EDI becomes much more economical as volume of trading partners increases. With telecommunications costs having a downward trend, electronic exchange of information is the way to go. Businesses are interacting with each other nationally and globally to leverage advantages that one trading partner might have over the other.

## INTER-ORGANIZATIONAL SYSTEMS AND INFONETS

Information sharing through the use of technology across organizations has lead to a general term for these network IT systems called Inter-organizational Information Systems (IOS). An IOS is an information system that is shared by one or more suppliers and customers. As discussed above, there are several advantages to IOS systems, including:

- Reducing paper-work and manual operations
- Reducing the stock levels
- Accelerating the product and material flow
- Standardizing of procedures
- Accelerating the flow of information about changes on the demand
- Reducing telecommunication costs

Furthermore, the advantages of using IT in an IOS can bring the following advantages:

- IT influences the nature, punctuality and detail level of the information shared by enterprises
- IT reduces the transaction costs, while it provides a better management of the risks
- IT reduces the co-ordination costs

Therefore, IT should be considered a resource to achieve the overall company goals. While technology itself is not enough to achieve an advantage, it can act as an enabler to accomplish the intended shared business objectives as well as enable cooperative behaviors and therefore should not be ignored. Technology can be a very important strategic instrument.

An IOS can bring with a compatibility problem in that not all companies may be able to easily integrate information systems and data since their respective systems could have been designed without accounting for any network integration. However, an IOS can also be effectively utilized to coordinate interdependent activities and thus provide an extremely important benefit to both parties. Furthermore, it can allow the accessible sharing of business objectives, experience, labor, and responsibility. This creates a great opportunity to establish economies of scope when both organizations follow a common objective through collaborative agreements. For instance, links can be used strategically to increase the competitiveness since it allows for customers and suppliers to be bound together.

Networks utilizing an IOS are sometimes called "Infonets" and contain the following key attributes:

- Speed and agility
- Lower overheads
- Ability to switch directions quickly
- Ability to discover new linkages between problems and solutions, wherever they may lie
- Few strategic brokers, problem identifiers and solvers work for high value enterprises

In effect, because of the possibility of these Infonets, it reduces the need for office space. Specifically, because of the elimination of borders through technology, the emergent organizational forms are relying more on regional cooperation than national affiliation and as an example, product designers in Oregon can now control activities of a network of factories throughout Asia-Pacific. IT basically eliminates barriers due to distance and makes location irrelevant. As is argued by Pitt, Berthon and Berthon in their Business Horizons [6] article, "For the distribution of many products- those that can be digitized, such as pictures, video, sound, and words—distance will thus have no effect on costs. The same is true for services. And for most products, distance will have substantially less effect on distribution costs." As an example, the location of Amazon.com is irrelevant to both buyers and publishers so that location is no longer central to most businesses due, in a large part, to technology and these networks.

## FINAL WORD

Technology has had a massive impact on the way companies do business as well as the buyer-supplier relationships between organizations. While some may argue that there is a privacy, trust, or possibly security issue with forming these types of integrated networks, clearly technology has not only transformed, but improved the way that organizations communicate and deal with one another. These interconnected organizations have proven to be more responsive and flexible to the rapidly changing markets and technologies and the rapid exchange of information has led to much greater market efficiencies as well as strategic advantages for these collaborative networks.

## REFERENCES

1. Bensaou, M., *Portfolios of Buyer-Seller Relationships.* Sloan Management Review, 1999. **40**(4): p. 40-42.

2. Chen, J.-C. and B.C. Williams, *The Impact of Electronic Data Interchange (EDI) on SMEs: Summary of Eight British Case Studies.* Journal of Small Business Management, 1998. **36**(4).

3. Dhillon, G. and J.D. Orton, *Schizoid Incoherence, Microstrategic Options, and the Strategic Management of New Organizational Forms.* M@n@gement, 2001. **4**(4): p. 229-240.

4. Hammer, M., *Reengineering work: don't automate, obliterate.* Harvard Business Review, 1990(July-August): p. 119-131.

5. Knoke, D. and J.H. Kuklinski, *Network Analysis.* 1983, Beverley Hills: Sage.

6. Pitt, L., P. Berthon, and J.-P. Berthon, *Changing Channels: The Impact of the Internet on Distribution Strategy.* Business Horizons, 1999(March-April): p. 19-28.

7. Subramani, M., *How Do Suppliers Benefit from IT Relationships.* MIS Quarterly, 2004. **28**(1): p. 45-74.

8. Taylor, W., *The logic of global business: an interview with ABB's Percy Barnevik.* Harvard Business Review, 1991(March-April): p. 92-105.

9. Zornoza, C.C. and R.L. Alcamí, *The Enabling Role of Information Technologies on the Emergence of New Organizational Forms*. M@n@gement, 1999. **2**(3): p. 251-261.

## DISCUSSION QUESTIONS

1. There are a number of organizational forms that support or constrain management processes. These arrangements generally include the structure, systems and culture of the organizations concerned. There is a continuing debate about the most effective form an organization should adopt to improve its internal efficiency and external effectiveness. Comment.
2. Volatile market conditions and intense competition are commonly cited drivers for such organizational changes. A significant feature of this changing business orientation has been the emphasis for more autonomy of subsidiary units where co-operation is emerging as the main characteristic with less centrally initiated control. Discuss.
3. You have just been hired by an Insurance company as a Manager of Outsourced Services. This insurance company has strong external relationships with at least 5 other companies, ranging from debt collection to underwriting. How do you think you will be able to balance pressures to collaborate with external parties and yet maintain integrity of the operations?
4. In order to truly understand new organizational forms, scholars need to develop a little less breathlessness and adopt a longer term perspective in which there has always been schizoid incoherence, there have always been accumulated micro-strategies, and today's new organizational form will always be tomorrow's old organizational form. Discuss.

# 3. INFORMATION SYSTEMS PLANNING

In a survey of 708 executives across 70 countries completed by Bain & Company, it was found that, on an average, companies used 16.1 tools. Eighty-nine percent of the respondents said that they used some strategic planning tool.

**Information Systems Planning in Action**

The $1 billion-a-year multinational company, Noble Corp. had a problem. How could it pay its suppliers in the 10 different countries? Ideally the company wanted to migrate from paper-check payments to electronic payments. However, there were concerns with the time it would take tying the core SAP financial system to that of the five banks processing Noble's transactions.

Noble evaluated services from a number of banks, but it seemed that Wells Fargo & Co. was the only one that offered what Noble wanted - an electronic-disbursements system. Today Noble's global payments are completed within 15 minutes at the press of a button.

Wells Fargo has been at the forefront of online consumer banking. Today, three-quarters of W ells Fargo business customers conduct at least some transactions online. Most of such online transactions come via the Commercial Electronic Office (CEO). CEO serves as a gateway to a range of commercial banking services. Tim Sunrise of FactPoint Research Group commented, "Wells Fargo is about as far out in front in using technology as any financial-services company."

It has been possible to achieve this coveted position simply by harnessing technology to get closer to its customers. In its relationship with Noble, there was no need to modify the SAP system. A team of Wells Fargo programmers developed custom code to make standardized transactions. Custom programming translates customer's preferred format to an internal Payment Manager format. This helps in validation, routing, and execution of the payments. Noble usually transmits a payables file from SAP to Wells Fargo. Thereafter Wells Fargo takes care of everything – notifying customers of their cash etc. There is an in-build fraud control system screening mechanisms, which make the system useful.

Recently, Wells Fargo has also launched an internal version of CEO. This allows for relationship managers to view customer details and hence interact with the customers in a more informed manner. The system requires minimal training and is therefore easy to use.

Wells Fargo has also partnered with BEA Systems Inc. This proves access to the WebLogic Portal developed by BEA. Such relationships ensure a services-oriented architecture, or Web services, for delivering banking services internally and externally. The bank has pioneered in providing online services, when most of the competitors were using dial up services. Very early on the bank realized that the only way they could retain an edge was by applying Web-services technologies for accessing services, especially with single sign on.

The innovative technology use gave Wells Fargo the first move advantage and they have never looked back since.

---

Until very recently, and perhaps to some extent even today, IS managers would groan on hearing the phrase 'strategic planning'. This was largely because most would be busy dealing with legacy system problems, understanding the changing technology or gearing up to become 'e' enabled. There were also pressures to cut costs or to be in a position to have successful implementation. Any call for strategic planning would result in increased resistance and be considered a shear waste of time. Although many discount the importance of IS planning, it is nevertheless important when significant change is on the horizon. It may be integrating the Bank of America and Nations Bank computer system following the merger, or the implementation of a computer-based system for the London ambulance, careful thought needs to go into the process and various contextual drivers.

IS planning, simply put, defines a portfolio of computer based applications that will help the company achieve its business goals. In order to develop a plan that would really work, clearly the CEO and CIO of the company need to come together and discuss various issues. If this happens, an organization is in a position to create a well-integrated business and IS strategy. This is opposed to merely stating, "We need to buy more PCs" or "Lets buy Oracle" or "Lets have a web presence". It is well worth communicating and assessing what the needs are and how various systems and applications fit in with existing infrastructure and the overall business strategy.

At times a company may create a well defined plan that may fit well with the business strategy, but there may be problems of culturally aligning the IS plan with the organization. A new computer-based system might change the way people do things or supersede a particular persons authority. A new system may also impose too rigid a work environment, while in the past people would come together and do things informally. All these are cultural challenges that need to be considered, if IS plans are to be successful.

Clearly developing a good IS plan is a key to the success of IS in organizations. This chapter focuses on concepts and tools that that will help in undertaking successful IS planning. However some of the key issues that need to be addressed in order to gain success in planning include:

- There needs to be a close alignment between the IS goals and the business strategy. This is possible when an IS plan goes beyond detailed system architectures and focuses on business benefits.
- Senior executive buy-in is essential for a successful IS plan. This is possible only when the IS plan helps the bottom line.
- A proper cost-benefit analysis should be an integral part of an IS plan. Intangible costs and intangible benefits are as important as the tangibles. There should clearly be options to improve and update the plan.
- The person responsible for developing and subsequently implementing an IS plan should be carefully chosen. Although it may be likely that a technology enthusiast close to drawing the specification may become the driver, it is only on rare occasion that such an individual may appreciate the business side.

In presenting material for this chapter we will logically classify the concepts into two parts. The first part will evaluate aspects of business strategies and the implications there might be for IS planning. Part two will focus on the process and tools and techniques available for undertaking IS planning.

## CONCEPTUALIZING ABOUT BUSINESS AND IS STRATEGIES

Clearly business strategies are needed when a firm wants to identify a direction it intends taking. The nature of the business strategy however is a function of the complexity of the environment (see table 3.1). In a relatively simple context merely meeting the budget would suffice. Such exercises are carried out internally in the organization and there is an emphasis to reduce almost everything to a financial problem However if there is need to predict the future, to say determine demand for a certain product, then some sort of forecast-based planning would be essential. This would involve establishing multi-year budgets, undertaking a gap analysis and perhaps allocating resources in accordance with the gaps identified. In forecast based planning a number of external parameters are considered, including economic and market research data. Based on the data, sales and market growth opportunities are calculated and their impact on income and expenses assessed.

There may also be a situation, most likely because of competitive pressures, that a firm may be forced to think strategically. Such a case would warrant situation analysis, evaluation of strategic options and a dynamic allocation of resources. The company might want to reconsider the market it currently operates in and may decide to reorient based on competitive forces. In yet other cases, a firm may use certain opportunities to create a whole new market. This would need a well-defined strategic framework and widespread organizational capability to think strategically. Good example of creating a new market can be found in the online brokerage firms like E*Trade and Ameritrade that ushered in a new concept of stock market trading. Companies that create a new market or a different context are faced with another challenge. They have to continuously innovate in order to stay abreast.

Classification of business strategies into four classes (table 1), affords some interesting observations and implications for IS planning. Clearly there are a number of situations where the business strategies and IS plans are not in sink. While an organization may be attempting to transform and create a new future, and many a times IS forms an integral part of the process, yet IS plans and strategies are considered in as class 1 or 2 activities. Consider the *Information Management* vision developed by Xerox. While the organization was attempting to transform the way in which internal information services were rendered, it considered IS as a cost and managed the technology resources as one would typically deal with class 2 projects. As a consequence, the mission of the organization and even the outsourcing deal with EDS where at odd purposes with each other.

During the late 1980s and early 1990s a general recession had forced firms to focus on the short term. This meant that any strategic project that would perhaps deliver benefits after a say two years was shelved. Companies wanted a shorter turnaround in order to justify the investment. This obviously forced many organizations to class 1 or 2. A similar phenomenon has been witnessed during early 2000s, essentially because of a recessionary environment. While the late 1990s saw a flamboyant economy, and companies ventured in to transform their businesses, the early 2000s because of lack of confidence in the market following demise of Enron and WorldCom, have been careful in their technology investment plans. IS has therefore been placed on the backburner and at best investments are being made that would bring in efficiency of current operations rather than transform the organizational processes for some future benefit realization.

*Table 3.1, Classes of business strategies (in part based on Gluck, Kaufmann, Walleck [12]).*

| | Nature of business strategy | Key activities |
|---|---|---|
| Class 1 | Meet the budget | Focus on meeting the annual budgets<br>Optimize internal functioning |
| Class 2 | Forecast the future | Consider past performance and develop multi year budgets<br>Undertake a gap analysis<br>Consider allocation of resources to fill the gap |
| Class 3 | Strategic orientation | Understand the situation<br>Evaluate options<br>Allocate resources for achieving strategic advantage |
| Class 4 | Transform and create a new future | Desire to undertake work innovatively<br>Well defined strategic framework<br>Well established business processes |

## BUSINESS STRATEGY TOOLS

In order to deal with class 1 and 2 business strategies, there are numerous economics and financial tools that come in handy. In such situations IS are merely a means to bring about efficiency. Discussion of such tools is beyond the scope of this chapter. However for strategies that are classified as 3 and 4, numerous tools and techniques have been developed that help in conceptualizing and realizing the business strategy. The different tools help in evaluating a particular dimension of the problem rather than present a generic overview. There obviously are a number of implications for each aspect of the tool. In the discussion below, we shall discuss two business strategy frameworks that have had a profound impact on strategy formulation and implementation. These are:

- The Boston Square developed by Boston Consulting Group
- Competitive forces framework proposed by Michael Porter

## The Boston Square

The Boston Square essentially brings together two concepts - product life cycle and relationship between market share and profitability. The product life cycle concept maps the demand for a product against time and identified four stages - initiation, growth, maturity and decline (see figure 3.1).

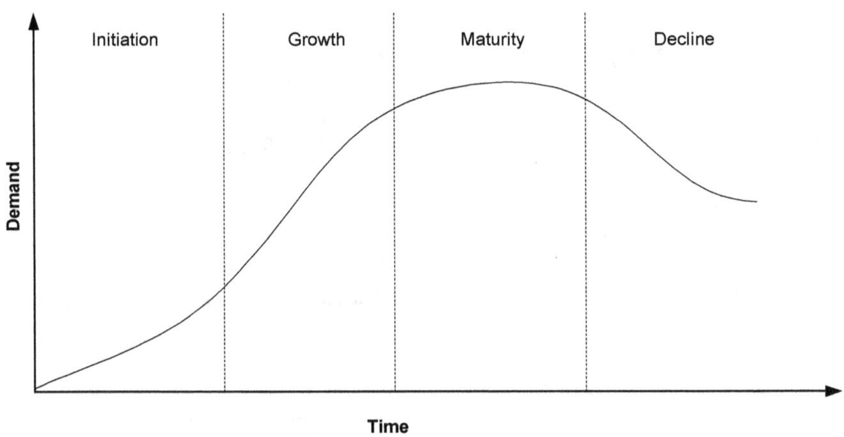


*Figure 3.1, A typical product life cycle*

The underlying argument in the product life cycle concept is that irrespective of the kind of a product, it generally goes through four stages. Unless an organization is in a position to identify the systematic position of its product in each of the stages and charts a future course of action, it will be difficult for that company to compete. Take the example of Iomega's zip disks. When the product was first launched, it took the company a few years to become a standard in storage media world. The 100 MB capacity disks were a real bonus to computer users who could take back up and move large files from one computer to the other. However other players were taking market share away from Iomega - viz. cheap alternatives in writable CDs and other high capacity storage media. In response Imogea launched the 250 MB drives and disks with backward compatibility. This allowed the company to extend its product life cycle. Imoega was successful since it not only recognized the external threats, but also understood that their 100 MB technology had reached maturity.

Related to the product life cycle is the concept that relates market growth with market share. Given different combinations of market growth and market share, four scenarios are possible. First, although market share might be low, potential market growth is high. This situation represents a situation, where a new product is being developed and it is anticipated that the market growth will be good, but obviously current market share is low. Such products are 'Wild Cats'. From a strategy point of view, we are never sure what direction such products will move in.

Second, in a situation where market share is high and the market growth is also high. In such situations there is obviously a lot of potential in the product or service being offered. These are our 'Stars'. Major revenues are sought from the 'Stars'. Businesses however need to be aware that competitors are going to catch up. Stars roughly correspond to the maturity stage of the product life cycle. Unless a company has ongoing research and development to 'create' more 'Stars', its market share and market growth is going to gradually dwindle. A good example of this case is the development of the drug Prozac by Eli Lilli. For the six months ended 6/30/02, net sales fell 9% to $5.34 billion. Net income fell 21% to $1.29 billion. These revenues reflect lower Prozac sales due to the August 2001 introduction of generic competition in the U.S. market. In the pharmaceutical industry, for every 10,000 compounds that might be considered as a potential drug candidate, only one or two might make it through the development and approval stages. It is anticipated that it takes approximately $500 million over 10 to 15 years to develop a successful new drug. Although Eli Lilly was aware that its patent rights on Prozac were for a limited time, yet after spending nearly $2 billion annually on research and development the company was unable to create another 'Star'.

After a product remains a 'Star' for a while, competition takes over. This is the stage that marks the maturity of a product. Market growth for a given products slows down and while market share still remains high. Such products and services are termed as 'Cash cows'. It will perhaps make little sense to pump in extra funds into 'Cash Cows', since they are never going to become or 'Stars'. Significant research and development would be needed. In rare cases where the brand has significant recognition, it is possible to make some improvements to elongate the growth phase of a product life cycle (c.f. the introduction of 250 MB Imoega drives).

Somewhere along the way 'Cash Cows' become 'Dogs'. This is when the market share significantly declines and so does the market growth. A very good example of 'Dogs' can be found in many of the products in the automobile industry. In July 2002 Ford announced that the Excursion Sports Utility Vehicle would be discontinued from 2004 onwards. It was anticipated that the Ford would sell 50,000 Excurions every year. However being able to average at about 15,000 only, it became a 'Dog' relative to the Chevrolet Suburban, which was a 'Star'.

The above concepts are diagrammatically represented in figure 3.2. The product portfolio model emphasizes a few key issues in business strategy.

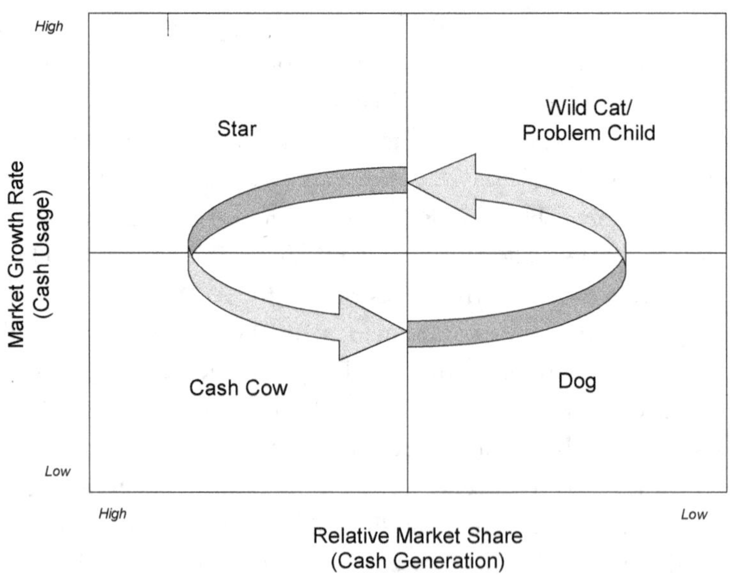


*Figure 3.2, Product Portfolio*

The product portfolio is a useful tool to begin thinking about a range of strategy issues. It emphasizes the need to manage products according to pressures in the market rather than internal factors. Implicitly it also suggests that net cash flows need to be diverted back into future product development. This will ensure future business success. There is also a need to have a well balanced portfolio. Over emphasis in one category may be detrimental to ongoing success of a product or service.

There are also a number of inherent weaknesses with the product portfolio. Clearly it is important to be aware of these if the product portfolio is to be used with confidence. One of the implicit assumptions of the portfolio model is that higher rates of profit are directly related to a larger market share. With respect to larger products, such as aircrafts by Boeing, there are usually high development costs that need to be taken into account. The product portfolio is normally applied to Strategic Business Units. It however needs to be noted that Strategic Business Units are business areas, not necessarily products. One might also end up assuming that there is going to be cooperation among various units. In reality however this may not happen.

## Implications for IS Strategies

Since the strategies for a product will be different for initiation, growth, maturity and declining stages, so would be the strategies and plans for IS. If a given product is in the low market share and high market growth category, success is going to come from a series of innovations leading to a clearly focused niche. In such a case the relevant IS strategy option is going to be in enabling the creation of such a niche. This strategy was evidenced by Amazon.com when the company first entered the market. Clearly there was an extremely low market for selling books online, yet the prospects of market growth were rather high. Innovative use of technology enabled Amazon.com to establish itself over a period of time. However since cash generated was low and cash used relatively high, very quickly Amazon.com ended up in a problematic situation. Since Amazon.com had to keep the investors and venture capitalists at bay, they were forced to diversify into selling a range of other products through their online store.

If a product falls in the strong market and high growth or attractive market category, the implication is that the product will play a leading role for the company. The impetus for IS will be towards customer orientation and ensuring sufficient revenue growth enabling a 'star' performance. Systems supporting products in this category help in handling greater volumes more effectively and also ensure good customer relationships. There are numerous examples of products and services that have come into being in this category. Over the years such products and services have not only defined and established new markets, but have also radically changed the way in which business has been conducted. In the 1970s and 1980s, American Airlines use of IT to tie together the operational side of the business in a common information stream and then extending it to tie together the business side of American, resulted in giving American Airline a significant advantage in the marketplace. InterAAct, as the resulting system came to be called was one of the earlier system integration efforts in the airline industry. Coupled with the success of SABRE, American Airlines became well poised to thwart competition from other airlines.

In the late 1990s, Harrah's Entertainment was involved in establishing an electronic customer relationship management system, that helped in capitalizing on the low rollers in the casino industry. At the heart of Harrah's eCRM system was the Winners Information Network (WiNet), which was a centralized database to value of casino customers. As a result Harrah's has saved $20 million a year in overall costs, while increasing same-store sale growth. The number of customers playing at more than one Harrah's property has increased by 72 percent, and cross-market revenues have increased from $113 million to $250 million. It is estimated that $50 million of the 1999 profit of $594 million are a direct result of cross-market visits.

Implementation of an extensive real-time training system by 3M is another example of an innovative use of IS to remain competitive in the marketplace. In the fiber-to-desk cabling market where 3M has to compete with manufacturers such as Lucent Technologies and AMP, 3M created this system, which not only provides training but also offers significant marketing advantage by demonstrating the products to potential customers and enables self learning necessary to install the Volition Cabling System. 3M was able to develop this product since they had the comprehension that Web based training will remove barriers of time and distance and will continually provide easy access to customers and sales staff.

If a product is in a strong market position in a mature, lower growth market, it becomes extremely important to develop systems and IS support that defends the current position of the product or service. This is usually done by ensuring lower costs (or same as that of the competitors) and fulfilling demands in a most optimal manner. In this category, it's important to remain productive while controlling the customers and suppliers. Therefore systems tend to be oriented towards business control rather than innovation. Good examples come from the use of purchasing cards by companies in order to reduce invoice processing costs. The St. Louis-based agro-chemical, Monsanto slashed its operating costs by issuing purchasing cards to its employees so they could pay for many non capital purchases. The company estimated that if a car is not used by the employees, it costs the company \$40-\$45 to process each transaction. By using the purchasing cards it has been possible for Monsanto to streamline its payment processes.

Finally if the product is in a weak position (low growth or declining market), there is obviously going to be less corporate interest in it. Companies tend to begin thinking about disinvesting the product. Therefore IS investments for products and services in this category should really be based on the business intent and the direction the business strategy advocated. Innovative use of systems is uncalled for and will perhaps not be looked upon favorably. However in many cases companies are forced to keep offering a product or service, which can rightly so be termed as a 'dog', just because it makes sense to loose money (or subsidize) on one product or service for advantages elsewhere. For instance, it costs Microsoft and Yahoo! Money to sustain their free email services (see Box 3.1).

Following the product portfolio framework, researchers have proposed the IT application portfolio model [30]; [22]. The IT portfolio defines the range of current and future applications. The applications could be high potential, strategic, key operational and support. The IT application portfolio is diagrammatically represented in figure 3.3.

**High potential IT applications.** These are generally applications related to a new business idea or a technological opportunity that are realized through the development and rapid evaluation of prototypes. An inherent ability to reject failure is the key guiding principle. Hence the intent is to refrain from wasting any resources. Individual initiatives may be in one part of an organization and are generally owned by one individual who might champion them. Therefore an understanding of the potential of applications in relation to the business strategy and the likely economics is the key. High potential applications are founded on the assumption that they demonstrate value, which forms the basis of deciding whether and how these could be exploited. Allocation of specific responsibilities and mapping out the exact way to proceed is essential for realizing high potential opportunities.

**Strategic IT applications.** Strategic applications generally come into being because of market requirements and competitive pressures. Such pressures are more likely to be externally driven, perhaps from the suppliers and customers. Strategic applications therefore require a rapid development to meet the business objectives within a given window of opportunity. In case of strategic applications, the business objectives, success factors and the management vision to achieve them is pretty clear. It is also important to sustain the advantage achieved. Therefore an emphasis on flexible solutions that can be adapted to meet changing business environments is the preferred route. In case of strategic applications, it always makes sense to link the applications to associated business initiatives or changes to sustain the business commitment to IS development.

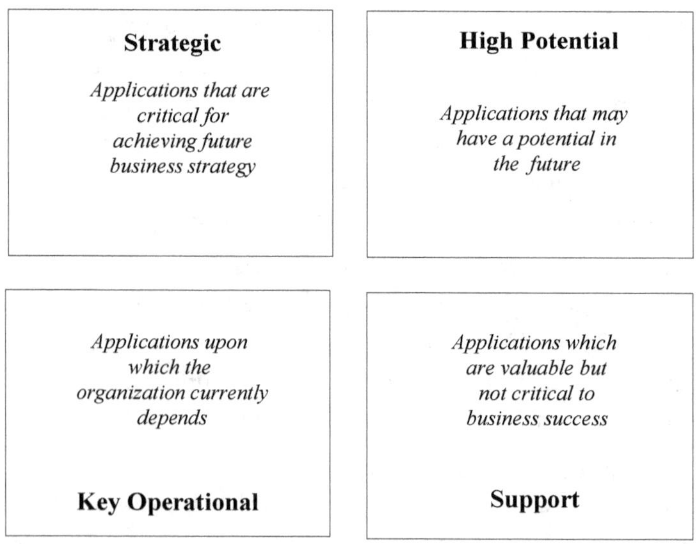


*Figure 3.3, The IT application portfolio (adapted from Ward, J. and P. Griffiths [30]).*

**Key operational IT applications.** Key operational IT applications are designed to improve the performance of existing activities in terms of speed, accuracy, effectiveness and economics. This is generally done by focusing on high quality solutions and effective data management. This ensures a degree of stability and reduced cost over a period of time. Key operational applications are largely founded on integrated systems, thus avoiding duplication and misinformation. Besides, risks because of inconsistencies are also minimized. This allows for balancing costs and benefits, which is so essential for an objective evaluation of alternatives.

**Supportive IT applications.** Support applications are founded on the principle of ensuring improved productivity and efficiency of existing tasks. Therefore low cost and long term solutions are sought. This often leads to selecting package software and at times compromising user needs because of solutions available. Many support applications are put in place because of the legal requirements which have to be met. Support applications are changed or modified not for strategic gain, but to avoid obsolescence given the pace of the IT industry. Management of support applications demands the cost effective use of IS funds and resources.

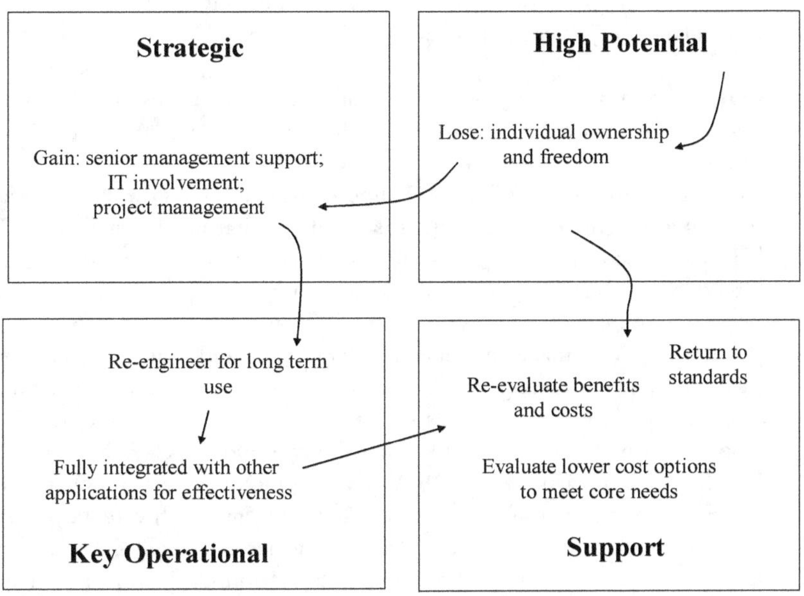


*Figure 3.4: Evolution of applications over time (adapted from Ward and Griffiths [30]).*

Clearly applications in the portfolio evolve over time. At any given time a firm may have more than one high potential initiative. Given the market dynamics and the viability of certain applications, a few high potential applications may become strategic. When this happens, there is usually a loss of individual ownership. While it makes sense to tightly control the development and expenditures associated with a high potential applications, it is perhaps wise to let go of the control and seek senior management support of there is any hope of an application becoming strategic. If the senior management decides that there is value on the application, it becomes paramount fort he IT department to get involved with project. Issues time, cost and intent management become very important.

## Box 3.1, Sustaining free Email services

**Hotmail**: In 1998 when Microsoft bought Hotmail in a stock swap, the general consensus was that it got more than what it bargained for. Microsoft had inherited nearly 8.5 million customers and considered it as an ideal means to direct Microsoft products at them. The intent was to sustain Hotmail by selling advertising space. In 2002 Microsoft had some 110 million customers, however advertisements were covering a mere 20% of the cost. It is costing Microsoft about a $1 per year to maintain each mailbox. For this reason, the company is now focusing on generating non advertising revenues that can sustain the email.

**Yahoo!**: Nearly 80% of the Yahoo mail traffic ends up using other Yahoo services including stock quotes, news etc. The portal has always considered email to be the means to sell advertising. Matter of fact in the fourth quarter of 2002 advertising accounted for $189 million of Yahoo's revenue. However Yahoo! Mail has been money looser for the company. It is estimated that like Hotmail, even Yahoo! Mail advertising covers only 20% of its costs. Largely because of the dot com meltdown, advertising revenues at Yahoo plunged 35% in 2001 to $717 million

**Other players**: Smaller players like Terra Lycos and Mail.com have been having a real problem sustaining the business model. It is costing Mail.com (a unit of Net2Phone) as much as 6 cents to send each message, while the cost for Hotmail is about a penny. In terms of sustainability options are rather limited for these players. On February 19, 2001 AltaVista announced discontinuance of its email service and concentrate on the search engine and software businesses. For this reason, smaller players are trying new strategies. Mail.com for example is offering an ad free option for $19.95 a year. Other options being offered include POP access and mail forwarding. *(Based on reports in Business Week, New York Times and CIO)*

Over a period of time however strategic applications loose their luster. By now competitors may have either copied these applications or the market has just simply moved on. At this stage it becomes important to consider ways and means in which strategic systems could be fully integrated into the business processes. This helps in achieving effectiveness. Applications generally get re-engineered for long term use. There are occasions in the course of evolutions of applications that key operational systems need to be re-evaluated for the range of benefits and costs. Obviously lower cost options that meet the core needs are considered. There is a focus on standardization as well. Given the context of use, if it makes sense, key operational systems may result in being support applications.

## Competitive forces

Michael Porter [25] in his seminal work of competitive strategies suggests three generic competitive strategies for a firm. First is a differentiated strategy that relies on providing superior value. In this case products are difficult to imitate or replace with substitutes. Hence they command premium prices. Second is the cost leader strategy where a lower cost structure is advocated. This enables competition on the basis of price. Third is the focused niche strategy where a particular player finds a small specialty market. This is protected by geographic isolation and historically tight working relationships between buyers and sellers. Porter believes that these strategies form the basis of any successful overall business strategy. Porter, while discussing the competitive strategies, used an industry structure framework to determine appropriate strategies for a firm. In this framework he identifies five competitive forces: new entrants, suppliers, customers, substitute products, and competitors. Accordingly a good strategy should enable an organization to do one or more of the following: erect barriers against potential new entrants; change the balance of power in supplier relationship in favor of the firm; increase switching costs for customers; change the basis of competition among rivals in the firm's favor. These are illustrated in figure 3.5.

In a market place, one or more of the forces may be at play. There may be rivalry between existing competitors on price or aggressive advertising. The traditional competitors may also be cooperating with each other and forming alliances simply to thwart external pressures or threats. Suppliers and customers may form alliances with the firm so as to substantially increase the switching costs thus preventing other firms to be able to enter a marketplace. It may also be possible for new firms to enter a market place by virtue of a disruptive technology and hence be a threat to established products or services. It is also possible for innovative firms to develop substitute products and services and hence be able to create a totally new market.

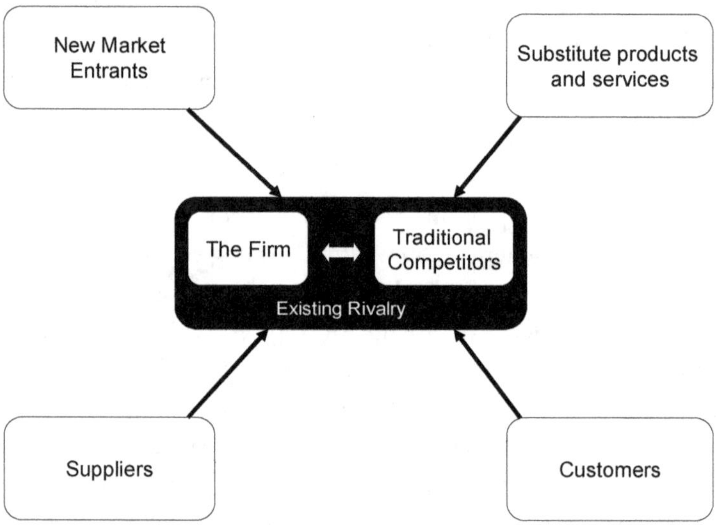


*Figure 3.5, Competitive forces*

Clearly if all the forces exert pressure at the same time, the business would indeed be in a dire situation. However if nature and scope of the forces is clearly understood and the potential impact adequately assessed, a firm would be suitably positioned to take on any competition. Technologies not only play a significant role in realizing some of the forces, but also in creating new forces. It is therefore important to understand the range of impacts of IS on competitive forces such that adequate strategies could be formulated.

More recently Porter has described how a firm's value chain can be used as a framework for identifying opportunities for competitive advantage. A firm's value activities are classified into two broad categories: primary and support. Primary activities are those that are involved in the physical creation of a product, its marketing and delivery to customers and after sale servicing. Support activities provide the inputs and infrastructure that allow the primary activities to take place. These are linked together to form a firm's value chain.

While discussing the role of IT in a firms' value chain, Porter and Millar [26] argue that IT is permeating the value chain, thus transforming the way value activities are performed, besides affecting the nature of linkages among them. The competitive scope and the way products meet customer needs are also affected. Every value activity has both a physical and an information-processing component. Each activity creates and uses information. The role of IT is to enable a firm such that it can better co-ordinate its activities thus generating greater flexibility in deciding the breadth of its activities.

## *IT and Sustainable Competitive Advantage: fad or hype*

It is argued that to create a sustainable advantage, one must either be blessed with competitors that have a restricted menu of options or be able to pre-empt them. This notion is further augmented by the research that illustrates competitive restrictions and unique factors such as macro-economic, political and regulatory, as having a potential to influence sustainability. Such restrictions can hamper a competitor from responding to a threat that it would otherwise answer. For instance, a company that is on the right side of public policy can exploit its position to build sustainability. This analysis on sustainability of competitive advantage can thus lead to a situation where the significance of the technological factor, needs to be explained in more realistic terms. As Clemons and Weber [4] questions, "IT -equipment, and services- is available to all firms and most applications can be duplicated. To what extent can we duplicate successes, find critical opportunities, or even predict the effect of new venture?" Hence it may not be possible to gain and subsequently sustain advantage from the use of IT alone. Indeed there is growing skepticism among practitioners and academics suggesting that opportunities for achieving sustained competitive advantage from early use of IT may be more difficult than originally conceived and that the number of 'silver bullets' are few. Clearly some innovations are widely copied but their benefits can be defended; others are copied with no strategic gains for any player.

This means therefore that it becomes uncertain whether to rely on technology as being the enabler of gaining competitive advantage. For instance, Automatic Teller Machines (ATM) in banking are almost universally available and have produced no measurable benefits for most early providers. And an introduction of IT may be a 'strategic necessity' to maintain current competitive position. Therefore the competitive use of IT must be a component of overall business strategy; its application depends more on understanding unique business opportunities than competitive benefits achieved through technological features.

## *Why IT by itself fails to provide any advantage?*

The proposition that technology can not be regarded as the only factor in gaining competitive advantage has been analyzed by many researchers. Cecil and Goldstein (1990), while discussing the predicaments of achieving sustainable advantage on the basis of technology, state that it is virtually impossible for major IT users (excluding vendors) to gain advantage based on IT alone. They suggest several reasons as to why information technology by itself fails to deliver a sustainable competitive edge:

- Peer competitors generally start with equivalent application knowledge: There may be differences after an application has been developed, but it's usually difficult to protect. Competitors can recruit key employees or use the same vendors and system integrators to take advantage of the leader's experience.
- Differences in IT developed capabilities among competitors can usually be evened out by vendors. For many applications, followers can purchase packages or hire systems integrators and end up with equivalent functionality at lower cost than the leaders.
- Larger scale rarely translates into a cost advantage. Larger companies generally have more complex requirements, increasing development costs. They are more likely to need (or think they need) customized systems instead of vendor-supplied packages.

Similarly Vitale [29] suggests that attaining competitive advantage through IT may be difficult. This means that in many cases the initial innovator may, in fact, even place his firm in a disadvantageous position. Moreover the innovating firm can find itself in a week competitive position. This may be because:

- There are no first mover effects or barriers to imitation to give advantage to the innovation

- The innovation becomes a necessity and the innovating firm lacks special skill in producing this necessity

Indeed many applications of information technology are in fact strategic necessities. Such systems radically change cost structure, relative bargaining power, or the basis of competition to an extent where most competitors are compelled to imitate them. However, because competitors often imitate them or otherwise respond before customers change their behavior, these systems seldom confer competitive advantage.

Likewise, Johnston and Carrico [17] argue that "virtually any corporation with a strong IS function can use the capabilities represented within that function as leverage to achieve improved competitive position in their industry". Therefore successful deployment is contingent to the presence of a set of external environment factors and in developing a set of internal capabilities that extend beyond the IT function.

## *Two Paradigms for Sustained Competitive Advantage*

In the strategy literature there are two major paradigms for explaining sustained superior performance of the firm. The first of these paradigms draws upon the concept of industrial organization economics. Traditional industrial economics emphasizes barriers to competition, and takes the position that industry effects will explain the greater part of persistent above-normal returns. Particular industries are more or less attractive because they contain 'structural impediments to competitive forces' and thus allow participating firms to sustain competitive advantage [24].

The second paradigm for gaining competitive advantage of the firms suggests an alternative perspective - that firms are fundamentally idiosyncratic. Hence firms accumulate unique combinations of resources and abilities over time. These allow organizations to garner rents on the basis of distinctive competence.

The nature of firms' idiosyncratic endowments of proprietary assets as mentioned above has been further studied by. All competitive advantages are limited to a certain period. Firms develop idiosyncratic resources, which can be further deployed to achieve competitive advantage. It thus implies that the quest for new advantages is a critical responsibility. At the same time a need to understand the processes by which firms accumulate and deploy resources at the business unit level to effect superior performance within the industry, has also been emphasized. Hence processes used to develop new sources of advantage are as important to the vitality of a firm as the content of the advantage.

Thus the sustainability of the competitive advantage poses a major problem for strategists to manage the development of new sources of advantage to substitute the sources that are deemed unable to yield return. A principal mechanism through which organizations develop new competitive advantages is through the pursuit of new initiatives - attempts to add new products, markets and technologies to its current portfolio. Initiatives can lead to advantage in a number of ways. McGrath et al. describe these as:

- A firm may utilize resources, which are already at its disposal to tap new market areas, entering the new markets with lower cost, with greater efficiency or with more attractive offerings than competitors.
- The intention of the new initiative might be to contribute to the absorptive capacity of the firm. By entering small, less challenging markets initially in order to learn, it can develop product, market or technology assets.
- Firms are sometimes fortunate, gaining competitive advantage through luck.

By undertaking new initiatives firms can capture advantage. However two aspects must not be ignored in this respect: First, competitive advantage can hardly evolve from an initiative unless those responsible can develop competence at what they are doing. Second, competence should be thought of as a purposive combination of firm-specific assets (or resources) which enables it to accomplish a given task.

Competence of firm is the ability of the firm to reliably and consistently meet or exceed its objectives. An increasing convergence between the objectives of an initiative and its result has been regarded as a useful indicator of the potential advantage. For unless such convergence is occurring, it is difficult to argue that the team is developing competence, and without competence there can hardly be any advantage.

## THE IS PLANNING PROCESS

IS Planning means the effective long term planning of IT applications in an organization. This section establishes the framework and process by which strategic IS planning can be undertaken. In order for IS planning to be successful, it is assumed that the process is closely aligned with business planning. It is also assumed that the outcomes of business planning will either inform or dynamically interact with the IS planning process. In organizational situations where there has been a limited exposure to IS planning it may be worthwhile to undertake an initial planning exercise in a few business area. This will help in fostering awareness and the importance of benefits delivery. There are however numerous barriers that hinder proper conceptualization and implementation of IS plans.

In research carried out by Basu et al [1] it was shown, consistent with prior research, that insufficient senior management involvement was detrimental to the IS planning process. It was also found that excessive organizational and team commitment did not result in an adequately planned IS implementation. This was an interesting finding of this research and perhaps contradictory to previous research. It suggests that there is an optimal level of organizational commitment that results in IS planning success. The success of IS planning increases until it reaches a maximum, following which if there are increases in organizational commitment, success decreases. This finding is clearly consistent with traditional thinking that too much planning can have a negative impact on success.

Planning for IS is a cyclical and an iterative process. A number of frameworks have been proposed that help in undertaking IS planning. Martinez [21] suggests that a significant amount of time should be devoted to creative thinking, which is followed by prototyping and experimentation. This sets the scene for design, development, implementation and rollout. A critical question that arises is as to how an organization will ensure creative thinking. It is important to ensure that the core of an IS plan is not constrained by the structured methodology. One effective means of ensuring creative thinking is to allocate substantial time to the thinking and avoid the use of any structured method. Prototypes may be developed, tested and later discarded once the purpose has been achieved. In due course as solutions begin to take shape, they need to be developed for actual business operations. This is the stage were effective project management and control techniques come to be used (see figure 3.6).

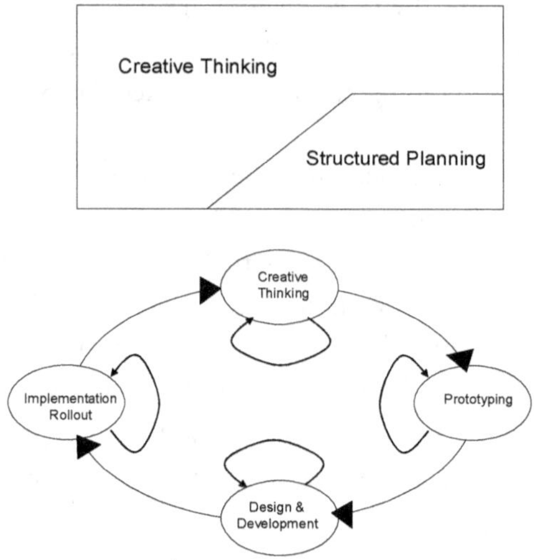


*Figure 3.6, Creative and structured planning (adapted from Martinez [21]).*

Creative thinking always plays an important role in IS planning . Since the very nature of IS projects is dynamic and new problems and situations arise at every stage, it is important to allocate sufficient resources to thinking about problems and potential solutions than dealing with situations in a reactive manner.

One of the major outcomes of IS planning is the development of a portfolio of IS applications. The application portfolio helps in realizing the business plans and in achieving the business goals. Organizations undertake IS planning to identify the right mix of applications in the portfolio. Typically applications are sought that provide higher payback, strategic significance and congruence with the organization's competitive needs. A long term view of IS planning suggests that the focus should be on improving organizational capabilities

Although the objectives of IS planning are generally well received, this does not mean that the adopted planning process is adequate. While some researchers have suggested a comprehensive rationally executed planning process, others suggest an incremental emergent process. Comprehensive planning is exhaustive and attempts to integrate a range of strategic decisions. Large groups of people from various organizational levels are involved in decision making. Extensive analysis is carried out. In order to manage a large planning group, some degree of formality is essential.

Critiques of comprehensive planning suggest that by focusing on formal planning methodologies and predefined criteria trivializes IS planning. This results in the IS planning exercise merely becoming a top-down activity. There are organizations however which do engage in incremental planning. In such cases the focus is on a limited number of themes and IS decisions are made on a one-by-one basis. Since the agenda is rather focused, it helps in keeping the team small, which in turns facilitates hight levels of informal communication. It often also becomes possible to experiment with new and innovative agendas. Table 3.2 summarizes the characteristics of comprehensive and incremental IS planning.

The Continuous Strategic Alignment model is perhaps the closest to the incremental method of IS planning [16]. The model has five basic axioms:

- Governance processes specifying decision rights
- Technology capability processes specifying IT products and services needed to support business strategy
- Human capability processes specifying skills necessary to support business strategy
- Value management process that allocates resources to maximize IT investment benefits
- Strategic control that maintains internal consistency

The notion of strategic alignment and incremental planning is based on the theory that organizations learn and benefit by adapting to the context. However there has been criticism of incremental theories on grounds that they fail to address critical needs. Based on extensive research carried out in Netherlands and Finland, Salmela and Spilb [27] propose the ***four cycles method*** of IS planning. The method divides the planning cycle into four distinct parts:

- Agreeing on planning objectives
- Aligning business objectives and information objectives
- Analyzing IS resources and IT infrastructure

- Authorizing actions

*Table 3.2: Comprehensive and incremental views of IS planning (adapted from Salmela and Spilb [27])*

| Planning characteristics | Comprehensive practices | Incremental practices |
|---|---|---|
| Plan comprehensiveness | Plans are generally complicated and integrate with the business strategy | Simple plans that are loosely integrated with the overall strategy |
| Approach to analysis | Formal multiple levels of analysis are used to arrive at plans | Personal experiences and judgments are used |
| Planning organization | Planning is based on a formal representation from various groups | Planning is based on informal networks of a few key individuals |
| Basis for decision | Formal methods and criteria are the basis of decisions | Shared group understanding if a few key people forms the basis of decisions |
| Plan control | IS plans are periodically reviewed and are adapted to changing circumstance | IS plans are continuously reviewed and changed to adapt to the context. |

The difference of the *four cycle method* from the traditional comprehensive method is that inputs from techniques such as mind mapping are added to the process. Furthermore the four steps are repeatedly applied over a period of time. The repeated application ensures that the existing strategies are monitored and updated periodically. The first cycle begins with an assessment of progress in implementing IS decisions and plans. New issues that require attention are also considered. If immediate action is required on any issue, then a special task force is set up. The second cycle begins with a review of current issues. Progress in implementing IS decisions and plans is reviewed. The main purpose of the second cycle is to undertake strategic thinking. Innovations in the planning process are considered and various business and IS plans integrated. There is an emphasis on identifying those IS projects that add value the business strategy.

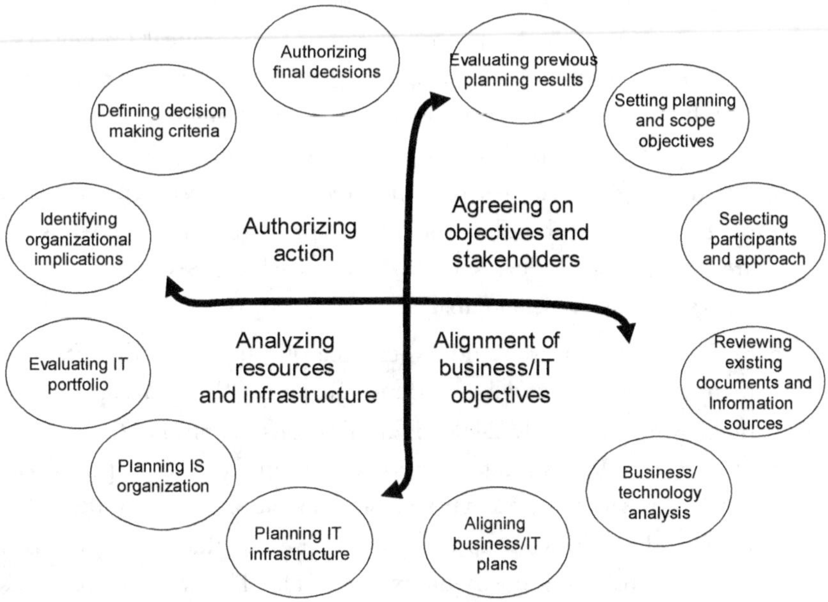


*Figure 3.7, The four cycle model (Salmela and Spilb [27])*

The third cycle begins with considering the progress to date. Specific attention is given to issues related to infrastructure planning, evaluating and establishing the organizational structure and development of a project portfolio. The fourth cycle focuses on establishing clear proposals for action. The intent is to ensure commitment of resources and mechanisms of acquiring such resources. Specific planning activities considered relate to identifying organizational implications; defining criteria for decision-making; authorizing final decisions. The ***four cycles method*** is illustrated in figure 3.7.

## CRITICAL REVIEW OF ASSUMPTIONS IN IS PLANNING[2]

In the previous sections we have reviewed some of the predominant methods for conceptualizing about strategy and means of undertaking planning. Over the years the variety of theoretical frameworks proposed have incorporated both business driven and creative approaches in the search for significant opportunities for gaining benefits from IT. These have included 'top down' ([30]), 'middle out' ([15]), 'eclectic' ([28]) and 'multiple' ([8]) methods. Incorporated within these approaches are a variety of tools and techniques, borrowed primarily from the business strategy area, including critical success factor analysis, SWOT analysis, five forces analysis and value chain analysis.

However, research and experience questions whether IS Planning in its many guises is actually working. Recent US research, for example, has highlighted that only 24% of applications recommended for development via a formal IS planning process were ultimately developed as organizations needed to carry out further substantial analysis post planning [19]; [20]; [13]. One study even went as far as to suggested that the whole process of IS planning may be a cosmetic exercise [11]. This was conveyed as a type of informal social consequence of traditional systems analysis and design.

The IS Planning process is grounded in a number of fundamental assumptions and in the remainder of this section these are surfaced and their validity is assessed.

### The organization has a business strategy

One of the major assumptions which underlies IS Planning is that there is a business strategy in existence; after all this is what the IS/IT strategy seeks to align itself with. We saw in the previous section that descriptive research has shown it to be sometimes emergent, often serendipitous and continually being renewed. This presents a challenge to IS Planning in that it must align itself to a moving target. The requirement is that IS/IT strategy must itself be dynamic. While it may be possible to articulate a flexible IS strategy, the paradox is that in order to develop an IT application

[2] Parts of this section are drawn from a the paper Peppard, J, Dhillon, G and Hackney R. (1996). Emergent Strategies, Strategic Renewal and Serendipity in Business Strategy Creation: The Challenge for IS/IT Planning. In proceedings of BIT '96, Manchester Metropolitan University, Manchester, UK. Used with permission.

a strong element of stability and predictability is required. In essence, we saw above that business strategy formulation involves an ability to articulate and capture a diverse, fluid and informal set or organizational characteristics which, to date, IT professionals regard as functional, quantifiable and certain. Cynically, one could argue that IS Planning represents the IT professionals' requirement for certainty in an uncertain world rather than to involve business managers per se in the process!

Paradoxically, the business strategy itself is often constrained by legacy IT systems, which represent that results of past strategies as articulated by the IS planning process. This restriction imposed by IT has led many companies to go down the outsourcing route in search of a more responsive IT capability. However, this practice is fraught with danger.

## Distinction between an IS strategy and business strategy

IS planning makes a clear distinction between a business strategy and an IS strategy. The message which this conveys is that IT is something which is bolted on and in some way is secondary to the business strategy. However, in many industries IT is often intrinsically linked to the success of the business, particularly in information intensive industries.

## IT is a source of competitive advantage

One of the principle assumptions underlying IS planning is that IT can provide a source of competitive advantage. The reality is that IT has become a commodity and in many industries today you cannot exist let alone survive without IT. The clear evidence is that IT alone does not generate sustainable competitive advantage rather it is through the business changes which it facilitates or its ability to leverage organizational capabilities. Recent research suggests that only IT managerial skills are likely to be a source of sustainable competitive advantage [5]; [6]. The implications of this analysis is that the search for IT-based sources of sustainable competitive advantage must focus less on IT, per se, and more on the process of organizing and managing IT within a firm.

## There are a class of information system called 'strategic IS'

The phrase strategic information system is now common in the lexicon of management. These are the systems which are seen as giving the organization strategic advantage. In reality, strategic information systems are in fact a misnomer. The so called examples of strategic information systems in fact represent a significant process capability which the organization has harnessed through IT. It is the process capability which is strategic to the business not the IT.

## The strategic applications of IT can be planned

By engaging in IS planning the underlying assumption is that the strategic application of IT can be planned. Clearly the focus should be on 'thinking' prior to any execution. Evidence however suggests otherwise. In an analysis of four of the most well known strategic IS, Baxter's ASAP, McKesson's Economost, American Airlines SABRE reservation system and the French videotex, Teletel, Ciborra [3] concluded that they were not fully designed top-down or introduced in one shot; rather they were tried out through prototyping and tinkering. This corresponds to Earl's [9] organizational perspective on IS planning. His research, further elaborated upon in Earl [7] concludes that 'effective [IS] strategies often emerge through implementation'. Planning is about programming not discovering [14]. It is about articulating a route map in the context of a defined strategy. This defined strategy is the result of creativity, innovation and foresight: of strategizing. This presents a contradiction of sorts in that organizations' engage in planning to develop an IS/IT strategy!

## The IS Planning process helps in organizational integration

The irony of IS Planning is that its supply orientation, with a strong focus on applications, can result in organizational fragmentation: exactly what IS Planning seeks to move away from. The assumption is that integration takes place at the technology level. While this may be the case, it is not always so. The end result, however, is usually more often about co-ordinating what results rather than integration. The implication of lessons from business process re-engineering (BPR) suggests that a strong process perspective should be adopted before any IT implementation is undertaken.

# CHALLENGES FOR IS PLANNING

The previous section questioned some generally held beliefs about IS planning. The discussion touched upon the confusion surrounding IS/IT strategy and IS/IT planning. In this section we take the argument further and review the primary challenges for IS planning. These challenges can be classified into three broad categories: reviewing benefits; managing business change; assessing organizational competencies.

## The challenge of reviewing benefits

One of the key challenges to IS/IT planning relates to inability of the business to reap benefits from IT investment. Part of the blame has been attributed to the mismatch between business strategy and the IS planning processes. It has been argued that if these are at tandem with each other, then there is a huge risk of benefits not accruing from IT investments. Hence it may not be sufficient to merely install an IT application and hope for the savings. At the very least, some training will be required, and probably changes in tasks, roles and responsibilities. This calls for a coherent understanding of the business strategy that may demand an investment, the IT strategy which may determine the nature and type of the system and an IS planning process which establishes a link between the business strategy and the IT strategy.

In the literature, it has been suggested that benefits of IT are often not realized because investment is biased towards technology (e.g. see Benjamin and Levinson [2]). This may occur because of inadequate attention being given to the management of change, organizational structures and culture. Benjamin and Levinson further argue that managing change enabled by IT is at least as important as bringing IT to the organization. Indeed the challenge of reviewing benefits is becoming increasingly significant primarily because of rapid changes in both the market place and the technology itself. Johnston and Yetton [18] bring out another interesting issue regarding benefits management and business change. Their notion of fit and compatibility suggests that the IT configuration of an organization should match the organizational structures. Although the main focus of the paper is on integrating IT divisions during a merger, the concepts seem to be equally relevant within an organizational context. Similar arguments have been proposed by other researchers as well, particularly those who have focused on strategic alignment. Prominent among these is the work of Henderson and Venkatraman [16].

## The challenge of managing business change

Organizations today are experiencing significant change. These changes have been afforded not only by advances in technology but also because of a competitive marketplace. This has resulted in the management of IS/IT related change emerging as a significant challenge for IS/IT planning. Indeed when an IT system is implemented in an organization, what actually occurs is change ranging from small scale and localized to major changes in the conduct of business and even major organizational restructuring. Change is not always welcome and can make or break organizations. It can be exhilarating or frightening but always creates uncertainty. Practitioners report that success rate for IT and change initiatives is well below 50%. Indeed some say that it's as low as 20%.

Research on Strategic Information System investments by McGolpin [23] showed that in successful investments, coherent change management approaches were an integral part of the projects. Such approaches were geared towards delivering business change and integrated business strategies with IT strategies. McGolpin found that more often than not, IS/IT was considered as a component of a business project and was the key enabler in delivering business changes. The research further found that less successful organizations were characterized by planning and implementation approaches that focused almost exclusively on the technology. Such projects did not address in detail the business change aspects of the solution.

## The challenge of assessing organizational competencies

The changing business environment coupled with a drive for getting benefits from IS/IT investments has generated a new challenge for IS/IT planning - the challenge of assessing future organizational competencies. An innovating organizations superior understanding of the technological and business aspects increases the likelihood that it will introduce competitively significant enhancements and thus sustain its advantage, despite innovation by rivals. This is becoming a key challenge in terms of IS planning, especially because of the prevalent disconnect between the business strategies and IT strategies. In the literature this disconnect has been related to the lack of organizational competence [5]; [24]. The inherent argument is that IT applications have the potential to lower costs or create differentiation across a wide array of activities that constitute firms value chain. When applications create a differential advantage, they affect the structural characteristics of the industry and become important to successful strategy and organizational performance [10].

Competence to exploit an IT opportunity is influenced by the prevailing management culture, experience, and satisfaction with IT. Beyond technological feasibility and customer demand, there must be an organizational infrastructure capable of developing and moving innovations to market quickly. The impetus to develop the IT application does not come through mere existence of firms technological strengths. Organizations at the same time need skills that can react effectively to changes in the business environment. An understanding of the potential strategic impact of IT and integration with business processes may lead to greater IT utilization, and hence the sustainability of competitive advantage. In essence a large number of factors can jointly shape an organizations propensity to utilize IT in its quest for sustainable competitive advantage. Among these, evolving business conditions, technical competence, consistent exploitation of opportunities can be regarded as the key components.

## REFERENCES

1. Basu, V., *et al.*, *The impact of organizational commitment, senior management involvement, and team involvement on strategic information systems planning.* Information & Management, 2002. **39**: p. 513–524.

2. Benjamin, R.I. and E. Levinson, *A framework for managing IT-enabled change.* Sloan Management Review, 1993(Summer): p. 23-33.

3. Ciborra, C., *The grass roots of IT and strategy*, in *Strategic information systems. A European perspective*, C. Ciborra and T. Jelassi, Editors. 1994, Wiley: Chichester. p. 3-24.

4. Clemons, E.K. and B.W. Weber, *Information technology and the changing nature of the financial services industry*, in *Collaborative work, social communications and information systems*, R.K. Stamper, *et al.*, Editors. 1991, Elsevier Science Publishers: Amsterdam. p. 93-116.

5. Dhillon, G. and R. Lambert. *Organisational competence for harnessing IT: the case of a major business transformation to leverage expertise.* in *First UK Academy for Information Systems Conference.* 1996. Cranfield School of Management, Cranfield, Bedford, April 10-12.

6. Dhillon, G. and J.D. Orton, *Schizoid Incoherence, Microstrategic Options, and the Strategic Management of New Organizational Forms.* M@n@gement, 2001. **4**(4): p. 229-240.

7. Earl, M., *Information systems strategy ...why planning*

*techniques are not the answer.* Business Strategy Review, 1996. **7**(1): p. 54-67.

8. Earl, M.J., *IT and strategic advantage - a framework of frameworks*, in *Information Management - the strategic dimension*, M.J. EARL, Editor. 1989, Oxford University Press: Oxford. p. 33-53.

9. Earl, M.J., *Experiences in strategic information systems planning.* MIS Quarterly, 1993(March): p. 1-24.

10. Floyd, S.W. and B. Woolridge, *Competitive strategy, IT and performance.* Journal of management information systems, 1990. **7**(1): p. 27-44.

11. Flynn, D.J. and E. Goleniewska, *A survey of the use of strategic information systems planning approaches in UK organisations.* Journal of Strategic Information Systems, 1993. **2**(4): p. 292-319.

12. Gluck, F.W., S.P. Kaufmann, and A.S. Walleck, *Strategic management for competitive advantage.* Harvard Business Review, 1980(July/August).

13. Gottschalk, P., *Implementation predictors of strategic information systems plans.* Information & Management, 1999. **36**: p. 77-91.

14. Hamel, G., *Strategy as revolution.* Harvard Business Review, 1996(July-August): p. 69-82.

15. Henderson, J. and J.G. Sifonis. *Middle out strategic planning: the value of IS planning to business planning.* in *The 1986 NYU Symposium on Strategic Uses of Information Technology, New York.* 1986. NYU.

16. Henderson, J.C. and N. Venkatraman, *Strategic alignment: leveraging information technology for transforming organisations.* IBM Systems Journal, 1993. **32**(1): p. 4-16.

17. Johnston, H.R. and S.R. Carrico, *Developing capabilities to use information strategically.* MIS Quarterly, 1988. **12**(1): p. 37-48.

18. Johnston, K. and P. Yetton, *Integrating IT divisions in a bank merger: fit, compatibility and models of change.* Journal of Strategic Information Systems, 1996. **5**: p. 189-211.

19. Lederer, A.L. and H. Salmela, *Toward a theory of strategic*

*information systems planning.* Journal of Strategic Information Systems, 1996. **5**(3): p. 237-253.

20. Lederer, A.L. and V. Sethi, *The implementation of strategic information systems planning methodologies.* MIS Quarterly, 1988. **12**(3): p. 445-461.

21. Martinez, E.V., *Successful reengineering demands IS/Business partnerships.* Sloan Management Review, 1995(Summer): p. 51-60.

22. McFarlan, F.W., *Information Technology changes the way you compete.* Harvard Business Review, 1984(May/June).

23. McGolpin, P., *An examination of the inter-related factors and issues affecting the degree of success with strategic information systems: throughout the application lifecycle*, .PhD Thesis 1996, Cranfield University School of Management: Cranfield, Bedford, UK.

24. McGrath, R.G., I.C. MacMillan, and S. Venkataraman, *Defining and developing competence: a strategic process paradigm.* Strategic Management Journal, 1995. **16**(4): p. 251-275.

25. Porter, M., *Competitive strategy.* 1980, New York: Free Press.

26. Porter, M. and V. Millar, *How information gives you competitive advantage.* Harvard Business Review, 1985. **63**(4): p. 149-161.

27. Salmela, H. and T.A.M. Spilb, *Dynamic and emergent information systems strategy formulation and implementation.* International Journal of Information Management, 2002. **22**: p. 441–460.

28. Sullivan, C.H., *Systems planning in the information age.* Sloan Management Review, 1985(Winter).

29. Vitale, M.R., *The growing risks of information systems success.* MIS Quarterly, 1986(December): p. 327-334.

30. Ward, J. and P. Griffiths, *Strategic planning for information systems.* 1996, Chichester: Wiley.

## DISCUSSION QUESTIONS

1. You have taken over as CIO of a large engineering and construction firm with contracts for building oil rigs in the North Sea, building a new airport in South East Asia and working with the US Department of

Defense on making substantial enhancements to buildings at a major US Air Force Base. The skill requirements for all the projects are diverse and requirements for safety, security and reliability considerably high. Although your company was successful in procuring the various contracts, sustainability of a leading edge industry position and containing the cost of operations are worries shared by most in the senior management. How do you think the company can (a) identify the right kind of skills necessary for being competitive and (b) how can the company harness the potential of IT to build a highly competent firm?

2. You are a founding member of a new firm providing educational, training and consulting services in the general area of Six Sigma. The operations are highly dependent on computer based learning and self directed study. Given that the firm is relatively new and various organizational processes are still being defined, how can you (a) ensure that the right kind of competencies are developed (b) the relevant IT competencies are sustained over a period of time?

3. Identify the implementation of any IT project is a firm and suggest how the company was able to (or not able to) balance the range of strategic and efficiency benefits.

4. Identify a firm in an information intensive industry. Comment on the range of competencies this firm possesses to harness IT to its advantage. Given our discussion in this chapter suggest how the chosen firm has been able to achieve success or failed in the process.

# 4. INFORMATION SYSTEMS PROJECT MANAGEMENT

A Standish Group report found that a staggering 31.1 percent of IT projects were canceled even before they were completed. Other reports have attributed the reason simply to poor project management (http://www.standishgroup.com/visitor/). According to project management analysts, forty percent of all IT projects fail, costing U.S. business approximately $100 billion annually. Thirty-three percent of remaining projects are challenged by cost and time overruns or changes in scope.

**Information Systems Project Management in Action**

Alaska is the largest of the 50 U.S. states. Because of this, many residents have had to travel hundreds of miles to one of only 44 state DMV offices for such things as license and tag renewals. Historically, the reward for such a long journey was a long wait in line followed by an equally long journey back home. In 1996, the wait in line at the Anchorage DMV office was measured at two and a half hours. Not only were the automobile owners tired of this system, but the process also caused the DMV employees to become demoralized over time. Because of the long wait in line, some customers were understandably characterized as "difficult." It got to the point where DMV employees had to receive counseling on dealing with difficult customers and violence in the workplace. The system's problems were not restricted to unhappy DMV customers and employees. There was also a significant cost to the old system that had to be covered by the Alaska taxpayers.

Faced with the task of addressing time, distance, and costs, a successful IT project was managed and put into place. The net result of the project was payback of the $300,000 project cost in four months, reduction in transaction cost from $7.75 to $0.91, potential reduction of transaction time from two and a half hours to under three minutes, elimination of the need for customers to visit DMV offices, and improved customer and employee satisfaction.

The first thing that went right was that the objectives and the scope of the project were correctly characterized prior to the start of the project. Boyer was able to identify the fundamental problems with the current system and was then able to systematically apply a strategy for each. For example, Boyer was aware of the geographical distribution of customers to the DMV. Because of this, he was able to allow Internet and telephone technology to bridge the gap between the DMV offices and the customer's homes. Also, since cost and time reduction was critical, Boyer realized that automation of certain processes would be necessary. With regard to project scope, it is important to note that Boyer used a stepwise approach. He defined the scope of the first step as basically a new way to pay for car registration. Once this step had been implemented, he shifted focus to other improvement opportunity areas.

The next thing that was managed properly within the process was clear and steady focus on the customers needs. Boyer could have managed the project from the perspective of having a computer problem. Instead, he managed the project from the perspective of having a customer service problem. At the end of the day, projects can be assessed on the basis of costs. In this case, the end-result on a cost basis would certainly be favorable. However, this is only part of the story. There are still the issues of time reduction and customer satisfaction. In this case, Boyer was able to maintain focus and direction on customer satisfaction by managing the project as a customer service problem rather than a computer problem.

Another thing that went right with the project was that Boyer was able to leverage the DMV's current core technology by utilizing new electronic venues. The manager of such a project could have made an assessment of the situation and then planned to throw out the existing mainframe system and reengineer the entire DMV. Had this strategy been implemented, there may have been another "Black Tuesday" similar to that which happened with the Nevada state DMV on September 7, 1999. There is a saying that goes, "if it is not broken, don't fix it." Boyer correctly identified the problem as a customer service problem, not a computer problem. He was ultimately successful in the project because he decided that it would be better to upgrade the existing system rather than build an entirely new application. In a sense, Boyer's success stemmed from the initial direction that he chose as a solution to the problem. He recognized that eliminating the need for people to have to visit the DMV was fundamentally important to reducing the line sizes and wait time. He was able to utilize existing technology (telephone and Internet) with the DMV's existing computer system.

Acknowledgements – Marc Rose.

---

Good project managers are in high demand because they play a critical role in the development and delivery of quality information systems. The topic of project management was traditionally covered under the discipline of production and operations management. In recent years, disciplines such as management information systems have recognized the importance of project management skills for information technology professionals. College curricula have been revised to incorporate courses that deal with project management principles. This set of skills is necessary for a team leader who is responsible for channeling collective team activities to produce an effective system in a timely manner.

As mentioned, the concept of project management has been around for some time and it has been a part of curricula for other disciplines. However, management of information technology projects requires additional knowledge and abilities that are expected of information system professionals. Rapid technology changes and enhancements require continuous self-training and self-learning. This rapid change also means that a project description and its features may change before the completion date not to mention the user expectations of the project outcome. All this requires the IT project manager to have a clear understanding of what information is, how it is generated, how it is used, how it is maintained, and how it is integrated with different functions of an organization.

Often end-users become a part of developmental activities in addition to the project team members who have specific responsibilities. It is important to understand this dynamic aspect of IT project management relative to the traditional project management function. An effective IT project manager must posses qualities and skills that relate to the management of Information systems functions as well as principles and concepts that relate to managing a project.

## PROJECT MANAGEMENT IN MODERN ORGANIZATION

Information technology has empowered workers by enabling them to be more productive and by giving them greater control and management of their tasks. This means organizations increasingly reevaluate job descriptions and add management responsibility to what traditionally was considered end-user level work. As a result, separate and distinct tasks in the traditional work environment are now integrated and managed by the same person through the use of information technology tools. This trend gradually reduced the need for middle level managers who were primarily responsible for work planning as well as horizontal and vertical communication with other middle level managers, subordinates, and superiors. These middle level managers also made sure that the left hand knew what the right hand was doing and thus avoided overlap, confusion, and work flow control.

As technology reshaped the role and definition of the work unit, it made ordinary tasks more abstract and in need of instant coordination with other tasks that were unfeasible to accomplish without technological help. In other words, technology has played a role in its own creation. Increasingly, jobs have become more abstract and involve sense making with an increased number of variables influencing decision outcome. This has created the need for more specialized careers that did not exist before. These new careers involve the need for greater technology application in the context of business mission, goals, and objectives. Integration of technology across functions and organizations has increasingly become a norm. In a way technology has influenced career options in different ways. On the one hand, it has increased the responsibility, influence, and complexity of most jobs and on the other hand has created opportunities for those with the know how to effectively use and manage it.

The growth of information technology and its increased application created the challenge of keeping up with system development needs. Delays and over-budget information system projects became the norm rather than the exception. A two-year backlog for a system development was considered normal in many organizations. Rapid development tools appeared to help timely response to system development needs. Technology was used to help technology application. The traditional system development process involved a dichotomous relationship between developers and system analysts on the one hand and end-users on the other. With the recognition of the user involvement phenomenon in system development activities, end-users played an increasingly critical role.

With the increased need for integrated systems that closely aligned with organizational goals and objectives and addressed the end-user expectations came the job of information system project management. While project management principles and techniques have been used in other disciplines such as operations management and the construction industry, its application for the development of information system is new and rapidly growing. Project management has become one of the most sought after positions in service as well as manufacturing industries in private as well as public organizations. The traditional job of information system analyst was gradually redefined to go beyond the responsibilities of requirement analysis, design, development, and implementation. Project management has gradually replaced the traditional middle management position. By its nature, the job of information system project management combines a set of responsibilities that span from understanding the technology to managing human resources to addressing organizational needs. It primarily involves managing all aspects of an information system development project from the beginning to the end and delivering it as specified on time and within budget. Therefore, critical project management dimensions relate to project scope, time, and budget.

## Project management portfolio

The rapid growth of information technology and the need for application development have caused many organizations to adapt, often by default, a short-term operational level response strategy. In the fusion of learning and managing new technologies (what type of technologies are available, how they help management and decision makers with pressing issues of cost and efficiency, and what is the best way to develop and implement applications) many organizations focused more on the logistical and operational aspects of technology transfer rather than its alignment with the organizational goals and objectives. This growth inertia that pushed developmental activities in response to immediate needs meant less planning and more action, less strategic alignment and more implementation, and less system development portfolio approach and more operational response activities.

This trend meant more technology transfer but at the level of task and unit rather than the organization. Ideas for new application development would often be initiated by individuals with technical skills who knew how the technology worked and how it could help solve problems at hand. These individuals were not necessarily able to assess the technology impact at the organizational level. In other words, initiators and planners were too close to the action, seeing the trees rather than the forest. This does not mean that individual applications did not help or they did not accomplish their purpose. In fact, they helped experimentation with technology fit, end-user training, and know how at the functional level. The effort to align systems selection and developmental activities with the overall organizational goal and objectives was lacking.

Some time later when demand and request for resources to develop and implement new technologies became a significant budget item, some high-ranking executive would pose a simple but important question - *what does all this technology investment mean to our bottom line?* That is a difficult question to answer and has appropriately turned into a long stream of research in this field. This question is important because information technology impacts all levels of management decision making and all types of activities, and therefore must be evaluated with an encompassing approach.

Traditionally, information system executives evaluated system success through the evaluation of system features such as convenience or ease of use, accuracy, integrity, speed, and format. This approach is appropriate for identifying strengths and weaknesses of an application and to that extent is useful to system development activities. However, it narrowly defines success and ignores broader issues of impact. Information system executives are increasingly required to explain and justify technology expenditure from a broader perspective that includes impact on work, the customer, and the organization. As a result, the evaluation of system success has over the recent years been expanded to include system use, task productivity, task innovation, management control, and the like.

Increasingly, organizations have developed technology selection and implementation processes using priorities that ensure congruity and alignment with organizational strategy. The strategic goals of most organizations are tightly linked with customer needs and customer satisfaction. Simple but important questions help set the course for identifying, selecting, and developing information systems that will satisfy the expectations of modern organizations:

- Who is initiating the project?
- Who is sponsoring the project?
- How does the project support the mission of the organization?
- What is the relative position of a project on the priority list of the organization?
- How does the project contribute value to the strategic goals of the organization?
- How does the project help meet current and future needs of the customer?

Responses to these questions help the information system project manager evaluate the contribution of a project to the organization. Questions concerning whether the project is doable or whether there are sufficient resources to accomplish project goals are all valid. First, the issue of strategic alignment must be addressed.

## What makes an effective IT project manager?

The skill set for a successful project manager includes a broad list of attitudinal and behavioral as well as individual and organizational traits. The following list describes important skills that make an individual an effective information system project manager.

- ***Communication***. This includes verbal as well as written communication. This is an important factor for managers who aspire to become top level executives in their organization. Often opportunities to reach top management level are lost because of communication skills that are less-than-adequate even for those who are otherwise highly qualified professionals. Effective communication with superiors, subordinates, and team members is critical for information technology project managers. Verbal communication is important where you need to make an immediate impression such as when you are presenting or defending a project proposal in front of a steering committee that can authorize funding support. In such cases, it is important to maintain focus, be clear, and be responsive. Written communication is particularly important where opportunities to expand or amplify through verbal communication do not exist such as when you need to report results of a project that will be distributed among several departments or divisions. In such cases, it is important to think of the target readers, keep the flow, be concise and to the point, and make it interesting. When writing a report, make sure it has a beginning where you describe why you did what you did, it has a middle section where you describe what you did and what you found, and it has an end where you describe why your findings are useful.

- ***Human interaction***. The project management task involves working with others. And the success of any project depends on how the team members work together and how they work with the project manager. The project manager is responsible not only for her/his interaction with team members but also for the interactions between members. An effective project manager understands the importance of being fair, consistent, supportive, and impartial in interacting with team members. An effective project manager not only adheres to these principles but also acts as a role model for her/his team members. Further, an effective project manager believes in standards that promote quality and in turn instill self-respect among team members. High standards and respectable quality will show and will have a positive affect on team members.

- **Creativity**. An effective project manager is knowledgeable about information technologies and their applications. It is one thing to use a tool for problems that others have used it for. It is something else to come up with a totally new way to use a tool. There are a variety of tools to help project managers in planning, communicating, controlling, scheduling, and implementing projects. With the development of more user-friendly software packages in recent years, the usefulness of these tools has increased. Often these software tools can be modified to address a unique situation and that is where the creativity of a project manager will come into play. Furthermore, there are situations where a project manager will not be able to use a standard tool or a standard procedure to address a unique problem. In such cases, the project manager must be creative and come up with a solution that is realistic, attainable within time and within resources, can be sold to team members, and above all it is effective.
- **Persistence**. The application of project management tools and concepts for information technology development is new. We used to do things differently and many people feel more comfortable with the way things used to be done. That is natural. However, as organizations modernize and more and more complex information systems are installed, our approach to the development and management of these large and integrated systems must be improved accordingly. Reluctance to change causes difficulties in managing a project. Difficulties by themselves should not deter a project manager from altering the course of project development. An effective project manager will persist and continue to guide and support team members in accomplishing what has been planned. This does not mean that whatever has already been planned should be rigidly followed without any revision. It simply means the project team must give its best effort to any plan or idea and requires persistence on the part of the project manager. The project manager also must show persistence in dealing with top management to obtain support and recognition for the project and its team members.

- ***Observation***. This is one skill that is difficult to learn from a book, but could be developed through practice. You probably know someone who will walk into a room and immediately notice what is changed or what needs to be fixed. On the other hand you may know someone who rarely notices what is changed around them. Similarly, some project managers notice immediately what is not right or what needs to be changed in a proposal or an idea. It is possible to study and learn key principles that any typical project should include and it is possible that a typical project will have a completely unique feature. The power of timely observation may save a great deal of hassle and inconvenience in the long term not to mention the possibility of saving resources. Observing the interaction among team members is also important. An effective project manager observes the subtle interaction between team members and intervenes appropriately when necessary to avoid long term personnel problems.
- ***Organization***. An effective project manager works in an organized manner and communicates that to her or his team members. Being organized enables the project manager to have easy and quick access to documents and resources that team members may need to consult on a short notice. In other words, an effective project manager is systematic about procedures and requirements. We all have friends, colleagues, or co-workers who tend to be very organized in their work activities. When you work and interact with these people, you tend to rely on them having things in a proper order. This makes you more relaxed when you know you may need to refer to a particular source, say the procedure to get something done. Try to put yourself in the position of a team member who has to work on specific tasks and deliver certain results. You like to do what you are supposed to do and not be worried about whether things you need will be there in time and in the right form. An organized project manager will give you that confidence and you know you can relay on your project manager. Consider yourself working with a project manager who is notoriously unorganized and unreliable and think about how that may influence your efficiency or effectiveness.
- **Outcome oriented**. Ultimately, what counts for those who

authorize a project and support it is the result and outcome of a project. And, to that extent the project manager must consider that important fact at all stages of project development life cycle. Outcome relates directly to the intent and expressed goals of the project. This perspective helps the project manager to provide more flexibility to team members. As long as team members deliver what is expected of them in a timely manner according to the plan it does not really matter how often they meet or whether they meet first thing in the morning or if they work late into the night. Some people tend to be more productive early in the day and some tend to work late into the night. What is important is that the team will work out a work schedule that is agreed on by all and produces the desired results. Through the power of observation that was described earlier, an effective project manager will develop a sense of how different individuals interact with each other. Even individuals with apparent opposing work habits can come up with a plan that enables them to accomplish their task. Many high tech organizations provide flexible work schedules in order to benefit from varied work habits.

- ***Distraction***. Most professional jobs such as information system project management deal with tight resources and deadlines; they need a pass-time that gives them the opportunity to get away from the day-to-day work activities and do something different. This is true even for people who like their work and enjoy working with their colleagues and co-workers. Your pass-time creates an equilibrium in your work-life. Life cannot be all work and no fun and it cannot be all fun and no work. We all need to produce expected results and productivity is not always a function of time input. You probably know of people who spend less time on tasks like studying and get good results. You also know of people who seem to be spending a great deal of time on a task but get little results. Part of that you may argue relates to work habit or competency. But that does not explain it entirely. What they do beside work and how they spend their non-working time also influences the productivity and efficiency of individuals. Remember you must enjoy your pass-time or hobby. If you play gulf just to network then that won't necessarily help you relax. A hobby takes a long time to become habitual and anything that you force yourself into doing is not a hobby.

## Writing an effective project report

Report writing is a form of documentation and, as you will learn in other courses such as systems analysis and design, documentation is very important. It is important because:

- it is an effective means of communication,
- it is an effective means of protection,
- it helps you carefully think through what you have done for the project,
- it is a means of getting credit for what you have done,
- it is a means of closure, and
- it is a source of reference.

A typical report will have several parts that more or less correspond with the following:

- Title
- Executive summary or abstract
- Introduction
- Background or literature
- Methods
- Analyses and results
- Discussion and conclusion
- Bibliography

***Title-*** The title should simply and clearly represent what is in the report. Try to make the title in less than ten words. To do that, one practice is to write down every word related to the topic and the project content. Then select a minimum number of words from your list that represents the essence of your report. The title must be accurate, it must capture the true essence of your report, and it should be easy to understand. Another important thing about the title is that it should be easy to remember.

***Executive summary or abstract-*** This section describes your report in a nutshell. It should not be too long, and in fact it can often be one paragraph. This section must briefly describe what you have done and what you have found. *Point out why your findings are useful and important in the context of your field or your work.* In this respect describe opportunities for follow-up studies built on your findings. Make your abstract or executive summary attractive for the reader to continue. Remember, busy people often only read this section so take advantage.

***Introduction***- In this section you need to accomplish only a few but very important points. You need to establish that the topic is important for your work or for your field and it needs to be addressed. Describe what has been done by others in this area and what you have discovered that has already been done. Then describe what has not yet been done and needs to be done in this area. This will lead into the next segment that describes what your project is about and how it fits into earlier works. Finally, tell your reader what to expect in your report. Make your introduction short and to the point. You may write one paragraph for each point and make your introduction within two pages.

***Background***- Depending on the type of project that you have done you may need to give a thorough review of the literature on the topic. Describe your study in the context of other works in that area and explain how cumulative work helped to prepare you for the current project. Identify the gap that exists in the current understanding for that topic. This should lead you into describing the rationale for the current project and the way it has been designed. *Make sure you do not promise what you cannot deliver.* Often readers will remember your promises and will judge your final results against the frame of reference developed reading your promises. In a way, you are shaping their expectations early on as you describe what has been done in that area and what needs to be done.

***Methods***- Describe as fully and clearly as you can the methodology that was used in the study. Present your methods in a logical sequence and think about how appropriate they are in the context of your work. Do not try to impress the readers with fancy methods. If the readers do not understand your methods they most likely will not buy them. Provide evidence that other similar works successfully used the same methods.

***Analysis and results-*** Describe your analysis first and then describe your results for each analysis. Sequence your results for a cumulative effect.

Use tables and figures and make sure you refer to them in your text. Make these tables and figures self-explanatory by providing headings and labels. Avoid referring your readers back and forth between tables or figures and the text. When presenting results be factual and minimize opinions on results. You can provide your opinions and interpretations under discussions.

***Discussions and conclusions-*** This is the section where you outline the contributions of your work. You can also interpret results as you see them and in the context of other findings. You want to make sure you do not talk down to your readers by telling them the obvious. People don't like to be told things they are supposed to know even if they don't know them. If your results do not support what others have found, then try to *explain your reasons for the discrepancy*. Describe opportunities for follow-up studies that could be based on your findings. Point out *limitations* of your study, particularly those that may relate to methodology, sample size, respondents, measurement, and so on.

***Bibliography-*** This is where you refer to all your information sources. It is important that you use a standard format such as the one used by the *American Psychological Association.* Using a recognized format will help consistency and ease of reference. Make sure the information about each reference is complete. Highlight the source such as book or journal; use italic, bold, or underline. Include only the references that you have used for your report. For multiple author references, give the full names of all authors.

## PLANNING AND CONTROL

The most important responsibilities of project management are ***planning***, ***executing***, and ***controlling***. A project plan maps out what is to be executed and controls are implemented to ensure proper and timely execution. Therefore, planning can be considered an activity that outlines objectives, policies, and procedures for a project. Planning enables the project manager to see the whole system, subsystems, key factors, and alternative approaches for accomplishing the task. In developing the project plan the intent should be to reduce uncertainty, increase operational efficiency, understand objectives, and set controls to monitor progress. The project manager must be involved with the planning phase from the beginning and get input from multiple functions that are affected by the project. In preparation for the planning process, it is important to think about fundamental questions such as:

- Environmental and organizational climate
- Top management attitude toward technology in general
- Current status of technology use and capability
- Potential resource barriers
- Potential personnel issues
- Existing strategic alliance with vendors
- End-user computer self-efficacy

In thinking about these questions, project managers will be able to evaluate where they are (current status), where they need to go (future place), and how they might get there (strategies). This is a pre-planning activity that paves the way for the development of a successful planning process. Specific components of planning activities are:

- *Goals and objectives*. What are the deliverables for each phase as well as the entire project?
- *Duration*. When does the project start and how long would it take to complete each phase or the entire project?
- *Budget*. What is the total cost to complete the project and accomplish objectives within the expected time limit?
- *Approach*. What are the principle methods, strategies, and actions that are expected to lead to a timely and successful completion of the project?
- *Milestones*. What are milestones and events that can be used to evaluate progress by a certain time?
- *Modules*. What are the principle components of the project that can be developed in parallel and with relative independence?
- *Authorization*. What are policies and procedures for releasing funds and authorizing expenditures?
- *Responsibility*. What are the duties and responsibilities of team leaders and key players and what is their authority?

- *Deliverables*. What are the minimum and acceptable deliverables and how is the quality of outcome assessed?
- *Control*. What are control mechanisms for schedule, budget, performance, and quality?
- *Contingencies*. What are contingency plans for shortfalls in personnel, resources, support, and the like?

Factors like budget, duration, and milestones are based on estimates. Contingency plans will be necessary because of these estimates and other events that are difficult to forecast. Some of these factors may be more critical to larger information system projects and some may be unnecessary for small projects. For example, modules and milestones are helpful for large projects that involve extensive resources and take long time to complete. Some of these factors are necessary regardless of project size. For example, all projects must have goals and objectives, deliverables, budget, and projected duration. Some projects may require greater control. For example, projects with strict deadlines or budgets or projects that must be completed in time so that they do not delay follow-up projects.

Plans are often long-term, forward-looking, and comprehensive and therefore must be unambiguous because they are used for vertical as well as horizontal communication and referred to as guiding documents. Because of its forward-looking nature, planning provides project managers with opportunities to be proactive when mapping alternatives. Because of its long-term perspective and its comprehensive focus, planning must go beyond departmental and operational issues and consider the strategic and organizational impacts of a new system.

Large projects may be broken down to smaller projects or subsystems. Project managers must be able to delegate authority to those key individuals responsible for subsystems. That means key individuals must be carefully selected and must have competency in technical as well as administrative areas. Once selected, it is important that these key players are involved with the planning process, are sufficiently supported, and understand that they are responsible for the outcome and success of their task. Therefore, planning becomes a part of the skill set for these key individuals; project managers must ensure that these individuals either have the planning experience or can be trained to make necessary contributions. Involvement with planning activities helps these key players understand and appreciate resource constraints, estimates and assumptions behind them, subsystem boundaries, the impact of deadlines on other subsystems, and stakeholder expectations. Involvement in the planning process also helps reinforce the authority and responsibility of these key individuals with project team members who directly work with them.

## Scope management

It is critical for the stakeholders and the project team to have a common understanding of the scope and boundaries of a project. Thus it is important for the project manager to clearly define the boundaries and describe what is and is not included as part of the project. The project processes and control mechanisms are also defined as part of the scope management. Many projects fail because they lack proper definition of what the project entails which in turn influences how expectations are formed. The project scope management is a part of planning activity within an organization and helps integration of the new project within the organization. These plans help identify objectives and the requirement for achieving those objectives. The scope management plan is used throughout the project development life cycle in identifying the risk management plan, in defining internal and external commitments, in time management, in project evaluation and acceptance, in procurement, in change management, in execution and control, and finally in archive and use for follow-up studies. Because of its broad impact, the project scope management is considered as a high-level big picture planning activity that includes components and subsections. Like other strategic and planning activities, project scope management looks at the long-term objectives and must be in sink with and supportive of organizational missions and objectives. A good project scope management plan will have the following characteristics:

- Defines project boundaries.
- Provides logical break down of the project.
- Provides organizational context for the project.
- Defines long-term objectives.
- Supports mission and objectives of the organization.
- Provides justification for the project.
- Describes the expected outcome.
- Defines success factors.

- Helps estimate resources.
- Helps determine completion date.
- Helps execution and controls.
- Helps define responsibility
- Helps measure performance.
- Can be used as a road map for the entire project.

Defining responsibilities is critical in evaluating performance. Project scope management, through modular break down of the entire project, helps provide a road map for defining responsibilities. It can also be used for horizontal and vertical communication as well as work planning. At milestones in the project development life cycle, when the project manager and the team members revisit with stakeholders to describe progress, the project scope management plan can be used as a reference document. User involvement and participation at the design phase of information system development is often cited as one of the most important success factors. User input and involvement is important as it influences user perception and attitudes toward the new system. The project manager must define the extent and type of this involvement and facilitate an appropriate level of interaction between team members and key users of the system. The project scope management and its plan components help the project manager determine this user input.

## Risk management

To a varying degree, all information system projects include risks because they involve individual and organizational commitment, internal and external resources, skilled personnel, management support, vendor commitment, and so on. An effective project manager must be able to understand and assess risks associated with an information system project. These risks may be problems, events, and occurrences that cause delay or prevent project completion. All risks must be identified even if some may be assumed away because the consequences are negligible.

Once the risks are identified, the project manager needs to determine the consequence for each risk as well as the probability of each happening. The project manager must carefully assess all risks and establish a contingency plan for each, especially for risks with serious consequences and high probability of occurrence. The IT project manager may use a variety of means for assessing risks and their probabilities including interviews with experts, use of PERT/CPM for estimation, previous case documentation, and computer simulations. Project risk management results in a security plan or insurance that provides confidence in the timely completion of the project.

To be effective, the IT project risk management must focus on three critical aspects of a project - project ***scope***, ***time***, and ***budget***. In other words, risks and their consequences must be evaluated in terms of their impact on the outcome of the project. Risks that are likely to change the project scope, cause serious delay, or result in undue budget overrun that hamper project success. Project risk management helps establish realistic estimates of time, budget, and support for current as well as future projects. Risks usually correspond with opportunities. That means there is a trade-off, the greater the payoff the higher the risk. The idea is not to eliminate the risk because often that is not feasible. The idea is to realize that there are risks involved with project development, understand and assess these risks, and take steps to be responsive.

Project managers who tend to totally avoid risks cannot expect to deliver high payoffs. On the other hand, project managers who tend to invite unnecessary risks or to ignore potential risks are also likely to be disappointed. The best approach is a balanced one that realistically examines opportunities and risks associated with a given information system project and develops contingency plans in anticipation. An effective project manager works to optimize opportunities and payoffs of a given project while minimizing risks associated with that project. To expect a totally risk free situation is often unrealistic and may result in procrastination and indecisiveness.

In order to have a comprehensive evaluation plan, information technology project risks can be classified as ***internal*** or ***external***, ***tangible*** or ***intangible***, and ***technical*** or ***behavioral***. Internal risks may include declining support from top management for the project or organizational restructuring. External risks involve vendor commitment or changing governmental standards. Tangible risks include budget and resource related issues while intangible risks may be human issues such as morale and dissatisfaction. Technical risks may include infrastructure or outdated equipment. Non-technical or behavioral risks include personnel issues such as motivation, security, integrity, attitude toward quality, and so on. Often three levels of low, medium, and high are used in evaluating risks. These three levels are also used to assign the probability or the likelihood of a risk event occurring. The results can be summarized in a table as below:

*Table 4.1, Risk profiles*

| **Potential risks** | **Potential consequence** | **Probability of happening** |
|---|---|---|
| Risk # 1 | High | Low |
| Risk # 2 | Medium | Low |
| Risk # 3 | Low | High |
| Risk # 4 | Medium | Medium |

The number of times a particular risk appears on reports and documents of earlier projects is an indication that it might happen. Some project managers keep a list of top ten most likely risks that they have developed over the years based on their own projects as well as those of others. This is similar to having a list of top ten most likely things that could go wrong, and if you believe in Murphy's Law that says what can go wrong will go wrong you will prepare a project risk management plan. However, project risk management is time consuming and is serious mental work. Depending on how a project progresses, a risk plan may or may not be put to the test. A project risk management plan can always be used for future projects even if it is not implemented in practice.

## Procurement and outsourcing

Most information system developments involve some kind of contract with external providers or vendors for the procurement of product and services. Some of these vendors have been working with the organization and the information systems team for a long time and many of the contractual issues are as a result established. However, rapid change in information technology capability and cost requires a fresh look at contractual issues for every new project. Important issues other than the cost of new technologies relate to vendor reliability and product quality. Procurement for a new information system project must be consistent with the organizational policy that is often meant to take advantage of volume discounts, reduce cash flow problems, centralize the purchasing process, and standardized procedure.

In order to achieve these goals, corporate procurement strategy often limits the number of suppliers for a given service or product. Procurement strategy for an information system project may deviate from that of the corporate strategy in exceptional cases when requirements are unique, supply is limited, or time is a constraint. Procurement strategies for information system projects must take a long-term perspective and develop mutually beneficial relationships with reliable vendors who provide quality product and services on time even if they are not the most financially feasible options. It is more cost effective in the long-term if product quality meets the standard and is delivered in time to help the entire project be completed on schedule. Therefore, important questions in information system project procurement are of two types: first, what to purchase, how much to purchase, when to purchase and second, how to purchase, how to select vendors, how to write contracts, and so on.

Information systems development projects often involve the decision to either develop the system in-house or outsource. A combination of these two is also possible when off-the-shelf software is bought and modified in-house to fit the team's needs. However, this latter option is not applicable for specific needs. Given the competitive business environment and rapid technological change, many firms opt to outsource all or part of their information system services including new information system projects. Outsourcing presents an opportunity to formulate faster responses to market change and competitive forces. The outsourcing vendor often posses a wider range of information systems know how and equipment that enable them to stay abreast with new developments. The outsourcing vendor is often used to replace inadequate and obsolete hardware and software at a faster pace than internally possible. Information system outsourcing is considered by organizations for several reasons:

- To provide a faster response to market and technology change
- To more efficiently replace problematic and obsolete software and hardware
- To concentrate on business strategies that cannot be

outsourced

- To focus end-user attention on core business issues
- To take advantage of a wider range of know how in information technology
- To control cost overruns
- To address a shortage of skilled information system professionals
- To reduce facility, asset, and other fixed costs (convert fixed cost to variable cost)
- To respond to the politics of information control and power issues

Some of these reasons are quite significant and could influence decision outcome more than others. For example, reducing cost may be critical for an organization that is faced with cash flow problems. Personnel issues and skilled information system professionals is another important factor that may influence cost decisions. Assessing the impact on some of the issues such as internal politics of information control and power may be difficult. As with any business decision, there are tradeoffs associated with information system outsourcing:

- Loss of internal information system expertise and experience
- Loss of internal control over information system services
- Lack of end-user experience in working with external providers
- Dependence on vendor expertise and experience
- Dependence on vendor commitment
- Risk of vendor insolvency
- Possibility of problem vendor after contract is signed
- Information system security risks
- Vendor limitations in providing non-standard applications, services, and support

Again, impacts of these issues vary depending on the individual decision situation. For example, loss of control over information system services or security issues is more critical for a financial firm or a pharmaceutical company than is required to maintain patient privacy. Reversal of outsourcing is often difficult especially when internal expertise is diminished and end-user attitude toward information system services is altered. Critical knowledge of current systems operation and the historical context of operating procedures may be lost when internal information system staff is replaced. End-users who rely on the expertise of internal information system staff may go through significant adjustment to work with the management of an outsourcing vendor. This could be a concern in the case of a large end-user population. Therefore, if a vendor is improperly selected it could result in higher information system risks and ultimately higher costs.

Probably the most critical concerns about the outsourcing of the information system are the wider issues of strategic control over information product and the security of proprietary information. This concern is greater when the users believe vendors are promising features they cannot deliver, or when the outsourcing vendor becomes non-responsive to user requests, exceeds agreed upon costs, fails to deliver systems on time, or delivers systems of poor quality and reliability. If the outsourcing is not properly planned, the firm may lose control over the vendor and as a result lose sight of the broader business issues that information system outsourcing was supposed to address. It may fail to achieve their financial objectives as well as compromise information security. This suggests the importance of a strategic partnership between the firm and its vendor for information system product and services. A true partnership between the two organizations will go a long way in addressing many of the difficulties that potentially can arise from the outsourcing decision.

## Cost control

Cost control is an important component and a critical success factor for information systems project management. Cost control management involves establishing appropriate guidelines, policies, procedures, methods, and control mechanisms that help on-going cost control of the project. These policies and procedures provide the project manager with up-to-date information on the cost and management status of a project and enable the project manager to foresee problem areas and prepare accordingly. This is similar to monitoring and assessing progress, performance, and schedule at predetermined milestones. Lack of cost control planning and monitoring will result in run away cost situations that take a life of their own and become difficult to resolve after a while. Cost control must be planned for during the initial planning stage and must be monitored throughout the project life cycle.

Effective cost control management requires knowledge of cost accounting, cost estimating, cash flow, and budgeting. The effectiveness of cost control management is also a function of good planning since cost is monitored against what was initially planned. An important part of cost control management includes estimating direct labor costs, overheads, and other project related costs. The failure to stay on target and within budget may be due to inaccurate estimates rather than poor control procedures. This necessitates proper documentation of how estimates were obtained and what assumptions influenced these estimates. When estimates are obtained from external sources such as vendors or consultants, it is important to include the estimating source as well as the reasoning behind estimates as part of documentation. When estimates are based on past experience or previous projects, it is important to critically evaluate these estimates considering changes that have taken place.

An experienced project manager understands that cost control management must be realistic, feasible, and easy to control. Important considerations for a successful cost control management can be summarized as:

- Plan cost control management early during the initial planning phase of the project.
- Make cost control management consistent with project plan.
- Establish and communicate policies and procedures for cost control.
- Document source and procedures for estimates.
- Use multiple estimates if in doubt.
- Use milestones for monitoring cost.
- Evaluate consequences of cost overrun.
- Communicate consequences of cost overrun.
- Establish authorization for expenditure

- Establish periodic review process.
- Emphasize commitments and responsibility for compliance.
- Use categories such as material cost, labor cost, overheads, and so on.
- Expect change and be prepared.

It is important to remember that management is interested in cost control relative to progress in schedule and performance. In other words, if cost is under control at a milestone but the project is 50% behind schedule then the overall success is not certain. Therefore, an integrated control that examines time, cost, and performance at milestones is necessary to provide the project manager with valuable information. At each predetermined milestone, time, cost, and performance are evaluated against the projected or estimated values in order to assess the success of the entire project. These evaluations are used as a base for project progress report to top-management and decision-making analysis for current and future activities. They will also provide an opportunity to prepare contingency plans early enough in response to possible cost overrun. Cost control and adjustment is easier in the early stages of the project development life cycle. Problems become difficult to resolve if they are ignored and allowed to continue and create snowball effects. Thus, to be effective, cost control must start early and be consistent, continuous, and timely.

## Quality management

It is too costly not to have proper quality control management. That does not mean managing quality is inexpensive. It is a lot more costly to take care of quality once the product is complete or is near completion. To avoid that problem, quality must be built into the developmental activities and be controlled at each stage of the system development life cycle. It must not be an afterthought event or a record keeping practice. Product quality translates into customer satisfaction more directly than any other factor. People are prepared to tolerate quality issues up to a point and will tolerate inconvenience to a degree. Most information system products tend to have direct and immediate impact on daily work and as a result their failure is more problematic. Thus it is critical that quality control management is an integral part of information systems design and development project.

It is important to plan for quality and to define quality in terms of requirements as part of that plan. The International Organization for Standardization (ISO) defines quality in terms of characteristics that meet and satisfy explicit or implicit needs. Meeting stakeholder specifications is therefore the main goal of project quality management. Fitness for use is considered one of the deciding criteria of success in many information system studies. Project quality plans must include control mechanisms to provide assurance that specifications and standards are being met. Project quality control activities continuously monitor outcomes to ensure compliance with previously agreed upon standards and to recommend corrective action when necessary. ***In that sense, project quality control procedures are preventive measures that save cost and time in the long-term.*** Remember, for a project to be considered successful it must be delivered on time, within budget, and meet user satisfaction.

Information system products are often implemented and put into use before all the 'bugs' are taken out and every user has a story to tell about that. This happens despite multiple tests that are carried out as part of the project development life cycle. Some of these quality problems are just difficult to see without extensive user interaction with the system. And the developers consider some of these problems as inconsequential and not serious enough to delay implementation or to miss the deadline. This judgment is based partly on experience, partly on the urgency of user needs, and partly for other considerations such as a timely integration of the project outcome with other systems that may be coming online. It is important for the project quality management to implement quality controls that result in continuous improvements not only for the current project but also for future ones. Project quality management must be considered as a tool for continuous improvement.

The success of project quality management depends heavily on how well it is communicated to and understood by everyone on the project team. While it is the responsibility of the project manager to make sure that quality is planned for, it is difficult to achieve qualitative objectives unless everyone buys into the idea that quality matters and they sincerely adhere to it. Project quality management starts early in the design phase and is continued throughout the project development life cycle. At the design phase, important variables that influence the final outcome of the project are identified and quality controls are established to assure compliance. Important factors that affect quality include functionality of the product, special features that are important to the user such as input forms or output format, system reliability and maintainability, and help functions. The user perception of system functionality and how it influences work and performance is probably the most important criterion for measuring quality.

Project quality management can benefit from established tools and techniques such as quality control charts, statistical sampling and tests. Statistical sampling and standard deviation is probably the most commonly used method for quality control. Statistical sampling refers to a method by which we select part of a population for quality inspection. The sample size and how it is selected (randomly or not) will influence the results. Another quality control tool is called Pareto analysis that helps identify the critical contributors of quality problems in a system so that control attention can be focused on those few causes of quality problems.

Tests of quality can be done for each unit or module as well as for the whole system. User involvement in testing the final product is important to ensure all features that are important to users are present and functional. Quality issues may not be limited to technical aspects. In information system project development and implementation quality problems may arise from management issues and cooperation with the user department. In other words, not all quality problems are of a technical nature. Often these non-technical or behavioral quality problems prove to be more difficult to monitor or resolve.

## Conflict Management

Most large information system projects involve conflict that if not resolved will cause the entire project to fail. In other words, conflict is a way of life for project managers and they must be able to manage it. Conflicts occur because of competing resource allocations, scheduling, strong and diverse opinions, administrative bureaucracy, poor communication, and differences in style. Some argue that personality conflicts are the most difficult ones to resolve. It is critical for the project manager to understand why a conflict has occurred and what the root cause is. Often when information about the specifics of a project and its objectives are not properly communicated it leads to different interpretations of the objectives as well as the responsibilities and that in turn leads to conflicts. Some projects tend to attract more conflict than others. These are projects that are not specific, have unreasonable expectations, receive insufficient organizational support, are given inadequate resources, involve intangible and hard to measure outcomes, and include multiple internal and external stakeholders and players.

An experienced project manager may be able to foresee conflicts given the initial project description and be able to make adjustments that help resolve some of the problems before they occur. For example, during the feasibility study phase of the system development, if resources are inadequate or skill levels are lacking then estimates may be reevaluated, alternative arrangements made, or objectives reassessed. This proactive approach helps the project manager to more carefully examine requirements against resources and communicate challenges to individuals and subgroups so that everyone can plan accordingly. Open and clear communication causes individuals to adjust their expectations and ultimately helps conflict resolution. It is important to:

- Identify clear objectives for the project
- Communicate specifics to all stakeholders
- Have realistic expectations
- Align resources with project goals
- Align project goals with organizational goals
- Have measurable outcomes
- Establish responsibilities
- Establish feedback channels
- Be proactive toward foreseeable conflicts
- Follow a consistent policy of conflict resolution

Sometime, conflict is inevitable because people do not accept change. This may not necessarily be a bad thing since it provides an opportunity for the project manager to examine and explain the reasons for change. Information technology is considered by most people to cause significant change in the way work is carried out, monitored, and evaluated. It is perceived to speed up the pace of work instantly and that in turn increases expectations. Information technology is expected to increase efficiency and reduce the need for resources simultaneously. This will result in considerable anxiety, resistance to change, and ultimately conflict. These concerns are often needless. Many systems lead to increased user empowerment, improved environment, customer service, work planning, innovation, and so on. In order to address these issues and reduce the possibility of conflict, a great deal of education is required before, during, and subsequent to the systems development project. Educational programs must correspond to the level of change that a new system will create and the influence that it will have on the individual.

An effective project manager does not ignore conflicts wishing they would go away. Often, conflicts do not go away and it is likely that they will intensify if ignored. Most conflicts are caused because of misunderstanding between team members or individuals who want the project to succeed. By just providing an opportunity for individuals to express their point of view or their concern, the project manager can take a step toward conflict resolution. Listening to alternative viewpoints and trying to resolve the conflict, new information is produced which in turn may enhance the decision-making process. In other words, an effective project manager is able to turn an adverse situation around and benefit from it. Some conflicts generate a domino effect in that they create further conflicts, some of which are open and obvious and some are subtle.

It is important to address the main conflict and deal with the root of the problem. For example, change causes anxiety that in turn causes a variety of attitudinal and behavioral problems some of which lead to conflict. It is important to address change through education and training within the organizational structure and treat it as a necessity and a response to competition, and growth rather than just as a policy issue that everyone has to comply with. Sometimes, as it is the case with information technology development, application, and penetration, it is not just the change but rather the pace of change that causes anxiety. In that case, the pace of change must be addressed and its necessity explained. People need to feel comfortable that they can cope with change and that they can cope with change without falling behind and that depends on their self-efficacy and their skill level.

Some conflicts, if ignored, may have long lasting effects that extend beyond the current project. For example, conflicts between managers of functional areas such as user departments and the project manager will impact future relationships. That means in order to build a relationship or to establish long term partnership some short term compromises might be necessary. In these situations, the project manager must carefully weight pros and cons of making compromises and make sure that the quality of the product and integrity of the process are upheld. Some short-term solutions cause long-term conflicts. For example, personality conflicts between team members must be resolved in a way that team members will be able to work together in future projects. It might be easy to drop a member from a team in order to avoid conflict, but that may not be a good solution if the expertise and experience of this member is needed for future projects and the same team members will have to work together again.

Sometimes rigid rules, inflexible situations, and stressful environments manifest themselves in individual behaviors and cause interpersonal conflicts. Again, as was mentioned earlier, it is important to address the problem at the source. It is difficult to prescribe one rule or one policy for all situations. For example, many computer programmers prefer flexible schedules and tend to work at odd hours while some are strictly 9 to 5 type. An experienced project manager is able to take advantage of these individual differences to produce the desired outcome within budget and in a timely manner.

## Change management

Many people fear change because they don't know what to expect. It is the responsibility of the project manager to remove fear and replace it with realistic expectations and provide individuals with the understanding to assess for themselves benefits of a new system. Managing project change is an important success factor for information system projects.

Project change can also alter outcome expectations. Some changes can be significant and as a result can alter the overall project outcome. This in turn may lead to change in the original expectations of owners, sponsors, and users. Project change may be perceived differently by different stakeholders. Some may see change as a useful development that improves the outcome product and some may see change as having a significant negative impact on the outcome. Some changes are proposed primarily to improve the developmental process while others are proposed with the intent to alter the outcome.

It is important to assess whether a change will alter the outcome of the project. It is critical to evaluate the effect of change on owners' expectations. It is important that project managers establish and communicate procedures regarding the change process. Forming a change management committee accomplishes several objectives: ***(a)*** to encourage useful and innovative change proposals; ***(b)*** to establish a review and approval process for change proposals; ***(c)*** to create a mechanism for administering approved changes; and ***(d)*** to establish a communication channel for updating stakeholders.

The change management committee can therefore become an effective means of managing expectations. The establishment of a change management process through an organization-wide committee has practical benefits that relate to receiving additional support to implement change or to release contingency funds. Expectations are often linked with due dates. Some change proposals may delay project completion. The change management committee can play an important role in informing stakeholders about possible delays and in providing them with rationale for such delays.

## Project success

The success measures of information systems project management may vary according to the evaluator's implied and expressed expectations. In other words, whether the project management is successful depends on how well it meets the expectations of different stakeholders. For example, the top management perspective of project management success may vary from that of end-users. Top management expects the project outcome to be consistent with strategic plans and be supportive of organizational goals, help decision rationalization, and facilitate management control. End-users on the other hand evaluate the outcome of an information system project in terms of its usefulness and impact on task productivity, task innovation, customer service, work planning, and so on. Therefore, for project management to succeed it must satisfy the needs of different stakeholders as identified in the initial planning phase of the project management. Several variables influence project management success:

- ***Customer satisfaction***. This is probably the most significant dependent variable for measuring information system success. User satisfaction exists when system utility in decision-making is enhanced, the output meets the user's information requirements, and interaction with the system is easy. Research studies have identified five dimensions for user satisfaction with computer-based applications namely information ***content***, ***accuracy***, ***format***, ***ease of use***, and ***timeliness***. User satisfaction with a computer application is expected to lead to increased use and consequently greater impact at the individual and organizational level. An information system that is delivered on time and within budget and runs according to specifications may or may not be widely used. Other factors such as ease of use may influence how well and how often users voluntarily use the system in their daily work. Systems that are not used are ineffective regardless of how well they are designed or developed. Required use may be effective for routine and well-structured tasks but it is not expected to be effective in generating new ideas or developing innovative applications. Users not only must need the system for work but they must also *like* to use it. Required use of a poor system or a difficult to use system may result in user resistance and ultimately conflict. Therefore, success is not measured simply through cost and time but is dependent on other factors such as user satisfaction. Several factors are expected to influence user satisfaction with a project outcome among which user involvement is said to be critical.

- ***User involvement***. This is probably the most important independent variable for measuring success. Because of considerable dissatisfaction on the part of system users and the cost of computer applications that do not meet organizational goals or user needs, information system researchers have looked at a variety of social science techniques, including user involvement in systems development, for solutions to these problems. User involvement in the design and development of computer-based information systems is widely accepted as one of the essential principles of information systems development. User involvement in system development may improve the quality of design decisions and resultant application, improve end-user skills in system utilization, develop user abilities to define their own information requirements, and enhance user commitment to and acceptance of the final outcome. The extent to which the user is involved in system development and the format (direct or indirect involvement) of involvement may vary among projects. For example, decision support systems require a greater level of user involvement for closer communication to define the specific needs of the user. User involvement in system development is expected to influence user satisfaction through three mechanisms called *value attainment*, *cognitive*, and *motivational factors*. *Value attainment* is accomplished through self-expression, ownership, influence, and independence. *Cognitive factors* refer to increased knowledge, understanding, and creativity. *Motivational factors* include increased trust and sense of control. In other words, user involvement gives users a sense of ownership and influence, increases their understanding and knowledge, and creates a sense of trust and control. However, user involvement is expected to be effective when users want to be involved and have self-efficacy that helps them contribute.

- ***Top management support***. This is probably the most important organizational goal for the project manager to obtain and sustain throughout the project development life cycle. Continuous and consistent support by top management facilitates coordinating efforts across departments, helps maintain structural flexibility for contingencies, acts as a buffer between the project manager and external entities, and suggests that the project is important for the organization. Top management support is critical not only for the availability of resources, the cooperation of other functional areas to name a few, but also for morale and the encouragement of project team members. The need for top management support is greater in larger and more diverse projects that extend across multiple functions and include outside entities. Top management support and involvement helps reduce planning problems facing project managers while providing necessary harmony between the project plan and organizational goals. Top management support is important for a broader reason than one project and that is to closely link organizational needs and technological opportunities. It helps develop better understanding and justify portfolio of technologies that contribute to organizational success.

- ***Competent team members***. The project manager must have the flexibility of selecting project team members and must carefully pick key members for the project. The project manager's experience with individuals is probably the most important source of information for identifying key individuals for a project. As part of project documentation, team members and key players are described and their contribution identified. This information is useful in assessing the qualifications of potential candidates for the project. Key players must have proven track records in the information system field, in team work and interaction with others, in contingency situations and problem solving, in working with end-users, and so on. The skills for team members and particularly for key members of project management include technical knowledge of information systems design and development tools and techniques as well as business knowledge of what the organization and its goals, objectives, and mission. Depending on the focus of the project and the expected outcome the project manager must determine an appropriate balance between the technical skills and business knowledge of team members. Careful assessment of skill levels for each team member enables the project manager to assign the right person to the right task. Probably the most important task at the outset is for the project manager to motivate team members to show commitment and develop a sense of mission for the project. Team members must feel responsible and understand their role in the overall success of the project and its impact on the organization as well as the end-users.

An effective and experienced project manager understands the significance of these issues and carefully plans for them. To be effective, compliance with these issues must go beyond understanding or documentation. For example, it is important to go beyond getting top management to say that they support the project and get them to show actual commitment throughout the project development life cycle. Commitments may not necessarily be carried out. It is important to develop an appropriate relationship with all stakeholders to ensure continued support. Often short and informal lines of communication are effective in getting things done on a timely manner. In communication with team members, excessive reporting and formalized interaction often backfires.

It is important to also realize that the most critical success factor for a project is the leadership quality and administrative skill of the project leader. It is the project manager who must bring everything together and plan for collaborative and effective teamwork and bring the entire project to a successful conclusion. Project management success is measured in terms of:

- Timely completion. This is the easiest thing for the user to measure.
- Completion within budget. This is a measure of planning and controlling for cost. It also suggests effective teamwork, coordination, and self-discipline.
- Meeting expectations. The answer to the question, what did the user expect?
- Managing expectations. The frame of reference for expectations is formed at the initial requirement analysis stage. These expectations, however, change and become unrealistic as stakeholders anticipate more results because of technology growth and development.
- Net present value (NPV). This is a more straightforward assessment of outcome based on calculating the net monetary gain or loss for a project.
- Return on investment (ROI). This also involves calculation and is equal to total benefits minus total costs divided by costs.
- Payback analysis. This involves determining how long it takes to recoup in terms of dollars invested in the project

## Ethics

Given the power and ubiquity of information technology and its pervasive influence in everyday work life, it is implausible to discuss information system development and management without discussing the role of ethics. Technology professionals design, develop, and implement systems that individuals and organizations use to gather data, generate information, analyze situations, and make decisions that influence every facet of work life. Invariably the outcome of system development projects includes consequences that were not planned for or expected. In her notable book, In the Age of the Smart Machine, Shoshana Zuboff suggests that "Technology is brimming with valence and specificity in that it both creates and forecloses avenues of experience." Information systems project managers must understand that a project's outcome will implicitly and explicitly influence the way users carry out work, rationalize decision, or create ideas and that some of this may be over and beyond what was initially intended.

It is important for information system project managers to understand and appreciate ethical issues of the information age. In a frequently cited article, Richard Mason suggests four ethical issues that relate to *privacy*, *accuracy*, *property*, and *accessibility*. ***Privacy***, he argues is about individual information and how much of that can be revealed and under what conditions. How can individuals keep private information to themselves and not be forced to reveal it? In fact the question has become increasingly more difficult to deal with in that one needs to go to a great extent to keep personal information private. It has gone from allowing personal information to be revealed to having to take steps to prevent it from being revealed. With the increased power of computing, communication, the ease of use, and manipulation this issue has become more important. Integrated systems make it easy to amass and combine a variety of information from various sources for decision-making, problem solving, surveillance, control, and so on. Often these integrated databases of personal information are formed and used without proper authorization from individuals. Individuals may authorize use of personal information to separate databases but not necessarily to merging of data about them, especially when it is difficult to foresee what new information may be revealed through this merging process. The ethical implications of merging or matching information on individuals are significant. On the one hand, the new information that is obtained through matching may be used to prevent fraud (for example, matching social security numbers and bank accounts). On the other hand, merging databases may provide information that can be used for political purposes that amount to invasion of privacy and abuse of integrated systems. This situation is more complicated when there is an error in the information.

The second issue, ***accuracy***, relates to the question of responsibility for authenticity and information content. Who is responsible when there is an error in information about the individual and what is the remedial procedure? In integrated systems where information about individuals is used as input for other systems and rapidly disseminated, it is difficult to measure the true consequence of an error. Furthermore, the corrective action is that much more difficult since in some cases it is not possible to evaluate how far the information is distributed. In a recent study for measuring the factors that influence e-commerce shoppers, information security was mentioned as a major concern. Respondents to the survey were concerned that once they input personal information such as name, address, credit card number, and so on, they could not control where that information would go. A major difference between shopping on the web and through the traditional stores is that for web shopping the customer is required to provide specific information such as their name, address, phone and credit card numbers. Accuracy of this information as well as its manipulation is critical since it can be stored, retrieved, merged, and shared with other entities.

The third issue, ***property***, relates to the ownership of information. Information is generated, stored, and exchanged through many sources. It is a commodity that is bought and sold just like other goods and services. The question is who should decide how much it is worth or how should the access to it be monitored or controlled? While some aspects of this issue are now clearer than when it was initially conceived still there are issues that need to be addressed. Intellectual property rights raised an important question for the information system professional and government agencies alike. Information is costly to produce initially and once it is produced it becomes easy to reproduce or transmit. This raises ethical and economic questions that require careful consideration. Information is considered a commodity that can be bought and sold but at the same time difficult to control and secure once it is produced. The ethical questions about information property have been present from the beginning. They have become more critical with the growth and complexity of producing, reproducing, and disseminating information product.

The fourth ethical issue relates to ***accessibility*** and the right to obtain information and safeguard it. This is important because information is the main ingredient for literacy and education. Our intellectual growth, innovation, invention and the like depend on information access. At the same time a certain level of computer literacy is required to enable one to benefit from the information product. In a way computer literacy becomes a means of access since without it there will be no gains even if information or access to it exists. Like radio, television, and newspapers, computers are means of communication and information handling. The access to information and its means is fundamental to democratic societies. Therefore, the ethical issue of access to information on the one hand and the right to protect it make this issue worthy of serious thinking. As societies grow more dependent on information means and information context and handling become more complex the issue of access and use become more critical and challenging.

## Closure

Closure facilitates the transition of a project into normal operation and the closing of accounts and books. It enables the project manager and team members to focus on other on-going projects and activities. Some projects require an integration phase into the normal operation and if so the integration may become a project by itself or an extension of the existing project. In any event the transition out of the existing project and into the integration phase can be facilitated through the steps for closure. The project scope defines the boundaries of a project and if integration into the normal operation of the firm is a part of the overall project, then activities involved with integration are included in the project schedule and the duration.

It is, however, feasible to consider the integration of a new project as a separate project especially if it involves a new organizational structure or restructuring of the existing organizational functions. This may be a necessary and useful approach if a totally new set of skills is required for the transition that involves a new team and a new plan. For example, consider a pharmaceutical chain that has traditionally been dispensing drugs through stores and now wants to offer the same service through the Internet. This project could be divided into two phases. Phase one involves the development and testing of an Internet system that puts the entire operation online. Phase two involves organizational restructuring that not only trains pharmacists to effectively use the new system but also establishes new billing, control, and reporting to take advantage of the new systems.

The project manager is responsible for and benefits from closure. It is a responsibility because a project should not turn into an on-going and ineffective undertaking that eventually dies due to lack of support and attention. Closure is beneficial to project managers in that it enables them to finalize, organize, and properly file away all documents and accounts. All lose ends such as final communications with vendors, contractors, consultants, and so on must be dealt with one way or another and final decisions documented for future reference. These documents are the clearest and often most appropriate evidence of activities, events, decisions, revisions, and so on that make a project complete. Time and again, you may need to refer to these documents for a variety of reasons. Personnel issues, performance evaluations, government and industry standards as well as compliance with these standards require proper documentation that is filed away as part of closure.

As part of closure, the project manager also seeks formal acceptance, user validation, recognition, acknowledgement, and the like. This enables the project manager to ensure deliverables are delivered and expectations are met. Audits are carried out and documented. Lessons learned during the initial phase of project transition and user reaction toward the new project are useful experiences to document for future use and to measure the project's success. Success is often measured through user satisfaction that is influenced by user expectation. Since user expectation was documented during the requirement analysis phase, it is useful to compare these expectations with user reaction to the final product. If the project outcome significantly surpasses expectations or fails to meet them, it is useful to investigate and document possible causes, be it administrative, resource, personnel, design, vendor, and/or others. Archiving these documents and reports helps maintenance of existing systems as well as development of new ones.

Documenting the interaction and the experience with vendors is a useful part of this archive. Often reliable and timely response by vendors directly influences the delivery of a project. This information is particularly useful since it relates to external entities for which appropriate data are not often readily available or at least data that directly link to one's own experience do not exist. This is valuable information for future project development and can save the project manager a lot of hassle. As a part of closure, project managers often examine the project results in terms of impact on work. For example, if the project was designed to improve certain processes it should be possible to evaluate how these processes are improved as a result of the new project. Often users request a new system that will help them eliminate a specific problem such as unexpected stock out. Again, it should be possible to evaluate the impact of the new system in terms of that problem. In general, research suggests that information technology can be evaluated in terms of impact on task productivity, task innovation, management control, and customer service.

## REFERENCES

1. Gary, C.F. and Larson, E.W. "Project Management: The Managerial Process." McGraw-Hill, 2000.

2. Kerzner, H. "Project Management: A System Approach to Planning, Scheduling, and Controlling." 7th ed., Wiley, 2001.

3. Lowery, G. and Stover, T. "Managing Projects with Microsoft Project 2000." Wiley, 2001.

4. Mason, R.O., "Four Ethical Issues of the Information Age." MIS Quarterly, Vol. 10, No.1, March 1986

5. Nicholas, J.M. "Project Management for Business and Technology: Principles and Practice." 2nd ed., Prentice Hall, 2001.

6. Zuboff, S. "In the Age of the Smart Machine: The Future of Work and Power." Basic Books, New York, NY. 1988.

## DISCUSSION QUESTIONS

1. Consider the following scenario. You have been working on a project to revise a large legacy system. It is important that you complete this project on time since the user department has plans to update the content immediately upon completion of your project. The project has been going according to the plan for the last three weeks. On the Monday of the fourth week, as you review your messages before starting your day, you notice that you have a message from the user department of another system that your team recently developed and installed. Based, on your knowledge of the installed system and what the voice mail suggests, you realize that this is not a quick fix and it will require at least one week of your time and may involve another member of your current team. It is clear to you that if you attend this problem

your on-going project will be delayed. Discuss the situation and describe (a) what you should have done differently regarding the previous system and (b) what you should you do.

2. Review benefits of project closure and develop a list of what you think should be lessons learned in a typical information system project. Break up your list in terms of management support, user expectation, vendor evaluation, administrative, personnel, and impact.

3. Discuss and list pros and cons of developing a project risk management plan. Describe how you would evaluate a good risk management plan, what are the quality indicators?

4. User involvement in systems design is considered an important success factor for information systems project as it plays a critical role in forming perceived usefulness. However, analysts, programmers, and system developers in general consider user involvement hampering to developmental activities. Assume you are the project manager for an information system that will eventually be used by great many users in your organization. Your project team members argue that users are not skilled to make contributions in the design and development of the new system and will only delay the project due date. In short, they are not happy getting users involved with the project. (a) Describe to your team members the merits of user involvement. (b) Suggest ways of getting meaningful input from users.

5. We have in this chapter argued that it is too costly not to plan for project quality management. Discuss why this statement is or is not true.

6. We have in this chapter suggested that projects that are not specific, have unreasonable expectations, receive insufficient organizational support, are given inadequate resources, involve intangible and hard to measure outcomes, and include multiple internal and external stakeholders and players are more likely to have conflicts. Describe how each case might be true.

7. Two of your programmers on your project team appear to have personality clashes and often take opposite points of view during the discussions regarding software selection, vendor selection, and so on. How would you address this continuing conflict that is hindering progress?

8. All procurements at your organization must go through the purchasing department. One of your main vendors for an on-going project that you lead almost always has conflicts with the point person in your purchasing department. This vendor provides you with reliable products in a timely manner and at competitive costs. You don't want to change the vendor at this stage of your project but have come to realize that the conflict between your vendor and your purchasing department is growing into a high maintenance activity taking a toll on your time. What are the possible solutions available to you?
9. Assume you are the project manager for a large information system that uses the Internet to integrate organizational databases. You have outsourced part of this project to an external company and have provided your project team members with guidelines to communicate and coordinate activities with this external provider. However, one of your key project team members seems to have personality conflict with the systems analyst at this company and tends to communicate with him through you avoiding direct communication. How would you resolve the conflict between your team member and the analyst at this company?

## DISCUSSION CASE: BELTECH INCORPORATED

Beltech Incorporated (BI) is a small firm that develops Global Positioning System (GPS) devices. BI's last year's sales were $3.1 million with a profit of $200,000. BI has a market share of 1% in a fiercely competitive market. BI's primary strategic goal is to gain an additional market share of 2% over the next two years. Like their competition, all of BI's products are proprietary in nature, using both proprietary software and hardware.

### Management

The small firm has 18 employees with a small team of highly skilled engineers who develop the hardware and software for their products. Many of the functions of the firm such as payroll and marketing are outsourced to other firms who have the professional knowledge to support BI. BI is committed towards developing high quality products. This is a necessary requirement due to strong competition from larger firms. BI promotes innovation and looks for ideas from all team members.

## Potential Opportunity

Recently, one of the employees presented an idea to management to use non-proprietary equipment for the basis of an innovative GPS product. The idea is to use common small handheld computers as a medium for GPS hardware. This would provide an advantage because, for the most part, the software and hardware is already developed. This would provide opportunities for a less expensive GPS and perhaps a quicker development cycle.

### PM Assignment

BI has assigned their Project Manger (PM) the responsibility to complete a feasibility study of the suggested product. The PM will need to perform research in order to complete the feasibility study. The PM will also need to coordinate within the company as well as their outsourcing partners to gain enough input for a comprehensive feasibility study. Additionally, some research will need to be performed to see how well the firm could utilize industry standard equipment, and which firms would best welcome a partnership with BI.

### PM Research

The PM has found that there is a mature Personal Digital Assistant (PDA) market with a small computer, which would be ideal for BI to base a hybrid device upon. There are several good hardware manufacturers willing to partner with BI. There are two very good operating systems (OS) available for PDA's from which to choose. One OS is provided by Microsoft and is well supported. The second OS is just as robust and possibly the dominant PDA OS which is provided by Palm. Both of the OS are very mature with strong support from their prospective companies, who are willing to partner with BI. The PM has also determined that the product can be developed in about 20% of the time a usual product requires. This indicates significant development savings. The device's projected retail prices will also be cost effective in comparison to current GPS products, and will offer additional functionality above the standard GPS. An additional bonus has been found in the fact that there is strong potential for 3rd party programmers to develop applications for the new hybrid device, allowing unprecedented opportunities for software development and growth. The major obstacle is caused bye the potential the new product may cause excessive erosion (loss of sales) to their current product line. To accomplish BI's strategic goal towards market share; Bi will need to be willing to gamble away their current product line for the new hybrid product. There is also a concern that BI's competitors may be working on a similar product.

### Management Decision

The PM has identified several opportunities for a new product to facilitate strategic growth for BI. There is high risk involved. However, there is also good potential in exceptional success of the new product. The risk of erosion to the current product line is found to be acceptable.

There is also risk that BI's competitor may be working on a similar device. BI needs to be first on the market with a hybrid device, or face the possibility of being forced out of business.

To summarize: BI's Management has decided to move forward with the project. Management is willing to support a new integrated PDA/GPS device, even at the risk of strong erosion of their current product line. It is anticipated that BI would gain strategic market share in the GPS market if they are first to market with a quality hybrid device.

## CASE DISCUSSION QUESTIONS

1. Did the project manager perform sufficient research for the feasibility study to complete the assignment?
2. Should Beltech's management have used a larger project team and gather more information due to the impact the project could have on the company's core competency and products?
3. What do you think are the project manager's tools for conducting this important assignment?
4. Should the project manager created and delivered more documents than the feasibility document mentioned?

# 5. EVALUATING INFORMATION TECHNOLOGY APPLICATIONS

A Forrester Research study found 63 percent of respondents as describing their business climate as okay to very strong. The other 37 percent described it as somewhat challenging or weak. Only 25 percent of respondents planned on spending more than what was budgeted. 56 percent planned on spending right on budget, while 19 percent expected to spend below budget.

**Evaluating IT in Action**

Harley-Davidson undertook an interesting project in 2001. An open IT town hall meeting was organized. The senior management always thought that everybody in the business knew exactly what IT was doing and that the rest of the business valued their contributions. However, when they were branded as "the big black box", it was an awakening call for the IT co-leaders Laurel Tschurwald and Reid F. Engstrom.

In response, the IT launched an internal evaluation and a marketing campaign. Senior business people were brought in to review and manage the IT project requests. Internal service-level agreements and IT financial audits were evaluated. And in order to communicate their activities to the rest of the business, they started publishing status reports. The reports recapped each business initiative and evaluated what all was done (or not done).

A similar approach is adopted by Tyson Foods. The CIO hired a change management vice president, whose responsibility, besides change management, is to oversee communication and internal evaluation. Tyson CIO admits that it is easy to assume that everybody has the same level of understanding. If one goes ahead with the changes and other projects, but does not evaluate and see if there is sufficient following, then it defeats the purpose.

There are clear benefits of internal evaluation. At least in the case of Harley-Davidson, evaluation and good communication helped IT to get quick project approval. This was possible, because the business understood the issues and could relate to them more easily than they were able to do so earlier on.

There is a marketing aspect of evaluation as well. At MetLife an aspect of evaluation is considered every year. One year it may be "Finding the R in ROI", while in another it may be "Moving IT to the Next Level." The themes not only help the company to focus, but also define a purpose in the evaluations. Such an approach allows for the projects to be showcased to other organizational members.

---

Organizations spending millions of dollars on information technology face the critical issue of evaluating information technology application and its impact on employees' performance and ultimately on the competitiveness of the organization. Increasingly information technology executives are expected to justify technology investment in terms of its impact on employees and their work. Information technology is expected to empower employee to improve productivity, service quality, work planning, communication, and the like. To the extent that information technology empowers end-users to do their job more effectively and more efficiently it can be considered successful.

Evaluating information technology application is always a complex process involving multiple criteria. There are at least two paradigms for evaluating information systems. The first paradigm has a strong tradition in the MIS field and calls for evaluating information systems relative to design specifications or user needs (this could be called design paradigm). Computer user satisfaction, typically defined as the extent to which the system's design meets the user's information needs, implicitly reflects the design paradigm. The second paradigm calls for performance-related evaluations that focus on outcomes (this could be called outcome paradigm). The outcome paradigm calls for evaluating information systems in terms of their consequences such as quality of service provided to customers.

This chapter describes system failures and reasons behind them. It will then describe system success and present several instruments for evaluating information technology applications. Some of these measures are developed based on design paradigm and some are developed using outcome paradigm. These instruments are widely used in practice and research to measure computer user satisfaction with a system, to measure the level and type of user involvement in information system development, and to measure impact and usefulness of information system outcome. This chapter also describes an instrument that measures customer value of the Internet commerce and identifies issues that influence online shopping decisions. The instruments described in this chapter can be used by information system executives to evaluate information technology applications as perceived by the end-user.

# INFORMATION SYSTEM FAILURE

Information system failure is rarely attributed to a single factor; often multiple criteria interact and result in system failure. Some systems fail so badly that the company goes out of business. Some systems fail and hardly anyone in the organization notices it. In most cases information systems are successful in some parts while fail in other. You would hope that the successful parts are greater and would overshadow the failed parts. A system is considered a failure if it does not meet stakeholders' needs. Every organization must have a profile of information system failure based on historical data. This profile helps system managers to monitor areas of concern and plan accordingly to improve the situation. This list must be updated as changes occur. The following Table provides an example of system failure profile for an organization.

*Table 5.1, An example of information system failure profile*

| System life cycle | Likelihood of failure |
|---|---|
| Initiation | Low to Medium |
| Development | High |
| Implementation | Low |
| Acceptance | Medium |
| Level of use | Medium |
| Infusion or full use | High |

Whether a system is successful or not depends on what stage it is in relative to its life cycle. For example, at the end of the development stage, a system may be considered unsuccessful if it is significantly over budget and behind deadline. At the end of acceptance stage, a system may be considered unsuccessful if, say, less than 50% of the potential end-users want it. The last two stages, the level of use and infusion or full use, differ in that one is a measure of quantity and another examines usage pattern. For example, the amount of time that users spend interacting with a system reflects the level of use for that system. Whereas the way a system is used (e.g., to server the customer or to improve work planning) reflects the pattern of use. Both measures are necessary depending on the system development life cycle stage. Some system's success is more appropriately measured through the level of use (e.g., data entry applications) whereas others may be more appropriately measured through pattern of use (e.g., decision support systems).

Depending on the circumstances, some system failures may be more acceptable than others. For example, some information systems are mission critical and as a result it may become necessary to go over the budget in order to ensure timely development. Such a system may still be considered a success, despite it budget overrun, if it satisfies mission objectives. This suggests that the tradeoff between extra cost and reduced development time depends on organizational needs and management assessment. Having the new system up and running one week ahead of the schedule may be worth a lot more than the additional cost. In situations like this, measuring system success may involve sponsors, customers, and top management.

Some MIS researchers have argued for system outcome measures where system success is measured in terms of its effective use; how it is used by the end user to create value for the organization. Others have argued that system outcome is a function of system features as well as individual skills and self-efficacy; poor business knowledge and ability limits how well the individual can benefit from a system. Given these arguments, it is prudent to measure system success in the context of its development stage as well as its original intent. If a system is initiated to help organizational goals and objectives then it seems appropriate to measure success in terms of how well the system helps organization rather than a specific task or project.

A system may fail at the development stage because of a variety of reasons. Information system specifications may change so rapidly that the developmental activities could not keep up. Rapid turnover of key and talented team members can cause system failure especially when recruitment cannot keep up with demand. This is a more challenging task for the management of information technology because of high demand for technology talents and expertise. Some systems fail simply because human expertise does not match system complexity. Large systems involve complex testing that requires metrics for all possible test conditions. Testing by itself may become a major task. Even if a solution is correct, it must be demonstrated that it is correct and that is not always easy. In general application development may fail because:

- Human issues
  - Employee turnover
  - Conflict
  - Motivation
- Technical limitations
  - Incompatible hardware and software platforms
  - Limited bandwidth for data transfer
  - Inadequate response time
- Political game play
  - By the individual to gain rewards
  - By the team to create rivalry
  - By the project manager to control
- Funding issues
  - Erroneous estimates
  - Poor budgetary control
  - Run away costs
- Leadership issues
  - In dealing with people
  - In dealing with technology
  - In dealing with processes

Experienced information technology managers often can come up with solutions for a given problem. They can detect when a system might fail. The following table provides a list of typical problems and possible solutions, especially during the system development process. This table also suggests ways of knowing if an information system development is likely to fail.

*Table 5.2, Examples of problems and possible solutions*

| Typical problem | Possible solution |
|---|---|
| Users cannot agree on business needs. This usually happens in the early stages of system development. | Use prototype to allow users see the impact of their decisions. |
| Users and developers do not communicate effectively. | Provide guidelines for communication. Try multiple means of communication. To encourage communication, you may need to link with rewards. |
| Users want a solution without fully understanding the ramifications. | Facilitate meetings to take users through various levels of the system. Share details with all parties to help understanding. |
| Developers and users resist change. | Document changes and assign priorities for them. Involve users and continuously monitor progress toward change. |
| Employee turnover, new hire with insufficient expertise. | Provide training. Encourage self-learning, it is an integral part of IS profession. Have technical 'gurus' go around helping others. |
| Stakeholders have unrealistic expectations; they want to fulfill a dream. | Clarify system scope. Avoid scope creep. Explain difficulties of making changes and the impact on cost and delivery date. |

## EVALUATING APPLICATION SUCCESS

Information technology executives have significant challenges and opportunities in modern organization. They face the critical issue of assessing the impact and influence of information technology applications on employees' performance and the organization's competitive strength. Information technology is expected to empower employees to improve task productivity, service quality, work planning, and communication. Increasingly, information technology executives are expected to justify technology investment in terms of its impact on employees and their work.

To the extent that information technology empowers end-users to do their job more effectively and more efficiently it can be considered successful. This section describes widely used instruments to measure end-user satisfaction with a system, to measure the level and type of user involvement in system development, to measure impact and usefulness of information system outcome, and to measure factors that influence e-commerce. These instruments have been developed by MIS researchers using field surveys and real world data. They are useful tools that assist management in evaluating system success as perceived by the end-user.

## Critical success factors

There are at least two perspectives for evaluating information systems. The ***first*** perspective calls for evaluating information systems relative to defined specifications or user needs. User satisfaction is typically defined as the extent to which the system meets the user's information needs. This definition assumes that user needs are accurately described, documented, understood, and reflected in the system development plan. The ***second*** perspective calls for performance-related evaluations and focuses on system outcome as it influences work and activities. This perspective assumes that the system is accepted by the end-user and is used to perform specific tasks.

These two perspectives are related in that customer needs and satisfaction is linked with system effectiveness and performance. However, there are several important management and leadership skills such as communication, coordination, conflict resolution, and interaction that influence this relationship and the outcome of any system use. There are several critical success factors that influence both perspectives of user satisfaction and system outcome. These critical success factors include user involvement, business knowledge, expectation management, and change management. Discussion of these factors follows.

- ***User involvement*** – user involvement in the design and development of information system is considered one of the essential principles of effective information system development. End-users are an integral part of the system development process. Users must be involved in all phases of the information system development life cycle especially during the specification and design phase. User involvement is critical in design of input and output forms, creation and test of prototype, and development of interface.

The management must ensure the involvement of users from the entire organization and include individuals that will directly or indirectly interact with the system outcome. Information system literature and research studies suggest a strong relationship between user involvement and user satisfaction. End-user involvement in system development is expected to *improve the quality of design decisions and resultant applications, improve end-user skills in system utilization, develop user abilities to define their own information requirements, and enhance user commitment to and acceptance of the resultant application.* In situations where users are only consulted regarding their needs with no direct involvement, user satisfaction with the resultant outcome is less likely.

The end-user population is characterized by great diversity in skill and motivation. Some users enjoy getting involved while others, concerned about the complexity of the technology or their ability to contribute, show little interest. Sometimes it is argued that user involvement will delay system development because of the users' inadequate skills. This is a short-term outlook at system development and system use. The management must create involvement arrangements that enable end-user input and contribution to the process of system development as well as assessment.

Individuals may be reluctant to get involved because it will take time away from what they perceive to be more important to their career development. Individuals may also be reluctant to get involved because their beliefs about the benefits and outcome of the system; they perceive little personal benefit for their efforts. The management must think of adequate rewards and incentives to facilitate user involvement. Involvement may be dysfunctional for individuals who are not motivated or see little benefit in getting involved in system development activities. Research studies suggest three involvement episodes that provide a useful perspective to the management.

- ***Involvement equilibrium*** – an involvement equilibrium situation exists where actual involvement equals or roughly corresponds to the level of desired involvement. Thus, in this situation there is correspondence between how much the user wants to be involved and the extent to which the user is required to be involved. Several factors may influence this equilibrium such as *individual skills and competency, career and promotional opportunities, and learning opportunity.* Within this frame of reference, perceived involvement, whether low or high, is expected to have a positive effect on the end-user. In such situations: ***(a)*** involvement is viewed by users as a means of getting what they want from their environment; ***(b)*** end-users are more receptive to learning about the system, improving their understanding of how to use the system, and making suggestions that might improve system quality; and ***(c)*** involvement enhances trust and contributes to a sense of ownership and control, improving system acceptance and commitment.

- ***Involvement saturation*** – an involvement saturation situation occurs when an individual's actual involvement exceeds desired involvement and the user's frame of reference regarding the value of involvement is altered. Thus, the individual desire or motivation to get involved plays a key role in creating the feeling of too much involvement or a *saturation situation.* Other factors such as *individual characteristics, opportunities of higher responsibility, and the nature and form of involvement* may influence whether, or at what point, saturation occurs. In such situations, involvement may be viewed as a time consuming interference with other activities; impediment to other opportunities to enhance. The more valuable users regard their other activities, the greater the likelihood of saturation; involvement in system development activities might be viewed as an imposition. Where users are more involved than they want to be: ***(a)*** involvement is unlikely to increase trust or sense of control; ***(b)*** end-users might be less receptive to learning about the system, improving their understanding of how to use the system, or making suggestions that might improve system quality; and ***(c)*** user satisfaction is less plausible as end-users see little or no value in being involved.
- ***Involvement deprivation*** – an involvement deprivation situation occurs when an individual's desired involvement substantially exceeds actual involvement and the user develops a sense of alienation. Thus, the individual has a high level of desire and motivation to be involved in systems development activities but does not get nearly enough chances of participating. Individuals in such situations feel either there is little regard for their talents and energy or there is insufficient

use of them. It is difficult to determine the exact point where an individual's perception regarding their level of involvement is altered to ***high deprivation***. This might happen even when there is a level of involvement but the user perceives it as too little or of inconsequential effort. Users often expect meaningful involvement that gives them opportunities for self-expression, respect, influence, and contribution. Users may resent nominal involvement considering it as an act of manipulation. In such situations: ***(a)*** end-users are unlikely to be receptive to learning about the system, improve their understanding of how to use the system, or make suggestions that might improve system quality; ***(b)*** resistance is increased and acceptance is reduced; and ***(c)*** user satisfaction is negatively affected.

These involvement episodes create opportunities and challenges for the management. Opportunities exist for identifying individuals who are motivated to be involved and providing them with the right level of involvement through appropriate arrangements. Opportunities also exist for avoiding dysfunctional situations such as creating ***high involvement deprivation*** or ***involvement saturation*** scenarios. Challenges exist for the management in evaluating the individual's competency, matching the individual's talents with task difficulty, creating appropriate involvement arrangements, and determining involvement rewards. Ultimately, individuals want to benefit from involvement arrangements and enhance their career opportunities. The management must seek avenues for providing user benefits through the involvement process and the organizational context.

Using field study data, Doll and Torkzadeh developed and recommended eight activities in which users may be involved in information system development. Table below provides these activities and suggests a 5-point scale for measuring the user's level of *desired* involvement. The scale reflects a range from not at all (1) to a great deal (5). These measures can also be used to measure *actual* involvement in system development activities. The management can use this survey instrument in preparation for selecting individuals for involvement in system development. This instrument also provides information on the type of involvement that the user may feel confident or prepared to undertake.

*Table 5.3, Measures of end-user involvement*

| Developmental activity | Level of involvement |
|---|---|
| 1. Initiating the project? | 1 ------- 5 |
| 2. Determining system objectives? | 1 ------- 5 |
| 3. Determining the user's information needs? | 1 ------- 5 |
| 4. Assessing alternative ways of meeting the user's information needs? | 1 ------- 5 |
| 5. Identifying sources of information? | 1 ------- 5 |
| 6. Outlining information flows? | 1 ------- 5 |
| 7. Developing input forms/screens? | 1 ------- 5 |
| 8. Developing output format? | 1 ------- 5 |

- ***Business knowledge*** – business knowledge and understanding is another critical success factor for information system development. There are at least two perspectives for business knowledge. The ***first*** perspective relates to the understanding of what the business is about, what the organizational mission is, and what its goals and objectives are. This perspective involves a focused understanding of the business over and beyond understanding of the respective industry. For example, while it is useful to clearly distinguish between service, manufacturing, healthcare, or insurance industry, it is critical to understand the business of the organization within a given industry. A system is developed, for example, for a business that is in the healthcare, insurance, or manufacturing. The management of information technology function must understand their industry in general and their organization in particular. Technical skills of an information technology manager are not substitute for their business knowledge and understanding.

The ***second*** perspective about business knowledge relates to the understanding of the organizational culture and processes. Organizations are run differently even within the same industry, and much of that depends on the culture of the organization and top management decision making style and viewpoint. The management of information technology must have a good understanding of effective ways for getting things accomplished within the prevalent organizational culture. Organizational culture reflects, for example, the level of organizational understanding and appreciation for new technology or the type of interorganizational relations that is necessary for system development activities and support.

Sometimes, information systems managers find themselves in a situation where they need to educate senior executives about potential and eventual benefits of technology application. This approach can be quite effective in situations where top management is skeptical of technology benefits but open to learning. This approach may not work in situations where top management is not only unenthusiastic about technology application but unwilling to learn. The management of information technology must use discretion in deciding what approach is effective to promote top management support and understanding of technology. The knowledge and understanding of organizational culture is an important factor in that determination.

- ***Expectation management*** – managing user expectation is a critical success factor for the management of information technology function. There are two levels at which this user expectation is influenced. The ***first*** level relates to the correspondence between the expectations of system sponsors and users on the one hand and those of the system developers and technical support personnel on the other. System sponsors describe their expectations via proposal for system development and in their initial interaction with system developers. Understanding business issues as well as effective communication skills are important mechanisms for creating the necessary correspondence between expectations of these two groups. In order to develop realistic user expectation, information technology management must avoid 'overselling' technology capabilities and benefits.

The ***second*** level of expectations relates to managing expectations relative to the original understanding between the sponsors and developers. System sponsors and users alter their expectations as system development activities progress and as they learn about new technologies. The management of information technology function must clearly communicate expectations to the developers and update sponsors and users through progress reports and regular feedback. It is important that project progress is communicated with respect to scope statement and in the context that the sponsors and users can see their original expectations realized. In other words, progress is expressed in terms of deliverables, milestones, and other indicators described in the development plan.

- ***Change management*** – managing system change is also an important success factor for the management of information technology function. System change can also alter user expectations. Some changes are significant and can alter the overall contribution of the system. This in turn may lead to change in the initial expectations of sponsors and users. System change may be perceived differently by different user groups or sponsors. Some may see change as a useful development that improves the outcome product and some may see change as having a negative impact on their work. Some changes are proposed primarily to improve work process while others are proposed to improve usage.

It is important to assess whether a change will alter the system's contribution to work and productivity. It is critical to evaluate the effect of change on sponsors and users expectations. It is important for the information technology management to establish and communicate the change process and reasons for change. Forming a change management committee is an appropriate way that accomplishes several objectives: ***(a)*** to encourage useful and innovative change proposals; ***(b)*** to establish a review and approval process for change proposals; ***(c)*** to create a mechanism for administering approved changes; and ***(d)*** to establish a communication channel for updating stakeholders.

The change management committee can therefore become an effective means of managing expectations. The establishment of a change management process through an organization-wide committee has practical benefits that relate to receiving additional support to implement change or to release contingency funds. The change management committee can play an important role in informing stakeholders about possible delays and in providing them with rationale for such delays.

## User satisfaction

Ideally one would like to evaluate information technology applications in terms of their degree of use in decision making and their impact on productivity, innovation, customer service, management control, and increased competitive advantage. In other words, information systems utility in decision making and problem solving reflects their benefits. However, this decision analysis approach is generally not feasible. End-user satisfaction is a potentially measurable surrogate for utility in decision making. User satisfaction is typically defined as the extent to which the system meets the user's information needs. An information system utility in decision making is enhanced when the outputs meet the user's information requirements and the system is easy to use. Ease of use or user friendliness is especially important for voluntary use of the system by managers and individuals who are not technology savvy.

In a voluntary situation, system use can also be a surrogate measure of system success. In situations where system use is mandated by the top management, perceptual measures of satisfaction may be more appropriate. Research studies have shown that user satisfaction leads to increased system use making it a critical factor for measuring success. Information system researchers have dedicated significant efforts to developing reliable and valid measures of computer user satisfaction. One of these instruments measures end-user satisfaction with different dimensions of information systems and is widely used in research and practice. The end-user computing satisfaction instrument was developed by Doll and Torkzadeh who used field study data in their research. This instrument measures end-user satisfaction with respect to content, accuracy, format, ease of use, and timeliness. These five factors capture important features of information systems that are important to the end-user and that influence user satisfaction.

Table below presents recommended measures for these five factors of user satisfaction. More than one measure is used to capture end-user belief about each factor. These factors collectively reflect the overall user satisfaction with a specific system. A 5-point scale is also recommended for these measures that range from not at all (1) to a great deal (5). This instrument could be a useful tool for information technology managers in assessing end-user satisfaction with a system. Mean scores of responses to these questions will provide the extent of satisfaction. This instrument also is helpful in deciding areas of strengths and weaknesses in a system.

*Table 5.4, Measures of end-user computing satisfaction*

| Measures of user satisfaction | Satisfaction level |
|---|---|
| ***Content*** | |
| 1. Does the system provide the precise information you need? | 1 -------- 5 |
| 2. Does the information content meet your needs? | 1 -------- 5 |
| 3. Does the system provide reports that seem to be just about exactly what you need? | 1 -------- 5 |
| 4. Does the system provide sufficient information? | 1 -------- 5 |
| ***Accuracy*** | |
| 5. Is the system accurate? | 1 -------- 5 |
| 6. Are you satisfied with the accuracy of the system? | 1 -------- 5 |
| ***Format*** | |
| 7. Do you think the output is presented in a useful format? | 1 -------- 5 |
| 8. Is the information clear? | 1 -------- 5 |
| ***Ease of use*** | |
| 9. Is the system user friendly? | 1 -------- 5 |
| 10. Is the system easy to use? | 1 -------- 5 |
| ***Timeliness*** | |
| 11. Do you get the information you need in time? | 1 -------- 5 |
| 12. Does the system provide up-to-date information? | 1 -------- 5 |

These five factors are intuitively appealing and seem relevant to the majority of information system applications. However, additional questions may be added to these measures to evaluate unique features of an information system. For example, if an information system application involves online database access through the web, additional questions that relate to communication channel and speed may be added to measure retrieval effectiveness. Similarly, one or more of these recommended factors may be dropped from a given survey if they do not seem to be relevant to the focus of the evaluation.

This is a short and easy to use instrument that can be administered at multiple points in time to all users of an information system product and to study the pattern of change in the level of satisfaction as well as the areas of concern. For example, the level of satisfaction for ease of use factor may increase as users are better trained while the level of satisfaction with content or accuracy factor may remain the same suggesting the need for system modification. In other words, this instrument can be used to compare end-user satisfaction with specific factors across projects. Multiple administrations of these measures at different times and for different systems will provide a framework for comparative analysis.

The sample data that were used to develop this instrument represented diverse information systems from 44 firms. The sample also represented a diverse set of applications for analysis, decision-making, engineering, planning, and control from 618 respondents. This cross organizational aspects of the sample and its characteristics made it appropriate to develop tentative standards. Percentile scores for the 12-item satisfaction instrument are presented in Table below. The possible total score for the 12 items is 60 given the 5-point scale used with this survey instrument. These statistics can be used as a benchmark to evaluate end-user satisfaction with a system.

*Table 5.5, Percentile scores for 12-item satisfaction instrument*

| **Percentile** | **Value** |
|---|---|
| 10 | 37 |
| 20 | 43 |
| 30 | 46 |
| 40 | 48 |
| 50 | 51 |
| 60 | 53 |
| 70 | 54 |
| 80 | 57 |
| 90 | 59 |

## Perceived usefulness

Information system executives are increasingly required to justify technology investment in terms of its impact on and usefulness for employees and their work. This perspective goes beyond design features to evaluate benefits in terms of outcome. The success of information technology from this perspective is measured through the impact on work at the level of the individual. The widespread use of information technology at all levels within organizations has increased its impact. Organizations that spend millions of dollars on information technology are primarily concerned about how their investment will influence organizational and individual performance.

Information technology researchers have shown increased attention to measures of information technology impact and usefulness. One research study has produced an instrument that measures perceived usefulness of information systems for the individual. It is argued that the impacts of information technology are quite varied in their nature and their levels, not only across different types of settings, but also across different computing contexts within comparable settings and even across different individuals. The set of questions presented in Table below relate to information system usefulness in terms of task productivity, task innovation, customer satisfaction, and management control. A five-point scale was used to develop this instrument where 1 = not at all, 2 = little, 3 = moderately, 4 = much, and 5 = a great deal. The instructions for respondents should ask them to indicate the response that reflects their current belief rather than their expectation.

*Table 5.6, Measures of information system usefulness*

| Measures of usefulness | Level of use |
|---|---|
| **Task productivity** | |
| 1. This application saves me time | 1 -------- 5 |
| 2. This application increases my productivity | 1 -------- 5 |
| 3. This application allows me to accomplish more work than would otherwise be possible | 1 -------- 5 |
| **Task innovation** | |
| 4. This application helps me create new ideas | 1 -------- 5 |
| 5. This application helps me come up with new ideas | 1 -------- 5 |
| 6. This application helps me try out innovative ideas | 1 -------- 5 |
| **Customer satisfaction** | |
| 7. This application improves customer service | 1 -------- 5 |
| 8. This application improves customer satisfaction | 1 -------- 5 |
| 9. This application helps me meet customer needs | 1 -------- 5 |
| **Management control** | |
| 10. This application helps management control the work process | 1 -------- 5 |
| 11. This application improves management control | 1 -------- 5 |
| 12. This application helps management control performance | 1 -------- 5 |

Individuals responding to these questions describe the extent to which an information system product impacts their work relative to these dimensions (*productivity, innovation, customer satisfaction, management control*). This instrument enables the information technology manager to study a system's usefulness and the areas of concern relative to the four dimensions. There may be different levels of interest for each dimension depending on system objectives. For example, if a system is developed to help employees improve customer satisfaction then the factor that measures this dimension will be more relevant to measuring system success and may be given more weight when analyzing data. This instrument can also be used to compare perceived usefulness across time, across user group, and across systems.

By identifying unique aspects of the end-user perception regarding a system's outcome, the management can more carefully allocate human and other resources to improve system success. The two success instruments presented in this chapter for user satisfaction and perceived usefulness provide good tools to gather data from the end-user and study areas of strengths and weaknesses. The involvement instrument is also useful in assisting the management for involving end-users in system development activities and evaluating the extent to which these end-users might be able to help with developmental activities. Management can develop other measures that are more closely related to a specific system. However, these instruments have been developed using widely accepted research methodologies for instrument development. They have high reliability and validity that makes them appropriate for decision making analysis. The use of instruments such as these suggests a systematic approach by the management for obtaining feedback from the end-user. Using a structured approach to system evaluation such as the use of a valid instrument has several advantages. It:

- Provides historical data for comparative analysis
- Enhances confidence in stakeholders
- Provides confidence in the reliability of the results
- Provides ease of documentation
- Can be used as additional means of communication

- Helps user acceptance of the system
- Provides evidence of system success
- Provides useful information to design training programs
- Provides useful information to evaluate team performance
- Maintains top management support

## E-COMMERCE SUCCESS

Internet technologies have and continue to influence management decisions for all types of organizations including for and not for profit organizations. Effective use of Internet technologies is considered a major determinant of competitive advantage, market penetration, innovation, technology transfer, and even management competency. The value of Internet commerce to the customer is an important factor that influences online shopping decisions. Information technology researchers have examined what customers value as they shop online. It is argued that the ultimate question about Internet commerce success may be more a function of customers' belief and perception of the net value of the benefits and costs of both a product and the processes of *finding*, *ordering*, and *receiving* it.

In an attempt to understand what customers value most, Torkzadeh and Dhillon surveyed 620 online shoppers and developed two sets of measures for *means objectives* and *fundamental objectives* that influence Internet shopping. Fundamental objectives are important in that they influence decisions on whether to shop online or not. Means objectives help organizations achieve fundamental objectives. Measuring these objectives helps us understand benefits and costs of what Internet offers to the customer in terms of products and services and how this offering can be better than what is available through conventional means. The set of questions presented in the following two Tables represent measures of fundamental objectives and means objectives for Internet commerce as perceived by online shoppers. A five-point scale similar to the one described for user satisfaction was used in this study.

*Table 5.7, Measures of fundamental objectives for Internet shoppers*

| Measures | Value level |
|---|---|
| **Internet shopping convenience**<br>It is important to:<br>1. Make shopping easy<br>2. Minimize time to select a product<br>3. Minimize queuing time<br>4. Minimize effort of shopping<br>5. Minimize personal hassle<br>6. Minimize payment time<br>7. Minimize time pressure when shopping | <br><br>1 -------- 5<br>1 -------- 5<br>1 -------- 5<br>1 -------- 5<br>1 -------- 5<br>1 -------- 5<br>1 -------- 5 |
| **Internet ecology**<br>It is important to:<br>8. Minimize pollution<br>9. Minimize environmental impact<br>10. Reduce environmental damages | <br><br>1 -------- 5<br>1 -------- 5<br>1 -------- 5 |
| **Internet customer relation**<br>It is important to:<br>11. Assure an easy return policy<br>12. Provide quality after-sale service<br>13. Provide an easy return process | <br><br>1 -------- 5<br>1 -------- 5<br>1 -------- 5 |
| **Internet product value**<br>It is important to:<br>14. Minimize product cost<br>15. Minimize tax cost<br>16. Maximize product value<br>17. Ensure quality of product | <br><br>1 -------- 5<br>1 -------- 5<br>1 -------- 5<br>1 -------- 5 |

These measures can be used to evaluate what influences Internet shoppers and to provide insight for making decisions about Internet commerce. These measures can be applied to a specific product or to develop the value proposition viewed by prospective customers. The concept of a value proposition helps us arrive at benefits to a prospective customer of purchasing a product or services on the Internet. The end-result benefits and costs of product and the processes of finding, ordering, and receiving it characterize this value proposition. Different customers may consider different benefits and costs in judging the net value of Internet purchases, and the potential value to the customer is influenced by the means of purchasing it. The alternatives for the customer include purchase through other means, such as mail order or store shopping. The customer can also decide to purchase from another site or not purchase. These measures can also be used to prioritize objectives and identify individual value trade-offs. For example, what is the value trade-off to the customer between Internet customer relation and Internet ecology?

*Table 5.8, Measures of means objectives for Internet shoppers*

| Measures | Value level |
|---|---|
| **Internet product choice** | |
| I like to: | |
| 1. Have greater product selection | 1 -------- 5 |
| 2. Broad choice of products | 1 -------- 5 |
| 3. Have maximum range of quality product options | 1 -------- 5 |
| 4. Have maximum product variety | 1 -------- 5 |
| 5. Have maximum product availability | 1 -------- 5 |
| 6. Have ease of comparison shopping | 1 -------- 5 |
| 7. Greater product choice | 1 -------- 5 |
| **Online payment** | |
| I am concerned about: | |
| 8. Who will have access to my credit card number | 1 -------- 5 |
| 9. Unauthorized use of my credit card | 1 -------- 5 |
| 10. Misuse of my credit card | 1 -------- 5 |
| 11. My personal information being shared | 1 -------- 5 |
| **Internet vendor trust** | |
| I am concerned about: | |
| 12. Vendor legitimacy | 1 -------- 5 |
| 13. Seller legitimacy | 1 -------- 5 |
| 14. How much I can trust the vendor | 1 -------- 5 |
| 15. Security for Internet commerce | |
| **Shopping travel** | |
| I like to: | |
| 18. Travel as little as possible to purchase | 1 -------- 5 |
| 19. Drive as little as possible to shop | 1 -------- 5 |
| 20. Minimize travel for purchase | 1 -------- 5 |
| **Internet shopping errors** | |
| I am worried about: | |
| 21. Receiving wrong products | 1 -------- 5 |
| 22. Shipping errors | 1 -------- 5 |

## CHAPTER SUMMARY

Measuring information technology success has been and remains one the challenges for technology executives. Organizations increasingly evaluate information technology investments in terms of its impact on work at the individual as well as the organizational level. The management of information technology function must consider system success from this perspective. Experience suggests a high rate of failure for information system development in terms of cost, time, and focus. Information systems fail because of human, technical, organizational, or leadership issues. A system's success is greatly influenced by issues of ***user involvement***, ***user satisfaction***, ***user expectation, business knowledge***, and ***change management***. User involvement is considered an important factor that influences user satisfaction and ultimately system use. This chapter describes an instrument for measuring user involvement in system development activities. This instrument contains eight questions and can be use to measure *actual* as well as *desired* user involvement.

Use satisfaction is considered as a surrogate measure of success in information technology research; it is an important factor in assessing technology application and in obtaining user feedback. This chapter describes an instrument for measuring end-user computing satisfaction in terms of ***content, accuracy, format, ease of use***, ***and timeliness***. These dimensions combined reflect the overall level of user satisfaction with a given application.

This chapter also describes an instrument for measuring perceived usefulness of computer applications for work in terms of ***task productivity, task innovation, customer satisfaction***, and ***management control***. Perceived usefulness is an outcome oriented approach for measuring information technology success. While the measures of end-user computing satisfaction evaluate a system from ***design perspective***, the measures of perceived usefulness evaluate success from an ***outcome perspective***. The first set of measures can help management assess technology transfer and user acceptance and the second set of measures can help management evaluate impact on work.

With the increased use of Internet technology, organizations have increased their attention for developing e-commerce applications. It has become evident that what the customer values is an important factor that influences online shopping. This chapter describes two sets of measures for evaluating ***fundamental objectives*** as well as ***means objectives*** for Internet commerce. The first instrument measures fundamental objectives in terms of Internet ***shopping convenience***, ***Internet ecology, Internet customer relation***, and ***Internet product value***. The second instrument measures means objectives in terms of ***online payment, Internet product choice, Internet vendor trust***, and ***shopping travel***. The two instrument help management evaluate customers' belief and perception of the net value of the benefits and cost of both a product and the processes of *finding*, *ordering*, and *receiving* it.

## REFERENCES

1. Doll, W.J. and Torkzadeh, G., "The Measurement of End-User Computing Satisfaction." ***MIS Quarterly***, Vol. 12(2), June 1988, 259-274.

2. Doll, W.J. and Torkzadeh, G., "The Measurement of End-User Software Involvement." ***Omega***, Vol. 18(4), 1990, 399-406.

3. Keeney, R.L., "The value of Internet Commerce to the Customer." ***Management Science***, Vol. 45(4), 1999, 533-542.

4. Torkzadeh, G. Dhillon, G., "Measuring Factors that Influence the Success of Internet Commerce." ***Information Systems Research***, Vol. 13 (2), June 2002, 187-204.

5. Torkzadeh, G. and Doll, W.J., "The Development of a Tool for Measuring the Perceived Impact of Information Technology on Work." ***Omega***, Vol. 27, 1999, 327-339.

## DISCUSSION QUESTIONS

1. Evaluating information system success is a complex task that involves knowledge of *business* as well as *technology*. Information systems can be evaluated from the perspectives of the user or the developer. What are some specific success features from the sponsor's perspective? The user's perspective?
2. Review items of the end-user satisfaction instrument presented in

this chapter. Why do you think there are multiple questions for each factor (*content, accuracy, format, ease of use, timeliness*)?

3. Review items of the end-user satisfaction instrument and propose additional factors that you think are important to end-users.

4. Review items of the user involvement instrument and discuss them in terms of system development life cycle. Do you see a pattern that fits the system development life cycle?

5. Review items of perceived usefulness and suggest additional factors that you think are important to improving work. Do you think that the recommended factors are applicable to most systems?

## EXERCISES

1. Studies of successful system developments indicate several success factors:

- User involvement
- Top management support
- Clear system objectives
- Good developmental plan
- Good change management
- Good scheduling
- Clear scope and requirements
- Effective communication with stakeholders

How would you rank these? What other factors would you add to this list?

2. Assume the percentile information for user satisfaction presented in this chapter is based on data gathered from users of different information systems within your organization. Develop a specific goal for information technology function using this percentile information.

3. Information technology research suggests a positive relationship between user involvement in system development and user satisfaction with the resultant application. Use survey instruments described in this chapter for user satisfaction and user involvement to collect data and test the relationship between the two.

4. This chapter suggests that the perceived usefulness of information technology applications is quite varied in nature and level, not only across different types of settings, but also across different computing contexts within comparable settings and even across different individuals. Use survey instruments described in this chapter for perceived usefulness, collect data in your organization, and test these propositions.

5. This chapter suggests relationships between factors of means objectives and fundamental objectives for Internet commerce success. Use the two instruments described in this chapter, collect data, and examine these relationships.

6. Conduct a survey in your class to determine the level of usefulness for each of the four factors (productivity, innovation, customer satisfaction, management control) given in this chapter. Ask your respondents to think of an application that they use most frequently as they answer your questions.

7. This chapter suggests that the two instruments that measure Internet commerce value for the customer can be use to prioritize objectives and identify individual value trade-offs. For example, they can be used to determine the value trade-off to the customer between '*Internet customer relation*' and '*Internet ecology*'. Design a study that involves data collection using these two instruments and analyze data to determine value trade-offs for online customers.

# 6. INFORMATION SYSTEMS OFFSHORING AND GLOBALIZATION

McKinsey Global Institute estimates that or every dollar US companies spend offshoring work to India, the US economy gains $1.14. India gets 33¢. The McKinsey calculation is based on the assumption that 69% of the displaced workers will find new jobs with a year. And they will earn at least 96% of their former wages. (As reported in Business Week, December 6, 2004)

**Outsourcing in Action**

Bradford & Bingley is in the business of real estate, mortgages and investment planning. With ambitions to grow, the company has a stated objective of improving shareholder value by increasing return on equity by 20 percent within the next five years. The company hopes to achieve this not only through an aggressive growth strategy in the retail business, but also through cost control. Some of this could be realized through cross selling between its estate agency and savings customers. Other significant aspects include outsourcing non core IT functions. In this regard Bradford & Bingley outsourced the management and maintenance of its information and communications technology (ICT) to British Telecom (BT).

BT was good choice since it helped the company move towards a single platform, enabling Bradford & Bingley fluidly cross sell and up-sell all financial offerings. This was not possible in the earlier setting because of independently operated businesses running disparate networks. In particular Mortgage Express, Black Horse Estate Agency and mortgage broker, John Charcol had completely different infrastructures.

The challenge therefore for Bradford & Bingley was to ensure how the separate businesses could be united culturally and technologically so as to optimize the combined assets. Clearly there was a benefit in having a common infrastructure. It would indeed cost less than separate upgrades with each change. A scalable infrastructure would also help in adopting new IT applications. It would also be possible to market new products and services faster, quickly and in a more informed manner.

Disparate networks and infrastructures were a consequence of new acquisitions. In 1998, Bradford & Bingley realized that it was time for them to rationalize their approach. With BT becoming their strategic partner, Bradford & Bingley strived to systematically streamline their network, ensue managed data and voice services, implemented collaborative tools, besides implementing a range of security and disaster recovery services. BT also provided management and maintenance of wide and local area networking, spanning more that 550 branches in the UK. Patchy email platforms were consolidated into a single platform, thus replacing a complex, inefficient message-handling service. To link businesses through ISDN lines, it transferred the dial-in structure to BT Business Port on a sliding, usage based tariff. This helped staff to have remote access to calendar, diary, email and the intranet. Such a service was a huge benefit to a mobile sales force that depends on remaining in touch with market developments.

By outsourcing its information and communication technologies, Bradford & Bingley was able to concentrate on its core business, thus enhancing its customer service. Rationalization of all technical costs and networks, the single platform ensure consistency across the group. As a result Bradford & Bingley was able to enjoy an efficient, state-of-the-art technology and communications service that BT would maintain and upgrade as needed. Bradford & Bingley felt that outsourcing enabled then to have a faster reaction to any demands for new services, thus ensuring best-value service at the cutting edge of technology.

Bradford & Bingley has also been able to reduce its in-house technology support team from 250 to 22. Greater cost granularity was instituted by replacing a base fee for each contracted IT-related service with a pricing model reflecting the group's actual usage. With the ability to see where the costs were arising, helped each business identify areas for cost saving.

Bradford & Bingley identified the following key results of their outsourcing relationship with BT:

- Enhanced opportunities for cross-selling and up-selling
- Group freed up to focus more on its core business
- New financial products and services brought to market faster
- A more dynamic pricing plan, giving the group greater cost control
- A scalable, future-proof solution

---

Globalization is about the monumental structural changes occurring in the processes of production and distribution in the global economy. These structural changes are responses by many global enterprises that confront tremendous pressures and fantastic opportunities presented by the increased application and integration of advanced information and communications technologies (ICTs) into their core business processes. Through the application of information and communications technologies, enterprises have the ability to diminish the impact of space, time and distance. Global companies can break apart business functions that were previously thought to be best collocated (i.e. within the same geographic area), and spread them across the globe in a globally disarticulated labor and production process. Because business functions are being spread internationally, globalization engenders a fundamental global restructuring that encompasses socio-cultural, economic, and political boundaries.

Due to the rapid emergence and tremendous impact of globalization, there has been an increased need for outsourcing. The idea of outsourcing has integrated itself into virtually every industry imaginable, especially information systems. Overall, outsourcing has become a means to:

- Cut costs
- Improve scalability
- Increase efficiency and productivity

Specific to information systems, outsourcing accomplishes a greater task; it becomes a means to an end when an organization lacks the necessary resources to advance in this technological age. Outsourcing information systems services allows the organization to focus in-house resources on core functions, improve the quality of information systems, increase access to new technology, stabilize information systems costs, re-engineer processes, and reduce obsolete technology.

As a consequence, a vast amount of services are being outsourced globally, a phenomenon often termed as offshoring. Table 7.1 depicts the primary services being offshored.

*Table 6.1, Primary Services Being Outsourced*

| | |
|---|---|
| Call Centers | System Integration |
| IT Consulting | Software Development |
| Financial Services | Billing Services |
| Application Maintenance | BackOffice Support |
| Networking Services | Software Testing |
| Customer Support | Technical Support |
| Product Support | Wireless Services |
| Data Processing | Design Services |

There are two kinds of outsourcing: Application and Business Process Outsourcing. Application Outsourcing (AO) helps companies manage their portfolios of business applications to gain greater value from their IT investments. It handles the full lifecycle of application services, from initial design development, and integration to on-going management and eventual retirement of software. On the contrary, Business Process Outsourcing (BPO) relies on third parties to manage and optimize labor intensive, repetitive technology-enabled business processes. BPO enables companies to reduce costs and gain efficiency improvements in non-core operational processes while freeing resources and management attention to concentrate on functions and processes that provide unique competitive advantage.

*Table 6.2, Average cost savings because of global outsourcing*

| Application Outsourcing (AO) | Business Process Outsourcing (BPO) | AO + Global Delivery | BPO + Global Delivery |
|---|---|---|---|
| • An average of 10-20% reduction in costs<br>• Improved IT performance<br>• Increased organizational flexibility | • An average of 10-20% reduction in costs<br>• Optimized processes<br>• Improved quality and business performance<br>• Increased organizational flexibility | • An average of 25-50% reduction in costs<br>• Improved IT performance<br>• Increased organizational flexibility | • An average of 30-60% reduction in costs<br>• Optimized processes<br>• Improved quality and business performance<br>• Increased organizational flexibility |

AO and BPO are effective on a domestic scale, however, when paired with globalization the effectiveness of each practically doubles. Table 6.2 displays how significant and cost efficient outsourcing on a global level is compared to outsourcing on a domestic level. Being able to demonstrate with financial evidence that pairing outsourcing and globalization is advantageous to an organization will propel this phenomenon into the future and increase global interconnectivity.

## GLOBALIZATION ISSUES

On a global scale, every country has its own socio-cultural, economic, and political values. Attempting to integrate these to accomplish outsourcing presents several obstacles that need to be overcome. Outsourcing challenges can be categorized into three areas: organizational challenges, business risks, and performance management.

## Organizational Challenges

In dealing with any agreement between two companies, organizational as well as cultural differences must be considered. These issues can cause communication breakdown and other work-related issues. The key to dispelling these occurrences is to establish trust, openness, and honesty between organizations as in the case of Xerox and EDS. Furthermore, change management must be implemented when planning to outsource any business function. In order to be effective on a strategic level, an organization must understand that outsourcing causes a great deal of change and precautions should be made to help soften the blow. Outsourcing also, impacts organizational structures, processes, job roles and responsibilities. There must be someone to take ownership of the outsourcing effort.

## Business Risks

There risks associated with outsourcing on a global level are magnified compared to outsourcing domestically. An organization must consider infrastructure risks, security risks, legal issues, and political and environmental disruption.

Infrastructure problems include power outages and disruptions in communication. Some necessary precautions that organizations must consider are backup generators and extra communication lines and network equipment. Security is one of the biggest issues because the outsourcing effort may give way to each organization's most sensitive and valuable data, which is another reason that establishing personal relationships and trust is imperative. The legalities of an international agreement are very intricate. Legal systems may differ and country standards may not be compatible. It is even more difficult to ensure that in a disagreement both parties are adequately protected. Apart from the organization, there are other external factors that can impact global outsourcing such as political affiliations and natural disasters. It is important that in planning the outsourcing effort that these situations are considered.

## Performance Management

The purpose of outsourcing is to get the desired result that one could not achieve in-house. Ensuring this from another company in another country is extremely difficult. In order for performance to meet expectations there must be equal effort from all parties involved. In order to accomplish this goal, performance management requires a combination of strong governance, well chosen measurements, and clear accountability.

## Trade Agreements

Advances in information technology, combined with free-market ideology, has given goods, services, and capital unprecedented mobility. If you look at it this way, then outsourcing globally is just a new way of doing international trade. There has to be an agreement that is fluid and mutually reinforcing and accounts for the economic, political, and cultural relationships that may be built from the global outsourcing effort. The trade agreement should also analyze the potential impact the trade agreement will have on globalization and international relations. Following is a list of organizations that facilitate trade agreements between organizations:

- **World Trade Organization (WTO).** Established in 1995 as a successor to GATT (General Agreement on Treaties and Tariffs), WTO aims to ensure free trade through reduction of tariff and non-tariff barriers.
- World Bank. The World Bank, an affiliated of the United Nations makes loans guaranteed loans to developing countries. Seven countries, United States, Germany, Japan, Great Britain, Canada, Italy and France, have 45% of the voting power.
- **International Monetary Fund (IMF).** The IMF is closely affiliated with the World Bank. IMF has a similar voting arrangement as that of the World Bank. IMF aims to maintain stable currency exchange rates between countries. IMF also issues loans to help countries restructure their economies.
- **NAFTA.** The North American Free Trade Agreement is an agreement between the United States, Canada and Mexico to integrate their respective economies through the lowering and eventual removal of tariff barriers.
- **Organization for Economic Cooperation and Development (OECD)** The OECD is a group of 30 member countries provides governments a platform to discuss, develop and perfect economic and social policy.

## OFFSHORE OUTSOURCING STRATEGY

Now that we have discussed various globalization issues and the importance of trade agreements, it is essential to discuss the need for companies to clearly define their outsourcing strategy before they put it into practice. Is the company pursuing an offshore outsourcing strategy because everyone else is? Has the company analyzed the short term and long term implications on their business processes? Has the company outlined their business requirements? These are just some of the questions, which have to be answered before outsourcing any project or department.

When a company or organization is trying to determine if they should use offshore outsourcing they need to base their decision on the same factors, which they use in managing their operations. Factors such as quality of work, risk, cost, understanding of local culture and business, and employee relations all need to be weighed in the decision. Each of the factors mentioned above can further broken down and analyzed.

**Quality** is the concept of creating software or other products with the smallest number of defects. Many techniques have been developed to minimize defects. Breaking a project into small well-defined tasks allows a company to create standards to ensure defects are eliminated. There are two main schools of thought with regard to quality. One school believes that quality should be part of the design process and not just tested for at the end of development. The next school of thought believes that the statistical approach to quality is best. This approach monitors the process and takes corrective action if too many defects are present. If a company takes the first approach and build quality into the design process many of the problems will be eliminated entirely. Some important factors include:

- **Risk** is the probability that some harm may occur due to a company's current decision or action. Managing risk is part of any company's day-to-day operations and their goal should be to reduce the risk associated with any project to an acceptable level. Off shoring work provides access to new highly qualified workers at a reduced cost. Also large companies reduce their risk level by distributing their work processes on a global basis. Failure, loss of intellectual property, and security of data are all additional risks that have to be assessed when outsourcing work.

- The **cost** of outsourcing projects can vary greatly. While large organizations can outsource entire divisions' small companies need to make sure they look at the total costs of outsourcing. Costs associated with personnel issues, travel, system infrastructure, telecommunications, productivity issues, and overhead should all be included. The economies of scale associated with a larger company may not exist for smaller companies when they try to develop an offshore project.
- Understanding the local **culture** and business processes of a remote country can be very complicated. Most companies lack the expertise and knowledge to effectively interact with other cultures. To help alleviate this problem companies are hiring consultants who can provide the industry expertise.
- As more and more jobs are outsourced overseas current employees may become less motivated. As the demand for skilled workers increase and as companies are pushed to decrease costs more and more work will be sent overseas. Employees will have to **upgrade their skill sets** to ensure they are not left behind in the global economy. Companies can help with this transition by training the employees who are with the company.

## CRITICAL SUCCESS FACTORS FOR OFFSHORE OUTSOURCING

Management of the offshore outsourcing relationship is critical for the success of the project. There is a direct correlation between the amount of time and care that is put into developing the relationship of the two companies and the overall success of the project. The more complex the outsourcing relationship is, in terms of services and alliances, the greater the demand is for establishing the management structure. The management team will have to interact with the outsourcing company at many levels. The factors which lead to the success of outsourcing decisions and the ensuing relationships can be broken down into four sections, strategy, evaluation process, contract agreement, and outsource management.

## Strategy

The long term plan of action designed to achieve a company's goals needs to be developed before a company out-sources any work or divisions. Therefore a company should have a clearly defined outsourcing strategy that identifies the business processes of the organization. Every organization has inputs, outputs, and methods, which have been developed over many years. These business processes are part of the larger organization and allow the company to succeed in its industry. By aligning the business strategy and outsourcing strategy a company can successfully develop new strategic alliances through offshore outsourcing.

## Evaluation Process

An evaluation process has to be developed and implemented to choose the best provider for a specific project. To start the process a company needs to know what is available in the offshore outsourcing marketplace. We have developed a list of offshore outsourcing companies, which we have included in an exhibit at the end of the paper. Each of the companies on the list has a brief description. After determining what the offshore organization's area of expertise is, it will be possible to develop a preliminary list of companies one may want to work with.

The next step in the evaluation process would be to request information from the company and ask for references from previous work. Offshore outsourcing has been in place long enough that most organizations in the business should have a long list of clients. One also needs to establish how long the company has been in business to ensure that the company has a successful business plan in place.

## Contract Agreement

A contract is a mutually agreed upon set of promises of which the law will hold both parties to. The contract should benefit both parties and it should be standardized so it can easily be copied. The contract must measure the performance of the offshore outsourcing company against the specified requirements. But the contract must have the flexibility built into it to change over time. The scope of the project, terms and conditions may have to be redefined as business conditions change. Therefore both parties must be willing to constantly adjust the relationship based on the needs of the company and strategy.

## Offshore Outsource Management

Management is the process of leading and directing a company and its resources. These resources include the financial capital, human capital, and intellectual capital. Management decisions have to be analyzed on a continual basis and measured against the goals of the organization. Offshore outsource management is the delegation of tasks or jobs from within the organization to an overseas company. If the company and the service provider are able to develop a disciplined plan they should be able to establish a successful outsourcing relationship. Offshore outsourcing projects require knowledge and time to successfully develop and implement. If the company does not have the knowledge or plan to support the implementation of an offshore outsourcing strategy the company should postpone the decision.

## Project Team Creation

Taking an IS project from identification through to implementation and ongoing management requires both structure and leadership: structure in terms of a repeatable management process that is understood and followed by all, and leadership in terms of executive sponsors, project team leaders, and effective project team members. Outsourcing looks very much like a divestiture, spin-off, or an acquisition. As such, it affects everyone, both inside and outside the scope of the specific services involved. It demands careful planning and implementation, not only at the operational level, but on people. Once implemented, the effectiveness of the ongoing management of the relationship between the companies is the ultimate determining factor of the results achieved.

Most outsourcing projects will require that a series of teams form and evolve over its life. These can consist of policy teams that work with senior executives to evaluate opportunities and identify corresponding projects. Another might be an idea team that looks across the organization to identify areas add value through project implementation. These are then presented to senior executives for review. There are many flavors of project development across organizations so for the remainder of this section, the focus will be on the creation of project teams after corporate sponsorship has been received and the project is kicked off.

A note on the role of consultants should also be discussed. Consultants often play an important role. They can bring templates for much of the work that is common project to project. They bring experience gained from multiple projects, which can enable the team to move forward more quickly and avoid common mistakes and pitfalls. Consultants often know the provider market extremely well and can speed the process of bringing the right providers to the table. They can also bring resources to the project, thereby reducing the amount of internal time needed for the project; time that might be better spent elsewhere.

At the same time, consultants bring their own biases to the process. Because consultants have looked at the market place and the issues many times before, they may not be as alert to new ways of doing things or new providers. At the same time, certain providers can have a natural affinity for or against certain consultants.

Eventually, the consulting engagement will end. Therefore, the customer must be, throughout the process, the one defining and shaping the relationship. In the final analysis, each project team needs to evaluate its skills and resources and the type and role they want and need external advisors to play.

Project team members must bring knowledge from key operational areas of an organization to add the value needed for the team leader to successfully deliver the project. Figure 6.1 illustrates a project organizational structure for an IS project in the financial services industry.

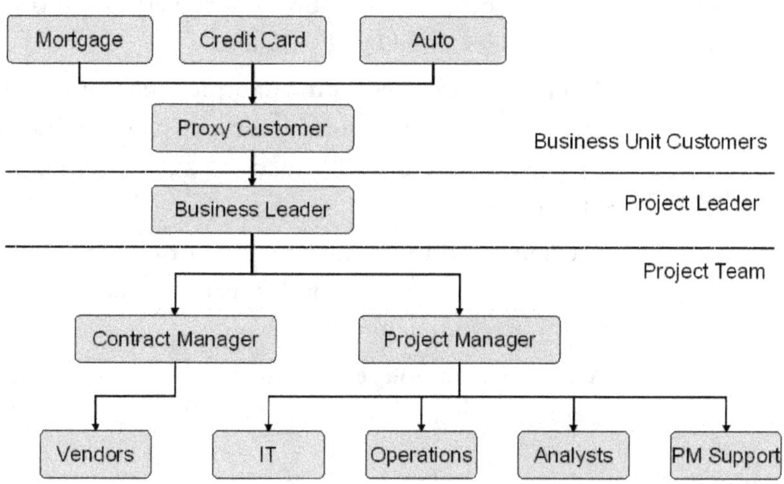


*Figure 6.1, Typical IS project management structure for a finance company*

In this example, there is an additional layer of management above the project manager. In many organizations, a business or project leader is required to focus squarely on the iterative process of defining the requirements between the internal customers and the operational specialists. The architecture of the requirements package must be specifications-based or performance-based. A decision between the two types involves a great deal of analysis and discussion of risks, institutional knowledge, and cash flow. The team leader works with the internal customers and senior management to make this determination. The requirements architecture is then communicated down through the project manager and once crafted, delivered to the contract manager for inclusion into the solicitation to vendors. In this case, the role of the team leader is independent of day-to-day generation of the project's scorecard which, consisting of cost and schedule information. That responsibility lies within the role of the project manager. It's also important to note that in this example, once the vendor is under contract, the business leader's role may be substantially reduced until the development phase is complete and the project is being rolled out. The integration of the system into the business units will then become the responsibility and focus of the team leader.

As apparent, the role of the project leader or manager is critical to the success of any project. In selecting individuals for this position, the following characteristics should be considered:

- **Ability to embrace and champion change.** They must be able to communicate not only what is happening, but also why and how it will benefit the organization, its customers, and its stakeholders.
- **Earned credibility across the organization.** To be an effective change agent, the individual must have a high degree of credibility across the organization.
- **A desire to manage, not to do.** The leader must be results-focused; excelling in the ability to accomplish results through others.
- **The ability to build trust.** Managers entrusted with evaluating and crafting outsourcing relationships need to have characteristics like principle-based decision making, and have demonstrated the

desire for both organizations to succeed.

- **Strong communications skills.** Communications is required throughout the process both externally and internally. Communications includes all media: written, verbal, small and large groups, traditional and electronic forms.
- **Strong negotiation skills.** Negotiating is not just a matter of getting the best deal, it's a matter of maximizing the value of the relationship for the client organization while, at the same time, fairly meeting most, if not all, of the needs of the provider.
- **Strategic planning skills.** A disciplined, consistent style in evaluating each decision as to its future implications is needed.
- **Project and team management skills.** The leader must be able to effectively bring both the customer sides and the provider sides together, keep them focused, recognize and reward each individual's contributions, and balance everyone's interests.
- **Marketing skills.** The leader constantly promotes the value of the project within the organization, ensuring that interest are understood and met, dealing with exceptions, and overcoming resistance
- **Process expertise**. The leader must have knowledge to the work being done, how the process works, what represents best-in-class performance, and how it is achieved.

Successful outsourcing efforts require support and leadership form the top of the organization; a well defined, forward leaning planning and implementation process; and participation of a multidisciplinary team. Organizations should not underestimate the complexity of the project or the level of internal resistance that a change of this magnitude can bring. Only a strong, fully supported process will overcome these challenges.

## FINAL WORD

Successful outsourcing and offshoring is indeed a function of how a given organization wants to focus (or refocus) its strategy. If the intent is to develop the core competencies and excel in delivering products and services that differentiate the organization from the other players in the market, clearly outsourcing and/or offshoring may be an option. However there should be a careful consideration of a range of financial, cultural and business process issues. Many a times it may make sense to outsource some of the functions, but a careful analysis may reveal that in fact getting others to provide some of the products and services may really not be an option. It therefore makes sense to develop organizational competence to define what needs to be outsourced and what needs to be kept in house.

In a final synthesis it is important to develop trust and ensure that the client and vendor fully understand the intricacies involved. It may be better to evaluate all pros and cons sooner than later.

## REFERENCES

**Further readings:**

Lacity, M., Hirschheim, M. (1993). Information Systems Outsourcing; Myths, Metaphors, and Realities. John Wiley & Sons, Inc. New York,

Kern, T., Willcocks, L. (2000). Exploring information technology outsourcing relationships: theory and practice. *Journal of Strategic Information Systems*. Vol 9, No. 4, pp. 321-350.

Amiti, M., Wei, S. J. (2005). Fear of service outsourcing: is it justified? *Economic Policy*, Vol 20 No. 42 pp. 308-347.

Langfield-Smith, K., Smith, D. Management control systems and trust in outsourcing relationships. *Management Accounting Research*, Vol. 14, No. 3.

## DISCUSSION QUESTIONS

1. You have taken over as CIO of a large engineering and construction firm with contracts for building oil rigs in the North Sea, building a new airport in South East Asia and working with the US Department of Defense on making substantial enhancements to buildings at a major US Air Force Base. The skill requirements for all the projects are diverse and requirements for safety, security and reliability considerably high. Although your company was successful in procuring the various contracts, sustainability of a leading edge industry position and containing the cost of operations are worries shared by most in the senior management. How do you think the company can (a) identify the

right kind of skills necessary for being competitive and (b) how can the company harness the potential of IT to build a highly competent firm?

2. You are a founding member of a new firm providing educational, training and consulting services in the general area of Six Sigma. The operations are highly dependent on computer based learning and self directed study. Given that the firm is relatively new and various organizational processes are still being defined, how can you (a) ensure that the right kind of competencies are developed (b) the relevant IT competencies are sustained over a period of time?

3. Identify the implementation of any IT project is a firm and suggest how the company was able to (or not able to) balance the range of strategic and efficiency benefits.

4. Identify a firm in an information intensive industry. Comment on the range of competencies this firm possesses to harness IT to its advantage. Given our discussion in this chapter suggest how the chosen firm has been able to achieve success or failed in the process.

# 7. ORGANIZATIONAL COMPETENCE IN INFORMATION SYSTEMS

Many organizations fail because of a lack of competence. Yet others are able to sustain themselves because they are able to leverage know-how and skills for competitive advantage. Ability to consider future competence and how information technology could be used is a useful organizations competence.

**Competence in Action**

John Brown was founded in the 1830's and by the time the company was acquired by the diversified Trafalgar House Group in 1986, it had built a global presence through a collection of relatively small offices around the world. With the addition of Davy International in 1991, a similarly long-established engineering company, the Trafalgar Group added complementary expertise to its Engineering Division and became the third largest E&C company in the world (measured on turnover), along with Bechtel (USA) and Fluor Daniel (USA). Acquisition of Davy increased the number of Trafalgar House Engineering offices worldwide to 182 (25,000 employees in 30 countries). John Brown's sites were small relative to those of the competition, whose sites were fewer, but of larger size. Generally each office offered a local service to local customers: *"the local offices had a lot of autonomy. The CEO was responsible for his own bottom-line and at the end of the Eighties, he really could have spent the budget however he liked. One used to joke that he could have bought a golf course with his annual budget."*

Offices had their own areas of expertise. John Brown management recognized the strength of the unique skills in these offices and tried to preserve them rather than rationalize or homogenize them into larger masses. But the size of many offices meant that they were restricted to bidding for small projects, or to taking on contract staff to man larger projects. Typically, a large project might require up to 40% extra temporary manpower, which was expensive and inefficient. Also, small offices rarely had all the skills required for large projects; finding these skills from other parts of the organization incurred travel and time costs for the rest of the Group.

IT systems had played an important part in the engineering task since the late 1970's. John Brown was no different from the competition in having large mainframes with proprietary systems available to enable projects to move through to completion. By the end of the Eighties, the company's systems were operating on a legacy infrastructure consisting of a dozen mainframes: *"We had made a lot of investment in IT during the first half of the Eighties and it really did not take us far. The mainframes we bought were very expensive, the CAD tools we invested in did not deliver, in general our systems were not cost effective."*

This realization became critical as cost issues surfaced in an increasingly competitive and recession-dominated economic climate. Driving the competitive climate was new, low cost, high-tech competition from the East, e.g. Hyundai and the Agip oil field project off the coast of Libya. A strategic initiative by the parent company at the beginning of the decade asked John Brown's business managers to list their needs for the future. High on their lists were ways to meet customer demands for reduced engineering man-hours per project; ways to reduce total installed costs of plant for the customer; ways to maximize customer satisfaction; and ways to stop the duplication of information. In addition, John Brown managers wanted to be in a position to take advantage of new opportunities that might become available as large oil and pharmaceutical companies outsourced 'non-core' activities.

Winning big projects from companies that were becoming more global was seen by John Brown as essential for the company's future. These were bread-and-butter contracts that allowed predictability in earning streams and cash flows back to John Brown. Compared with the competition, John Brown was not in a good position to win big contracts. Fluor Daniels and Bechtel generated sales close to double that of John Brown. These same competitors, plus M W Kellogg, the Wood Group, ABB Global and perhaps three other major players had better revenue-to-staff ratios. John Brown had a lot of staff, but they were spread over many small offices around the world resulting in mass without scale, and costs without the consistent ability to take on the big projects. The local presence, however, provided John Brown with good 'shop window' visibility, and knowledge of local requirements and peculiarities. To get more global contracts, John Brown would have to change: *"Toward the end of the Seventies, through most of the Eighties, the relationship with the customer was very adversarial. On projects, there was man-for-man marking! For example, on a design and fabrication contract there would be 150 John Brown engineers and 150 of the client's engineers checking our work."*

If the global client was the target, the global office was the way of creating scale without mass. IT would be at the heart of building project teams of people with unique skills from John Brown offices around the world without them having to leave their desks. It was a risky strategy for John Brown. In the late 1980's the company had tried to take advantage of a low-cost, English-speaking labor force in India by establishing an office in Bombay, which would contribute resources to larger, distant projects. This had failed, largely because communicating with other offices proved very cumbersome, especially when the majority of project work traveled by courier between offices. John Brown's top management learned that virtual teams could only work with the right foundations.

The new vision was to link all the disparate and far-flung offices around the world using open systems to build a global network of engineers. Using "electronic corridors" through which engineers could access, update or amend project data, CAD drawings, proposals, project management information, teams of specialists from around the world worked together without having to change their desks, offices, or cultures. Offices could retain their specialties because the IT systems became so common that engineers, wherever they were in the company, could use the same tools to complete the engineering cycle. "Our IT strategy was -- open systems, with a preferred approach to buy packages where possible. By using open systems with distributed databases there was no need to build a central system, but when engineers log-on and call-up the Engines system, for instance, it is the same system with the same functionality and the same engineering practices. For instance, there is a 200 man team in Charleston - USA, their experience is in maintenance and shut-down type work for process plants. The intention was not to turn that office into the full services of: design, procurement, commission, build. They were not equipped to do it, but they can use our tools for whatever part of the cycle their strength lay in. This expertise is now available worldwide; the systems enable anyone to use it."

The first step was the development of John Brown International Network (JOIN), a global, high-speed network, which provided the electronic corridors to the global office. The network had to accommodate client/server computing between 8000 PCs, 700 CAD workstations and over 170 corporate UNIX servers in 40 locations. John Brown worked with 3Com, the US computer networking company to develop a form of advanced data compression, enabling cheaper and quicker information transfer along JOIN. The company boasts that JOIN responds within half a second, even between London and Melbourne – "*any longer and users would not feel they were in the same office*." The primary benefit of JOIN is the cost-effectiveness and time-saving it can offer the client. Traditionally, prior to JOIN, amendments to engineering project drawings were manually created, copied, reviewed and transported by mail from John Brown's offices to the client - a time-consuming and costly process which could be required many times over. By using JOIN, this process is carried out electronically and is therefore compressed dramatically. By making the software applications that run on JOIN compatible as well, John Brown is able to extend the benefits of concurrent engineering and round-the-clock working still further. John Brown's advanced system enables engineering drawings and video images of the construction site to be transmitted in seconds to the client and the home office project team. As a result, problems can be discussed in a "live" on-line situation, amendments made and technical issues resolved by the original designer within a matter of hours.

---

Over the years, the issue of gaining benefits from IT (Information Technology) services within an organization has received much attention [1, 2, 3, 4, 5]. It is important to address this issue since the use of computer-based systems permeates most aspects of business life. Predominant emphasis has however been on assessing the user satisfaction, information quality, and individual/organizational impact as key determinants of success of organizational IT operations. DeLone and McLean [6], through a comprehensive literature review of IT success measures, observe that "in searching for an IS (information systems) success measure, rather than finding none, there are nearly as many measures as there are studies" (p.61). These researchers developed an integrated view of IT success by defining six major dimensions: systems quality, information quality, use, user satisfaction, individual impact, and organizational impact. Later, Delone and McLean [7] developed the initial framework and added the concept of service quality and net benefits. The concept of net benefits may reflect the positive or negative impact of information systems on customers, suppliers, employees, organizations, markets, industries, economies or even society.

In addressing a similar issue, our intent is to take the debate a step further by considering concepts rooted in the strategy literature to assess the ability of an organization to deliver IT benefits. In furthering this aim, we have adopted the notion of competence to interpret the ability of an organization to deliver satisfactory IT services.

Developing and managing IT service delivery is an important process within organizations since it enables an organization to be successful over a long period of time and it is a precursor to creating value for the stakeholders. This objective is achieved through two inter-related activities. First, by managing the current operations successfully. Second, by having an ability to change in the face of ongoing challenges and future demands.

In this paper, based on substantial research, a set of organizational competencies for delivering IT services are presented. An overarching framework for organizational competencies is developed. Such a framework will help in evaluating the current level of organizational competence in providing IT services. The framework can also be used as a planning tool to think about the future abilities that an organization needs to develop.

## CONCEPTUALIZING IT COMPETENCIES

The concept of competence assumed particular relevance with the development of the resource-based view of the firm. Resource-Based Theory (RBT) emphasizes the importance of resources of the firm that are valuable, cannot be easily purchased, or require a long learning process as an essential way to achieve superior performance ([8], [9]). RBT has been used in the information systems literature to explain the strategic impact of IT in organizations and understand business benefits from IT investments, more particularly how IT can influence firm performance [3, 10, 11, 12, 13].

One of the key challenges of RBT is defining the concepts of resource, competence and capability [14]. These concepts have been deeply discussed in the literature and a wide range of definitions can be found with a significant lack of consensus [14]. Srinivasan et al. [15] define resources as specific know-how or assets while capabilities include skills exercised through organizational processes that enable firms to use their assets.

Some researchers consider the concept of competence at the level of individual skills [16]. McGrath et al. [17] have considered the notion of competence emerging from an understanding of the business processes and individual skills. Peppard and Ward [18] argue that competence is an organizational concept that reflects a bundle of skills and technologies while capabilities are related to the strategic application of competencies in order to achieve business objectives. Caldeira and Ward [19] argue that in order to develop an organizational competence, it is essential to have not only the technical and managerial IT skills, business and general management skills, but also organizational processes to exploit those skills. Such exploitation allows an individual to apply his own personal characteristics and knowledge to resolve a particular task.

In the literature a few frameworks for IT competencies, resources and capabilities have been proposed. Peppard and Ward [18] based on the previous work of Peppard et al. [20] present a detailed framework of 26 IS organizational competencies that are important to achieve an IS capability. In the context of Peppard and Ward's paper [18], capability is a meta-construct, referring the strategic application of competencies to achieve organizational goals. The 26 competencies identified are divided in six major macro-competencies: strategy, defining the IS contribution, defining the IT capability, exploitation, delivery solutions, and supply. Dhillon [21] have also classified competencies into strategic, exploitation and supply. Caldeira et al. [22] developed a framework of information systems competencies that are relevant for SMEs (small and medium-sized enterprises).

Feeny and Willcocks [23, 24] introduced a model of the IT function with nine core capabilities. However, the concept of capability in Feeny and Willcocks [23, 24] is similar to the concept of competence of Peppard and Ward [18]. Core IS capabilities are, according to Feeny and Willcocks [23], "those necessary and sufficient to ensure that an organization can exploit changing markets of technology and services – to achieve business advantage through IT over time" (p.20). These are: IT leadership, business systems thinking, relationship building, architecture planning, making technology work, informed buying, contract facilitation, contract monitoring, and vendor development.

Using a knowledge-based perspective, Bassellier et al. [25] developed a "model of IT competence" with two major dimensions: Explicit IT Knowledge and Tacit IT Knowledge. They argue that "to address the emerging role of IT in organizations that goes beyond the simple execution of a task and requires a broader awareness, attention to non-task-specific competences is needed….bringing knowledge into the competence definition broadens the concept by making it dynamic and interactive" (p. 163-164). Explicit knowledge includes: technology, applications, systems development, management of IT, and access to IT knowledge. On the other hand, Tacit IT Knowledge involves experience (personal use of IT, IT projects, and management of IT) and cognition (process view, and vision for the role of IT). Montequín et al. [26] also present a framework of key success factors, for knowledge management, that is strongly based on competences.

By conducting an extensive literature review on previous research and using RBT principles, Wade and Hulland [14] present a typology of "key IS resources" (p.107). This typology includes: manage external relationships, market responsiveness, IS-business partnership (manage internal relationships), IS planning and change management, IS infrastructure, IS technical skills; IS development, cost effective IS operations. However, to Wade and Hulland [14] (p.109), resources are "assets and capabilities that are available and useful in detecting and responding to market opportunities".

Although presenting relevant similarities, the frameworks, models and typologies analyzed in the literature also show significant differences. This can be explained, not only by the different objectives and contexts where the research was conducted (for example, Caldeira et al [22] framework was developed studying SMEs, while Peppard and Ward's [18] was designed by analyzing large companies), but also due to the different levels of abstraction and detail involved in the analysis of the data and definition of competencies. For example, Dhillon [21] conceptualizes organizational competences for harnessing IT, using the case of John Brown Engineering. The competencies presented by Dhillon are at a higher level of abstraction than the ones presented in this paper. We use multiple case studies to develop a mechanism to operationalize competencies is organizations.

In a synthesis of the literature, we found that there are many competencies that an organization might need (e.g. in marketing the products and managing its people). However, an ability to seek benefits from IT for the internal user community is critical to determine the relative success or failure of IT adoption. We therefore argue that there is a group of competencies, termed as facilitating competencies, which are necessary for an organization. In the literature a lot has been written about strategic and core competencies that help organizations to be differentiated from their competitors. It has also been argued, based on resource-based theory, that asset specificity is the primary means for defining strategic differentiation. While externally oriented competencies are essential, an organizations internal ability to define a strategic agenda for IT use is equally important. We term such competencies as fundamental competencies. As can be well appreciated there is always a need to introduce guidelines for IT professionals to interpret the competencies that might be necessary for delivering good services internally. Dhillon and Lee [27], for instance, define value-based objectives that organizations need to adhere to in ensuring that benefits are delivered. In research by Dhillon [4] and Ward and Daniel [5] a "benefits management" is presented as a possible means to establish such linkages. We call these linkages exploitation processes. Bundled in the exploitation processes are the competencies for delivery of IT benefits to an organization.

Mainstream strategic management literature has also argued for competencies along similar lines. Mahoney and Sanchez [28], for instance, articulate the notions of fundamental competencies and facilitating competencies as "dissociation of espoused theory and theory-in-use", which according to them is so prevalent that it is unknowingly or stoically accepted by managers (p. 56). Along a similar vein, Orton and Dhillon [29] term these as "meso-strategic" options.

Based on our synthesis of literature, in figure 7.1 our conceptualization of organizational competencies necessary for delivering IT benefits is presented. We equate fundamental competencies and facilitating competencies with the espoused and in-use theories respectively of Argyris and Schön [30]. We also argue that espoused theories correspond to the thinking loop. This is where much of the theorizing takes place.

Theories in use represent the doing loop. This is where most of the action is taken. However in order for successfully articulating the competencies for delivery of IT benefits, it is essential that focused exploitation processes get developed. Argyris and Schön [30] call this double loop learning. In our research we used the fundamental competencies, facilitating competencies, and exploitation processes to define very specific competencies that might be necessary for delivery of IT services and necessary processes to link both competencies. The next section presents the methodology used in achieving this purpose.

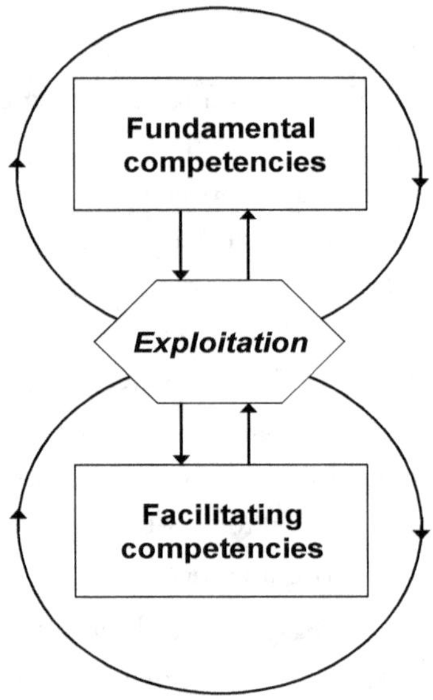


*Figure 7.1, A synthesized perspective on IT competencies*

## Fundamental competencies in delivering IT benefits

Our research identified six fundamental competencies that a firm needs to have to deliver good IT services. See appendix for methodological details. These include the:

1. ability to conduct IT strategic thinking and planning;
2. ability to align IT with business processes and objectives;
3. ability to deploy cost effective applications and systems;
4. ability to conceptualize the maintenance of data integrity and confidentiality.
5. ability to facilitate behavior enrichment for technology

adoption;

6. ability to ensure compliance with standard IT methods and procedures;

In the paragraphs below, each of the fundamental competencies is discussed in detail:

1) Ability to conduct IT strategic thinking and planning - Although the ability to conduct IT strategic planning is often preached as the cornerstone of good systems analysis, design and implementation, and many organizations consider themselves to be competent in this area, our research found that the majority of the firms studied were lacking this competence. Out of all our cases, there were just a few that could be classified as having the ability to undertake adequate planning and foresee the inherent problems emanating from sub-standard service delivery. This does not mean that companies don't have the skills to undertake planning and hence provide adequate services. In fact some of the case study organizations (e.g. Motorola ECID and a US based hotel and casino) perhaps had the best people. Problems arose when there was a lack of a process to facilitate the realization of any planning effort.

To properly conduct IT strategic planning it is important that managers (especially IT managers) are able to look at the external IT environment and understand the opportunities that may be inherent in redefinition of business processes and use of new IT. Many times, organizations tend to make future plans without any consideration to the nature and scope of IT usage within their firms. The converse of this is also true. Having a responsive strategy group or well aware IT people does not necessarily mean that the ability to consider future options with respect to internal IT use would prevail.

In one of the case studies conducted for this research, John Brown Engineering, the CEO proposed a strategic vision that was concerned with developing a global capability to leverage expertise. At the same time, it was however recognized that the current IT systems, advanced as they might have been, were not in a position to realize the CEO vision. This resulted in a concurrent effort to develop the IT infrastructure to support the strategic plan. Such a situation was at tangent to what was found in the case of Horizon Hospital in UK, where considerations for future option were completely divorced from existing practices in IT use. The strategic vision foresaw an elegantly networked hospital linked to the National Health Services network, while in reality various hospital departments saw a mushrooming of islets of automation. The differences between the strategic vision and the internal IT use could never be resolved, which resulted in wasted expenses. Clearly a good linkage between the choice of future options and internal IT use is a precursor to the overall ability to deliver IT services internally.

In the few medium-sized enterprises studied, IT strategic planning was very informal, without the use of formal IT planning methods. However some successful firms using and adopting IT clearly perform strategic thinking with respect to IT issues. At least, that was the case of a mould manufacturing firm that planned and started using 3D CAD/CAM in an innovative way.

2) Ability to align IT with business processes and objectives – Aligning IT with business processes and objectives is a common topic in the IS literature [40, 41]. However, IT systems are frequently adopted and their future use planned without any due consideration to the current procedures and business processes. It has been found, as was in the case of Reuters (UK), that if consideration is first given to the process of delivering services and products, and IT use is considered as a consequence, then applications tend to have a higher degree of success. This has a knock on effect on the manner in which the IT services are delivered within an organization. In one telecommunication company, there was poor knowledge on the existing business processes and many redundant software applications coexisted. The company had a large number of software applications and frequently when a new application was implemented, the previous one was not discontinued. As a result, there were multiple applications and data for the same purpose, thus leading to data redundancy and inconsistency.

3) Ability to deploy cost effective applications and systems – This competence reflects the ability to deliver software applications and implement systems on time, on budget and according to the business requirements. The literature suggests that a high percentage of IT projects fail. According to the Chaos Report (Standish Group Int.) [42], only 35% of software projects, started in 2006, in the US, can be categorized as successful, meaning they were completed on time, on budget, and met user

requirements. In order to deliver effectively software applications it is critical to have good project management skills. Some researchers argue that project management skills are an organisational competence not a specific IT competence [23]. However, it is not feasible to manage IT projects without IT knowledge. In our research some cases (e.g. a garment manufacturer in Hong Kong and a telecommunications company in the UK) clearly provide evidence of problems in project management because project managers did not know much about the technology that the organization was trying to implement, thus having to rely on IT experts who were too technology driven and not always providing the necessary input to understand the project as a business project. Hence, this is a fundamental competence in delivering IT services and a major concern to most IT managers. This competence is even more relevant for IT managers because frequently top managers see IT managers as fully responsible for the delivery of IT solutions, not considering the organizational issues relevant in an IT project.

4) Ability to conceptualize the maintenance of data integrity and confidentiality – This competence emerged as another critical competence that organizations need to have. Maintaining the integrity of corporate data is clearly fundamental to the successful conduct of business. The loss of data may bring serious problems to the organization. In one of the cases, the hospital that implemented a paper free software solution, important clinical data was in a digital format. Maintaining data integrity and confidentiality was extremely important for top management, and the ability to ensure data integrity and confidentiality was definitely a fundamental IT competence. Any problem with data integrity and confidentiality is likely to significantly affect patient healthcare, hospital reputation, and result in significant financial losses (for example, as a result of legal problems and cases brought to court).

5) Ability to facilitate behavioral enrichment for technology adoption. Behavioral skills are important to ensure successful deployment of IT. Training IT staff on business skills and user training on desktop management skills are no doubt very relevant in healthy assimilation of IT. But, the underlying theme of such education should result in an appreciation of each other's discipline, which is equally important in maintaining a good user-IT relation. IT, by itself, doesn't bring any benefits to organizations. Business benefits come from the organizational changes

introduced in business processes (although enabled by IT). However, to introduce organizational changes, it is important to adapt and involve users in these new processes. IT professionals are, very often, still perceived as 'techies' far removed from business realities. Proper training and an understanding of the nature and scope of the training are important aspects that need to be considered in any organization. In the case of Nevada DMV, although the managers and consultants alike recognized that training had to be imparted, the training itself was a half-hearted effort. There were no follow-ups and only a sample of the user population was given access to the intensive training facilities. This not only resulted in a lot of disgruntled employees, but at the time of the crisis, no one was able to deal with the situation.

*Table 7.1 - Case study summary: evidence showing the need for fundamental competencies.*

| **Case/Project studies** | **Key Findings** | **Fundamental Competence (FU)** |
|---|---|---|
| Motorola ECID | Lack of linkage between skills and business processes. Although there were highly skilled individuals, their work was not necessarily linked to the available business processes. | FU1; FU2 |
| US Hotel and Casino | There were highly skilled professionals but their work was not fully incorporated into the existing business processes. This resulted in lack of compliance to standards or in playing lip service to standard compliance. | FU1; FU2; FU6 |
| John Brown Engineering | Excellent linkage between strategic intent, sourcing of information and its exploitation. | FU1 |
| Horizon Hospital | Lack of linkage between strategic intent and execution. Absolutely no emphasis on getting benefits from IT implementations. Procedures for security patient information. | FU1; FU2; FU4 |
| European Hospital | Data integrity and confidentiality is seen as critical for the hospital. | FU4 |
| Mould Manufacturing Company | Innovative use of technology to assure competitive advantage. | FU1 |

| Reuters | Initial consideration of business processes resulted in successful implementation and adoption of IT. | FU2 |
|---|---|---|
| UK Telecom Co. | Understand of business processes in light of strategic choice. | FU2 |
| European Telecom Co. | Inability to plan options for supply of services resulting in data redundancy, inconsistency of business processes. Lack of subject matter expertise leading to poor project management. Strong need to implement IT standards. | FU2; FU3; FU6 |
| Portuguese Public Administration Org. | Poor strategic planning for IT. Inability to align IT with business processes and develop cost effective applications. The cost of software applications was very high, when compared to other organizations with similar systems. | FU1; FU2; FU3 |
| Garment manufacturer | Lack of subject matter expertise leading to poor project management. | FU3 |
| Nevada DMV | Ill conceived training program, no change management. | FU4; FU5 |
| Nevada FamilyTRACS | Detailed consideration of checks and balances ensure compliance to various social service requirements. | FU6 |
| Educational Institution | Poor project management led to lack of effectiveness of software applications. | FU3 |
| Wine Manufacturing Company | Inability to deploy cost effective applications due to lack of knowledge on project management. | FU3 |
| London Borough Council | Compliance to standards. | FU6 |

6) Ability to ensure compliance with standard IT methods and procedures - Clearly having a set of standards is one thing and ensuring compliance is another. In the IT field, it is important the use of tested methods, techniques and procedures to ensure that IT systems are well structured and decrease the cost of systems maintenance, which is significant in many organizations. In the case of a US based casino and gaming software firm, although a number of standards were adopted and developed internally, the organization lacked the ability to ensure compliance. This was because most of the time was spent on 'fire-fighting' tasks. The organization demonstrated a 'who cares' attitude. Such a

situation may not be disastrous, especially when adequate processes and procedures have been developed, as was in the case Nevada FamilyTRACS system. In this case, since individuals were bypassing the standards in the delivery of systems, the detailed procedures that had been developed, helped the organization to maintain an adequate level of services.

## Facilitating competencies in delivering IT benefits

Our research identified 17 facilitating competencies. Such competencies are abilities of an organization that would, in some way, support the fundamental competencies. More often than not, an idiosyncratic combination of the facilitating and fundamental competencies would result in an emergent capability of the organization to deliver IT services. The facilitating competencies identified were the:

1. ability to select and manage IT staff;
2. ability to provide on going IT training;
3. ability to get top management support in IT projects;
4. ability to design business processes for effective use of IT expertise;
5. ability to maintain systems' consistency;
6. ability to involve users in IT projects;
7. ability to institute SLAs (Service Level Agreements) with IT suppliers;
8. ability to identify and set IT standards and procedures;
9. ability to develop software in-house;
10. ability to select and contract IT vendors and IS consultants;
11. ability to decide on software sourcing strategies;
12. ability to maintain or decrease systems' response time;
13. ability to ensure user application knowledge;
14. ability to identify business IS requirements;
15. ability to increase the credibility of the IT department;
16. ability to increase service accountability;
17. ability to develop an IS architecture

1) Ability to select and manage IT staff - The development of in-house knowledge was important in most organizations studied. This knowledge in

used not only to develop applications in-house but also to contract out IT products and services. Selecting IT staff is an important competence of the IT department rather than rely on traditional human resources functions. For instance, in the case of a UK Telecom company, it was important to bring in people who have prior experience or had the ability to manage vendors in India. This was a difficult skill to come by, especially if the hire was made within the UK context. The company however had the ability to go beyond the UK to recruit an individual who had been involved with multiple business process outsourcing projects. Besides, it is important to evaluate technical skills and ensure that the "best people" for the job are selected. Another relevant issue, is managing career expectations and motivate people to give their best on IT projects. This is especially critical when we consider the strong dependency organizations may have on software and computer programmers. In one educational institute studied, a new expensive software project was lunched because two computer programmers decided to leave the organization and no one else, in the IT staff, was able to understand and manage properly the existing software applications used in core business processes.

2) Ability to provide ongoing IT training – The development of staff skills to use computers and software applications is important in order to get benefits from IT in organizations. If users feel comfortable with the business software they use, resistance to change will be reduced and the probability of success with IT adoption is higher. The ability to provide IT training is an important competence to increase users' application knowledge.

In the case of Nevada DMV, inadequate training resulted in utter chaos when the system went live. As a consequence the success of Project Genesis, which was a seven-year $34 million effort to design a new system, was not only stalled, but was on the verge of complete failure. The State of Nevada had to take dramatic steps to rescue the project. In a mould manufacturing company, on the other hand, careful planning and implementation of the software resulted in successful adoption of the technology. Therefore, an ability to train individuals in the use of technology and provide ongoing support, and training, are important facilitating conditions for successful IT use in organizations.

3) Ability to get top management support in IT projects – The

importance of top management in IT projects is well known (see for example [43], [44]). In the firms that showed higher levels of satisfaction with IT adoption and use, top managers were involved in IT adoption processes. In some cases, the whole board of directors was fully committed to implementing IT in the firm, showing its importance to the organization and transmitting that commitment to all users. Top management involvement is critical to reduce resistance to change [19],[44]. Lack of involvement from the top usually resulted in significant problems to IT projects. One relevant facilitating competence is the ability of getting top management trust and support to IT projects. This needs to be worked on by IT managers. Top managers must be told of their critical role in IT adoption and use within the organization and convinced to include IT in their priorities. Evidence from the cases studied shows that it may be the difference between success and failure. Organizations have a political dimension and this is a facilitating competence important to successfully deliver IT services.

For instance in the case of John Brown Engineering the involvement of the top management to implement a global network for virtual work was critical in transforming the company. On the other hand a lack of commitment by top management in the physical security management system, resulted in an ill-conceived system, which had to be later abandoned.

4) Ability to design business processes for effective use of IT expertise - Our research found that although there were a large number of rather skilled individuals in organizations, yet the organizations were finding it difficult to leverage them for their benefit. This was particularly evident in the case of Motorola and the UK Telecom Company. One possible explanation is the radical changes experienced by the companies in the past decade that resulted in pooling of resources across departments and divisions. Although such a move resulted in bringing efficiencies, the subtle connections so essential in linking expertise to business processes were lost.

5) Ability to maintain systems' consistency – Hardware or software problems affect the normal execution of business processes and the credibility of the IT department. In many organizations that are heavily dependent of IT, any systems' failure may represent significant losses. The ability to maintain systems' consistency is a common and necessary

competence in all the firms studied. This demands that organizations engage in developing business continuity plans. In undertaking research for this study we found that many organizations (e.g. Garment Manufacturer and Horizon Hospital) did not consider business continuity plans to be integral to their IT planning. This is clearly a weakness that needs to be addressed.

6) Ability to involve users in IT projects – Significant problems may occur when users are not involved in IT projects. The ability to involve users, not only in systems development processes, but also IT planning is important for IT success. Although in the literature a number of calls for user involvement have been made and organizations studied for our research seem to have taken this aspect on board, in many cases, user involvement in systems development has been carried out in a very mechanistic manner. In two of the case studies, a UK hospital and a Hong Kong manufacturing firm, the project manager sampled out his 'friends' and 'sympathizers' as individuals who would provide input for the systems development process. When user involvement takes this form, it does more harm to the requirement elicitation process than any good. User involvement in the IT planning process was virtually non existent in the organizations studied. Although there is no denying the fact that user participation in the IT planning process is useful, especially in meeting the expectations of the stakeholders, rather than introducing plans and policies in a top-down manner. In one of the cases studied it was decided, without any user involvement, that Lotus Notes would be introduced in the whole organizations. The intent was to essentially meet the email needs of the firm. Clearly Lotus Notes affords far more functionality in groupware and collaborative work, than just email. None of the planners considered the requirements or involved the users. As a matter of fact, it was clearly stated that the organizational expectation was to use Lotus Notes for more than just an email package. One of the memos stated, "… it is an expectation that users should exploit the full potential of this software. Rather than using it for emails alone, the collaborative work options would be extremely useful and should be used". No one in the organization considered it for a moment that collaborative work is not the norm. It was an idiosyncratic research environment and most individuals competed with each other for funding and grants. This minimized any chance of fruitful collaboration. A mere involvement of the users and various stakeholders would have helped

the planners to orient their decision towards a more suitable application package.

7) Ability to institute Service Level Agreements (SLAs) – The complexity of IT and the possibility of outsourcing IT services, to reduce costs and focus expertise in the core business processes of the organization, leads to the need of defining service level agreements. The establishment of service level agreements, and its control, is an important competence to ensure that IT performance will not be bellow acceptable levels. This was evidenced in the case the UK Telecom Company.

8) Ability to identify and set IT standards and procedures - Nowadays, it is possible to identify many industry standards and frameworks for operational performance and organizational processes (for example: ITIL – Information Technology Infrastructure Library, COBIT - Control OBjectives for Information and related Technology, TAM – Telecom Applications Map, SID - Shared Information/Data Model, eTOM - Enhanced Telecom Operations Map, ...). Unless or until an organization is in a position to assess the current state of IT services and compare it with industry benchmarks, it will not be in a position to make any improvements. As a consequence, there is no reference monitor. In the field of IT service delivery, essentially because of the rapid technological changes, there are limited standards. Therefore organizations need to constantly understand the evolving nature of technologies and the business processes to support the technologies and hence have the ability to establish generally accepted practices. In the case of Nevada DMV's Project Genesis, one of the research sites, it was found that an inability of the organization to suitably scan the environment and adopt adequate standards resulted in the lack of competence at two levels. First, in designing the system and second, in supporting the users when things went wrong.

9) Ability to develop software in-house. Nowadays, a significant number of organizations have decided to outsource or contract out software development. However, for others, in-house development is critical, especially when business requirements are constantly changing and the organization needs to react very fast. In these cases, contracting out maybe very expensive and outsourcing not acceptable. Several organizations studied avoided outsourcing their core business applications, especially when these may bring some competitive advantage. Even if the

organization does not develop software in-house, the ability to do so will help negotiating contracts and selecting implementation services, hence it is recognized as a relevant facilitating competence by many IT managers interviewed. In our study this ability was clearly illustrated in the case of Motorola and the Mould Manufacturing Company.

10) Ability to select and contract IT vendors and consultants – It is very difficult to manage IT projects without proper contracts with IT vendors or consultants. The contract must establish what the duties of each vendor are. If the contracts are not adequately written, the organization may become a hostage of its suppliers or consultants. In one case study, a Portuguese wine manufacturing firm that implemented an ERP system for administrative and manufacturing purposes, only after the contract was signed and the project started, the firm noticed that the IT vendor did not have much expertise on the software and there were few (and expensive) consultants available with the necessary expertise to customize the product. Since the contract was not favorable to the manufacturing firm, the project significantly failed in terms of budget, delivery time, and filling business requirements. The situation in SMEs can be even worse than in large enterprises because, in many cases, managers do not even have a clue about which IT firms or IT experts could help them implementing a new software system.

11) Ability to decide on software sourcing strategies. Software sourcing strategies may include custom designed applications, use of software packages, or outsourcing IT services. This is an ability that many organizations lack. As a consequence, wrong choices for systems are made. This usually results in problems at two levels. First, besides issues of monetary loss, it becomes rather difficult to configure the newly acquired systems to fit in with the existing organization. Because of the lack of fit and compatibility of the systems and organizations, service delivery to the users is compromised. Although it may seem that ability to decide between what needs to be custom designed and where packages could be used would have little impact on service delivery, however our research has found a strong relationship. Examples were found in several organizations, for example: Nevada DMV, federated IT infrastructure project at a London Borough Council, and food and beverage systems in a Nevada Hotel. Another sub-set of this ability, especially when implementing ERP (Enterprise Resource Planning) software is being able to understand the

proper level of customization of the software that is going to be implemented. Using the standard solution may not cover many business requirements and a deep customization may lead to problems in software maintenance, including the adoption of new releases, besides an eventual dependency on the implementation consultancy firm. This was also a problem in several of the organizations studied. Another option to consider is outsourcing IT services instead of software development (in-house or contracted out).

12) Ability to maintain or decrease systems' response time - In improving the level of IT service delivery, the most commonly used standard in many of the organizations studied was response time. Essentially this time is calculated as the difference between the time when the actual service call is made and the time when the original request was made. Although response time calculated in this manner is a reasonable means to consider if IT services are being delivered in a timely manner, it however does not mean that the service is being delivered in an effective manner. Therefore besides having an ability to decrease the response time in IT service delivery, complementary competencies for bringing about service accountability and developing service level agreements need to be developed. In most of the organizations studied for this research, service accountability and service level agreement issues were dealt in an ad hoc manner (for instance Nevada DMV and the London Borough Council). This was specifically the case when the IT function was internal to the organization. However in case of outsourced IT departments, accountability and service level were defined more clearly.

13) Ability to ensure user application knowledge - An organization's ability to ensure and subsequently increase the application knowledge of its staff is an importance competence that goes a long way to ensure good service delivery. This competence not only supports the key ability to undertake proper planning but also enables an organization to set standards and facilitate compliance. Very often, there would be individuals in an organization, who would have only a high level understanding of the application, but lack the ability to deal with the 'nuts' and 'bolts'. The obvious solution is to provide training. However even instituting a training program or establishing a process to impart training is a competence in itself. In one of the cases studies for this research, the concerned organization, a hotel and casino, introduced an IT system to control

inventory for its food and beverage department. On installation, the users were given only cursory training and a few experts in the IT department were expected to help the users with any problems, if and when these arose. The organization did not give any consideration to the complexity involved and when the system went live, the IT department was in no position to solve the concerns. This was a consequence not of their technical incompetence, but of lack of training. There was no established procedure to train (or even make aware) IT personnel on the new software. This not only resulted in substandard service delivery, but affected the credibility of the IT department.

14) Ability to identify business IS (information systems) requirements – It is extremely important that an organization is able to understand business needs and establish business requirements for IT development, both in contracting out software or developing in-house. Users' involvement in defining business requirements is usually very important. The existence of an IS architecture implemented in the organization that show existing processes and applications will help. A good definition of business requirements is also critical to align IT with business needs. Many of the firms studied, although having processes to define business requirements and understanding its importance, showed significant problems to provide a good description of its business requirements for IT development. Although the definition of business requirements requires a strong involvement from key users, the IT department must have a lead role in bringing up those requirements. In one of the cases studied, a Portuguese Public Administration organization, there were significant problems in the quality of applications, because IT people did not understand their role in identifying business requirements. They were completely relying on users to do so. Therefore, many requirements were incomplete and informally transmitted (frequently by phone). They were latter completed by IT people according to their own beliefs without consulting and checking those with key users. As a result, many software applications developed did not fit organizational needs.

15) Ability to increase the credibility of the IT department - Maintaining the credibility of the IT department is a competence that needs to be developed within organizations. Credibility, for instance, cannot be increased solely by improving communication between user departments and the IT function. As it emerges from the hotel and casino example

above, credibility increases by virtue of the right kind of skills and the process to realize the delivery of the service. A highly skilled programmer, for example, may not be very well versed with each and every aspect of IT service delivery. As a matter of fact, at least in the organizations' studied in this research, the misconception existed across the board. The emergent view in most organizations was that if a firm is able to hire technically competent individuals, particularly those skilled in programming, the organization would perhaps be in a better position to provide IT related services to the users. Clearly this is naïve. Rather than helping an organization to improve IT service delivery, such a preconception not only hurts the credibility of the IT function, the divide between the users and the IT department widens. Not only the organization ends up hiring the wrong people for the wrong job, the general morale of the concerned individuals dips, which, in itself, is detrimental to the firm. This competence is important, both to involve users and top managers, in IT projects.

16) Ability to increase service accountability – In order to improve IT in the organization it is important to measure its performance and use. Service accountability will enable managers to know what they need in terms of IT resources and evaluate IT performance. Although some companies have well established service accountability programs (e.g. Hotel and Casino), but such service accountability measures are restricted to very specific functions (e.g. gaming). Clearly IT services are important across the board and it is important to define corresponding measures for IT service accountability.

17) Ability to develop an IS architecture – The concept of information systems architecture was mainly introduced by Zachman [45] and further developed and discussed by several other authors [46][47][48][49]. Approaches to information systems architecture generally present frameworks to manage and integrate several interrelated dimensions of the enterprise: business processes, data, IT infrastructure, software, and organizational structure. An IS architecture (sometimes referred as "enterprise architecture" – see [50]) is a structural reference to the development of IT in an organization. The development of an IS (enterprise) architecture framework is an important step to align IT with business processes and organizational objectives [48][51]. This was a concern found in several firms involved in this research. In one Portuguese telecommunication company, there was poor knowledge on the existing business processes and many redundant software applications coexisted.

The company had a large number of software applications and frequently when a new application was implemented, the previous one was not discontinued. As a result multiple applications for the same purpose coexisted, thus leading to data redundancy and inconsistency.

*Table 7.2, Case study summary: evidence showing the need for facilitating competencies.*

| **Case/Project studies** | **Key Finding** | **Facilitating Competence (FA)** |
|---|---|---|
| Motorola ECID | Lack of linkage between business processes and individual expertise. Ability to develop systems in house. | FA4; FA9 |
| US Hotel and Casino | Lack of top management support in implementation of the system resulted in it getting abandoned. Lack of clarity as to what needs to be custom designed and where vendors should be used. There was no established procedure to train (or even make aware) IT personnel on the new software. Too much faith in the technical fix resulted in jeopardizing the credibility of the IT department. Lack of IT related service accountability | FA3; FA11; FA2; FA13; FA15; FA16 |
| John Brown Engineering | Excellent top management support helped the company transform its operations dramatically | FA3; FA4 |
| Horizon Hospital | Training imparted, but an emphasis on radical change resulted in acontextualizing the training effort. Lack of a well conceived business continuity plan. User involvement in system development is essential. | FA2; FA5; FA6 |
| European Hospital | Data protection and data ownership | FA5; FA16 |
| Mould Manufacturing Company | Lack of a well conceived business continuity plan. Importance of service level agreements. Ability to develop systems in house. | FA5; FA7; FA9 |
| Reuters | Clarity of business processes | FA5 |
| UK Telecom. Co. | Lack of linkage between business processes and individual expertise. User involvement in system development is essential. | FA4; FA7 |
| EuropeanTelecom. Co | Lack of an IS architecture, leading to poor IT management. Inability to design business processes and integrated IT into those processes | FA4; FA17 |

| | | |
|---|---|---|
| Portuguese Public Administration Organ. | Poor identification of business requirements for software application development. | FA14 |
| Garment manufacturer | Importance of user involvement in system development. | FA6 |
| Nevada DMV | Lack of proper training. Training was imparted on the Beta version of the system. Lack of standardization. Lack of clarity as to what needs to be custom designed and where vendors should be involved in the project. Service accountability and service level agreement issues were dealt in an ad hoc manner. | FA2; FA5; FA8; FA11; FA12;F16 |
| Nevada FamilyTRACS | Knowledge of the application | FA13 |
| Educational Institution | Lack of support to hire professionals with requisite skills. Poor involvement of key users in the IS project. | FA3; FA6 |
| Wine Manufacturing Company | Different perspectives of top managers on IS adoption led to insufficient top management involvement. Lack of IT staff and knowledge. Ill-defined contract resulting in inability of the firm to terminate the arrangement. IT people did not understand their role in identifying business requirements. | FA3; FA9; FA10; FA11; FA14 |
| London Borough Council | Lack of clarity as to what needs to be custom designed and where vendors should be used. Service accountability and service level agreement issues were dealt in an ad hoc manner. | FA11; FA12 |

## Orchestrating competencies

After the identification of fundamental and facilitating competencies, it is important to understand how these competencies are related and integrated. Competencies are not isolated in terms of operability, there are dependencies, especially in what concerns facilitating competences, relevant to understand why a firm can became capable of successfully delivering IT services. The realization of all or a subset of the competencies would make the firm more capable in providing service or function/facility that falls within its remit.

The conceptualization presented in figure 7.2 considers competence as an outcome. However in the literature it has been argued that in situations where the organization might have realized a particular competence, either accidentally or in a planned manner, the stakeholders may enact a reality where they genuinely believe that they did all the right things (e.g. see Weick, 1979). As a consequence, an outcome is considered to precede retrospective rationalization of the causes.

This paper adopts a causal mode and suggests the combination of skills and processes to enable an emergent competence. The links between the competencies are critical to understand the concept of exploitation presented in this paper. Gaining business benefits from IT adoption is only possible if the firm has a set of interrelated organizational competences established. Business benefits do not come directly from IT adoption but from organizational processes that are improved by the use of IT. The competencies presented in figure 2, identified in the cases studied, enable the effectiveness of IT in the organization. The level of granularity presented in figure 2, especially in the facilitating competencies, helps us to understand how these competences may interact to provide fundamental IT competencies to the organization and the delivery of business benefits.

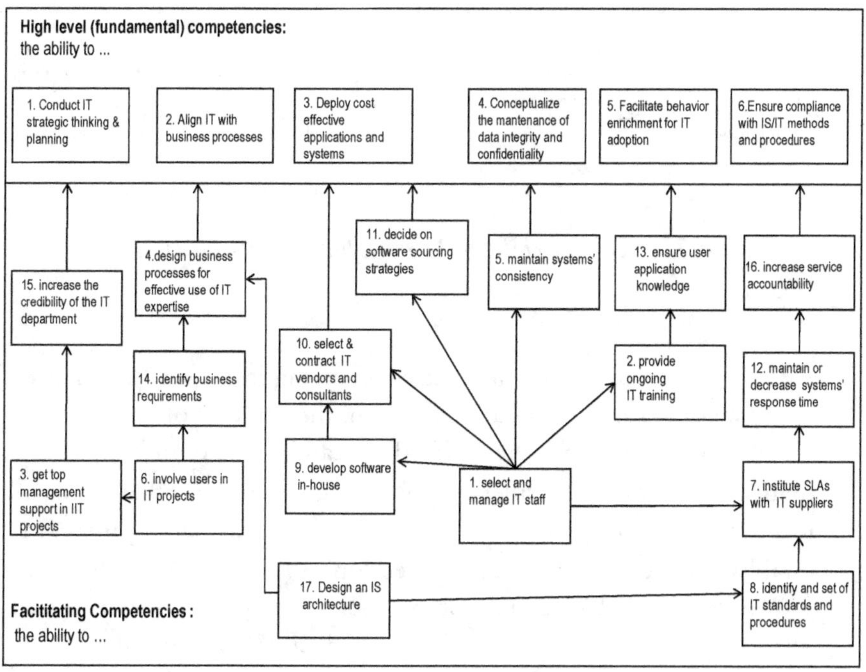


*Figure 7.2 – A network of competencies.*

In the research presented in this chapter, the bundle of fundamental and facilitating competencies has been identified and articulated. Although both, skills and processes, are inputs to develop a competence, skills must be incorporated into processes in order to be effective.

Organizational processes enable the exploitation of individual skills. An organization may have skilled human resources, from a technical and managerial perspective, but it is also necessary to design and implement proper organizational processes, for example, integrating people and offering adequate working conditions, so that those skills can result in organizational competences (see figure 7.3). However, the existence of IS competencies in a firm is not enough to successfully deliver IT services. It is important that top management supports IT projects and decides to affect resources (viz financial) because a capability of an organization to deliver IT services is based on effectiveness, not only on the potential efficiency of its processes.

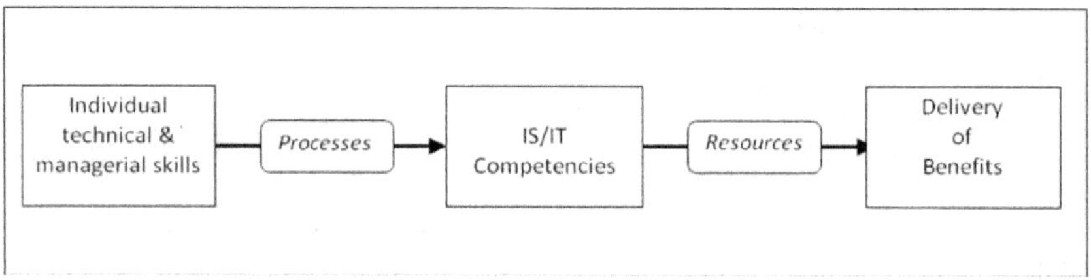


*Figure 7.3, How to deliver IT benefits (adapted from Caldeira and Ward [19])*

Irrespective of the competencies emerging in a causal manner or as an outcome of retrospective rationalization, the findings of this research make valuable contribution. They afford researchers and managers a starting point to proactively consider the kind of competencies that need to be put in place and then work on the necessary skills and processes to be established. If Weick's [52] conception is true, even then a study of fundamental and facilitating competencies being realized over a period of time (longitudinal study) would help in identifying the kind of skills and processes that come together for the ultimate realization.

## CONCLUSIONS

In order to gain business benefits from IT investments organizations must develop competencies to exploit IT. These competences involve individual skills and organizational processes that enable those skills to be effectively applied. In this paper we identify 23 competencies categorized into fundamental and facilitating competencies that firms need to have in place if IT services are to be delivered adequately and business benefits achieved. We also developed a network of competences based on the data collected in the 16 cases studied. As has been argued these competencies come together in unique ways so as to define success. The network of competencies (figure 1) helps in evaluating how a given firm may be performing with respect to the standard competencies. The relationships also help in establishing plans for further execution. The development of organizational competences to deliver IT services will reduce the risk of IT projects not being completed on time, cost over budgeted, not fulfilling business requirements, and not bringing significant business benefits to organizations.

## REFERENCES

1. A.Ragowsky, M. Stern, and D. Adams, Relating Benefits from Using IS to an Organization's Operating Characteristics: Interpreting Results from Two Countries, Journal of Management Information Systems 16(4) (2000) 175-194.

2. D. Staples, I. Wong, and P. Seddon. Having expectations of information systems benefits that match received benefits: does it really matter? Information & Management 40 (2002) 115-131.

3. T. Ravichandran, and C. Lertwongsatien. Effect of Information Systems Resources and Capabilities on Firm Performance: a resource-based perspective, Journal of Management Information Systems 21(4) (2005) 237-276.

4. G. Dhillon. Getting Benefits for IS/IT Implementation: Interpretations from case studies, International Journal of Information Management 25(6) (2005) 502-515.

5. J. Ward and E. Daniel. Benefits Management – Delivering Value from IS & IT Investments (John Wiley & Sons, Chichester, 2006)

6. W. DeLone and E. McLean (1992). Information systems success: The quest for the dependent variable, Information Systems Research 3(1) 60-95.

7. W. DeLone and E. McLean. The DeLone and McLean Model of Information Systems Success: A ten year update. Journal of Management Information Systems, 19(4) (2003) 9-30.

8. J. Barney. Firm resources and sustainable competitive advantage. Journal of Management, 17(1) (1991) 99-120.

9. G. Hamel and C. Prahalad. Competing for the Future (Harvard Business School Press, Boston, 1996).

10. F. Mata, W. Fuerst, and J. Barney. Information technology and sustained competitive advantage: A resource-based analysis, MIS Quarterly 19(4) (1995) 487-505.

11. A.S. Bharadwaj. A resource-based perspective on information technology capability and firm performance: an empirical investigation, MIS Quarterly 24(1) (2000) 169-196.

12. G. Bhatt and V. Grover. Types of Information Technology Capabilities and Their Role in Competitive Advantage: An Empirical Study, Journal of Management Information Systems 22(2) (2005) 253-277.

13. W. Oh and A. Pinsonneault A. On the Assessment of the Strategic Value of Information Technologies: Conceptual and Analytical Approaches, MIS Quarterly 31(2) (2007) 239-265.

14. M. Wade and J. Hulland. The resource-based view and information systems research: review, extension, and suggestions for future research, MIS Quarterly 28(1) (2004) 107-142.

15. R. Srinivasan, G. Lilien and A. Rangaswarny. Technological Opportunism and Radical Technology Adoption: An Application to E-Business, Journal of Marketing 66(3) (2002) 47-60.

16. R. Boyatzis. The competent manager: a model for effective performance (John Wiley & Sons, New York, 1982)

17. R.G. McGrath, I.C. MacMillan and S. Venkataraman. Defining and Developing Competence: A Strategic Process Paradigm, Strategic Management Journal 16(4) (1995) 251-275.

18. J. Peppard and J. Ward. Beyond strategic information systems: towards an IS capability, Journal of Strategic Information Systems 13 (2004) 167-194.

19. M. Caldeira and J. Ward. Using resource-based theory to interpret the successful adoption and use of information systems and technology in manufacturing small and medium-sized enterprises. European Journal of Information Systems 12(2) (2003) 127-141.

20. J. Peppard, R. Lambert and C. Edwards. Whose Job it is anyway?: Organizational information competencies for value creation, Information Systems Journal 10(4) (2002) 291-322.

21. G. Dhillon. Organisational competence for harnessing IT: a case study, Information & Management 45(5) (2008) 297-303.

22. M. Caldeira, P. Cragg and J. Ward. Information Systems Competencies in SMEs, Proceedings of the United Kingdom Academy for Information Systems (UKAIS) Conference, University of Gloucestershire, UK, 2006 (published on CD).

23. D. Feeny and L. Willcocks. Core IS Capabilities for Exploiting Information Technology. Sloan Management Review 39(3) (1998) 9-21.

24. D. Feeny and L. Willcocks. Re-designing the IS Function around Core Capabilities. Long Range Planning 31(3) (1998) 354-367.

25. G. Bassellier, B. Reich and I. Benbasat. Information technology competence of managers, a definition and research model. Journal of Management Information Systems 17(4) (2001) 159-182.

26. V. Montequín, V. Fernandez, V. Cabral, and N. Gutierrez. An integrated framework for intellectual capital measurement and knowledge management implications in small and medium-sized enterprises, Journal of Information Science 32(6) (2006) 525-538.

27. G. Dhillon, and J. Lee. Value assessment of IT service provision within organizations, Thirteenth International Conference on Information Systems (Brisbane, Australia, 2000).

28. J. Mahoney and R. Sanchez. Competence theory building: reconnecting management research and management practice. in Competence-based strategic management. A. Heene and R. Sanchez. (Chichester, John Wiley & Sons, 1997).

29. J. Orton and G. Dhillon. Macro-Strategic, Meso-Strategic, and Micro-Strategic Leadership Processes In Loosely Coupled Networks. Sharing Network Leadership. LMX Leadership: The Series Volume 4. G. B. Graen and J. A. Graen. Greenwich, CT, Information Age Publishing,

2006.

30. C. Argyris and D. Schön. Organizational learning: a theory of action perspective (Addison-Wesley, Reading, 1978)

31. R. Yin. Applications of Case Study Research (Sage Publications, Newbury Park, 1993)

32. R. Yin. Case Study Research, 2nd edition, (Sage Publications, Newbury Park, 1994)

33. I. Benbasat, D. Goldstein and M. Mead The case research strategy in studies of information systems, MIS Quarterly 11(3) (1987) 369-386.

34. M. Miles and A. Huberman. Qualitative Data Analysis, 2nd edition (Sage, Thousand Oaks, 1994)

35. M. Patton. How to use qualitative methods in evaluation (Sage Publications, Newbury Park, 1987).

36. R. Sanchez, A. Heene, and H. Thomas. Towards the Theory and Practice of Competence-Based Competition, in Dynamics of Competence-Based Competition: Theory and Practice in the New Strategic Management, Sanchez, R., Heene, A., and Thomas, H., Editors, Elsevier: Oxford (1996) 1-35.

37. R. Keeney. Creativity in Decision Making with Value-Focused Thinking, Sloan Management Review 35(4) (1994) 33-41.

38. G. Torkzadeh and G. Dhillon. Measuring factors that influence the success of Internet commerce. Information Systems Research 13(2) (2002) 187-204.

39. C. Emory and D. Cooper. Business Research Methods (Irwin, Boston, Mass, 1991)

40. G. Philip. IS Strategic Planning for Operational Efficiency, Information Systems Management 24 (2007) 247-264.

41. J. Ward and J. Peppard. Strategic Planning for Information Systems (John Wiley & Sons, Chichester, 2002)

42. Standish Group Int. The Chaos Report, 2006 (www.standishgroup.com)

43. M. Caldeira and J. Ward. Understanding the successful adoption and use of IS/IT in SMEs – An explanation from Portuguese manufacturing industries, Information Systems Journal 12(2) (2002) 121-152.

44. T. Somers and K. Nelson. A taxonomy of players and activities across the ERP project life cycle. Information & Management 41 (2002) 257-278.

45. J. Zachman. A framework for information systems architecture, IBM Systems Journal 26(3) (1987) 454-470.

46. J. Sowa and J. Zachman. Extending and formalizing the framework for information systems architecture, IBM Systems Journal 31(3) (1992) 590-616.

47. Y. Kim and G. Everest. Building an IS Architecture: Collective wisdom from the field, Information & Management 26 (1994) 1-11.

48. M. Lankhorst et al. Enterprise Architecture at Work: Modeling, Communication and Analysis (Springer, New York, 2005)

49. M. Caldeira and C. Pedron. Why CRM doesn't work – An enterprise architecture perspective, Proceedings of the 4th International Conference on Enterprise Systems, Accounting and Logistics July 9-10 (Corfu, Greece, 2007) (published on CD).

50. S. Spewak. Enterprise Architecture Planning - Developing a Blueprint for Data, Applications and Technology (John Wiley & Sons, New York, 1992).

51. A. Scheer and F. Habermann. Enterprise resource planning: making ERP a success, Communications of the ACM 43(4) (2000) 57-61.

52. K. Weick. The social psychology of organizing (Addison-Wesley, Reading, 1979)

## APPENDIX

### Methodology used for deriving the competencies

The study was carried out in two phases. Phase 1 involved conducting 16 extensive case studies. Case study methodology employed followed guidelines provided by Yin [31, 32] and Benbasat et al. [33]. Case studies were a suitable means to collect the data since the notion of competencies in delivering IT benefits has not been well understood in the literature. By analyzing and understanding the particular situation and factors in each organization in an in-depth manner, we developed a sound interpretation of the abilities that organizations need to have in place to deliver IT benefits.

Key stakeholders for each organization were identified and interviewed. The interviewees included top managers, IT managers, IT suppliers, and key users. All the case studies were conducted and documented over a period of four years. The 16 case study organizations were representative of a broad range of businesses in four countries: UK, Portugal, Hong Kong, and US. The cases studied included: four telecommunication companies, four organizations in the public administration sector, two hospitals, two engineering firm, one wine producer, one University, one hotel & casino, and one firm in the apparel industry.

Semi-structured interviews were complemented by an analysis of the documents provided by the firm. Semi-structured interviews are able to generate rich data that allow an understanding of the research topic according to the perspectives of the key actors involved. Between three to six people were interviewed individually in each firm, using a check-list to assure that all relevant topics would be discussed. The interviewees were free to introduce into discussion any issue that they considered relevant. Hand notes were taken and most interviews were recorded on tape. In the interviews that were recorded on tape, informants were not asked to review the statements provided. All organizations also provided access to internal documents describing the business activity and details related to IT systems and projects.

Data were later coded and analyzed using tables highlighting the most relevant issues (as suggested by Miles and Huberman [34]). The time spent by the researchers transcribing the data also enabled them to have a deep knowledge about the statements provided by each interviewee, making it easier to find, analyze and compare statements, in order to identify competencies and understand their relevance in the case. Data triangulation was executed by comparing the data provided by the different interviewees (as recommended by Patton [35]). When different perspectives were found, the researchers tried to find further evidence, usually by interviewing the same people (in some cases, also others) in order to clarify the situation and find a plausible explanation. In a few cases, informal telephone conversations were held to clarify some statements previously given in the interview. The fact that there are a reasonable number of cases, in different industries, showing similar patterns and that data were collected through relatively open interviews, reduces the probability of the phenomena under study being explained by other variables than the ones identified and used in the research

The output of phase 1 was a list of 23 competencies that organizations need to have in place. These competencies were classified into two categories – fundamental and facilitating (based on previous research, [36, 37]). Fundamental competencies were the ultimate abilities, which possibly could not impact another competence. These are the major concerns of people responsible for IT delivery. Facilitating competencies, on the other hand, could possibly result in another competence. Although important, these are more means than ends. Finally a network of competencies was developed, using interviewees' perspectives, and trying to explain relationships between competencies. We argue that organizational competencies in delivery of IT benefits are not independent but interrelated. One contribution of this paper is trying to show the different level of competencies (facilitating and fundamental) and their relationships.

Then, an important question that arises is as to how these competencies should be orchestrated. Merely establishing policies or strategies for the respective competencies or hiring the skilled individuals would not be enough. In the second phase of our research we established a panel of 8 experts representing manufacturing, customer service, hotel, consulting, telecommunications, and health care industry to comment on the initial set of competencies identified and to present their personal opinion in orchestrating the competencies. This process allowed us to not only validate and improve the initial listing of competencies, but also provided an insight into a generic method that could be put in place for realizing the competencies. Such an approach to establishing categories and relationships has been extensively used in IS research (e.g. see [38]) and has been considered a standard approach for establishing content validity (e.g. see [39]).

The respondents identified a large number of options that could help in orchestrating the competencies. An initial list was developed from the interview responses. Although the respondents had identified the values that they felt would be beneficial in realizing the competence, of relevance to our paper are the two emergent views. First the respondents felt that identifying, hiring and grooming the right kind of skilled individuals would certainly be necessary if IT service delivery were to be improved. Second, a need for a process to be put in place was felt. This would distinctively combine the skills and the processes for the delivery of an IT service.

# 8. INFORMATION SYSTEMS SECURITY

Organizations that have a well established security training program and make a conscious effort to train at least one in four IT employees in security are 20% less likely to suffer a security breach. – A survey undertaken by TNS Prognostics for the Computing Technology Industry Association (CompTIA).

**IS Security in Action**

Consider the case of illicit activities of Joseph Jett who defrauded Kidder Peabody & Co out of millions of dollars over a course of more than two and half years. Jett was able to exploit the Kidder trading and accounting systems to fabricate profits of approximately US$339 million. Jett was eventually removed from the services of Kidder in April 1994. The US Securities and Exchange Commission claimed that Jett engaged in more than 1000 violations in creating millions of dollars in phony profits so as to earn millions in bonuses. During the course of Jett's involvement with Kidder, he amassed a personal fortune of around $5.5 million and earned himself upwards of $9 million in salary and bonuses. In 1993 alone, he made nearly 80% of the firm's entire annual profit of $439 million.

Prior to joining Kidder, Jett was aware of the manner in which the brokerage business was conducted and the specific conditions at Kidder. Jett realized the shortcomings of the accounting system and began tinkering with it. The management overlooked Jett's actions, especially because he seemed to be performing very well and was adding to the firms' profitability. Jett had been hired to perform arbitrage between Treasury bonds and Strips (Separate Trading of Registered Interest and Principal of Securities). Kidder relied heavily on Expert Systems to perform and value transactions in the bond markets. Based on the valuation of the transactions, Kidder systems automatically updated the firm's inventory and Profit and Loss statements. Jett found out that by entering forward transactions on the reconstituted Strips, he could indefinitely postpone the time when actual losses could be recognized in a Profit and Loss statement. Jett was able to do this by racking up larger positions and reconstituting the Strips. This resulted in Jett's 1992 trading profits touching a $32 million record, previously unheard of in dealing with Strips. Jett's personal bonus was $2 million. The following year Jett reported a $151 million profit and earned $12 million in bonus. It was only in March 1994 that senior management started looking into the dealings. This was because Jett's position included $47 billion worth of Strips and $42 billion worth of reconstituted Strips. Clearly basic safeguards had not been instituted at Kidder. Although the junior traders at Kidder were aware of Jett's activities, the senior management did not make any effort to access this information. These factors certainly influenced Jett's beliefs and his intentions regarding the advantages and disadvantages of engaging in the illicit activities. As a consequence Jett manipulated the accounting information system and deceived the senior management at Kidder.

As is typical of many merchant banks, bonuses earned are intricately linked with the profitability of the concern. Kidder offered substantial bonuses for individual contribution to company profits. Even within the parent company, General Electric, CEO Jack Welch had told his employees that he wanted to create a 'cadre of professions' who could perform and be more marketable. This resulted in the employees being subjected to intense pressure to perform and having a focus on serving their self-interest. As a consequence, General Electric did not necessarily afford a culture of loyalty and truthfulness. The employees were inadvertently getting the silent message that they should 'look after themselves and win at any cost'. Critics claim that there was a certain hollowness of purpose beneath Welch's relentlessly demanding management style.

Reports of ethical violations had also marred some of General Electric's traditional lines of business. There had been allegations of conspiracy with De Beers mining company of South Africa to fix prices of industrial diamonds. The FBI has also been investigating charges that General Electric had repeatedly ignored warnings about electrical problems that could compromise the safety of aircraft engines. Jack Welch has dismissed these charges and has contended that had General Electric not acquired Kidder Peabody, such discussions would not have surfaced. Irrespective of the nature of defenses put up by the General Electric senior management, the fact remains that a dominant culture to win and an aspiration to be number 1 or 2 in every market, created an internal context within the organization such that unethical practices could be overlooked.

Prior to Jett joining Kidder Peabody, no significant ethical problems had been reported at Kidder. Over the past few years the bank had been striving to perform satisfactorily, because at some stage the CEO wanted to dispose off the loss making brokerage unit. It had stayed clear of all sorts of rogue dealings, a phenomenon so common to any merchant bank. In fact lessons had been learnt from dealings in 'junk bonds' elsewhere. For example, the horror stories surrounding the demise of Drexel Burnham Lambert Inc haunted every major bank involved in the derivatives market.

Kidder Peabody and the parent company General Electric were determined to court political and business acclaim by recruiting a large number of people from ethnic minorities. The bank considered this to be a means of paying back to the society and perhaps gaining esteem from others by lending a helping hand to certain under-privileged sections of the society. Various investigative reports following the Kidder Peabody swindling case have reported that the only reason why Jett got selected was because he happened to be a Black American. There are claims that Jett had falsified information on his vitae, thus making it extremely impressive. The personnel department at Kidder took this information on face value and did not make any attempt to verify it. It follows therefore that Jett's risk taking character and involvement in unethical deeds may have influenced his beliefs, ultimately leading to the demise of Kidder.

---

In the past decade two developments have brought information system security management issues to the fore. First has been the increased dependence of organizations on information and communication technologies, not only for key operational purposes but also for gaining strategic advantage. Second, abetted by information and communication technologies, the whole business model for many organizations has been transformed. Whereas in the past companies could rely on confining themselves to a particular geographical area to conduct their business. Today companies are increasingly becoming location independent and are finding themselves to be strategically disadvantaged if they are confined to a particular place. The consequence of advances in information technologies and the changing boundaries of the firm have brought the importance of data and information to the fore. This is because it is information that helps companies realize their objectives and helps managers to take adequate decisions. In the business model of the past, data and information to a large extend was confined to a particular location and it was relatively easy to protect it from falling in the hands of those who should not have it (i.e. maintain confidentiality). Because information was usually processed in a central location, it was also possible to ensure, with a relative degree of certainty, that it's content and form did not change (i.e. maintain integrity) and ensure that it was readily accessible to authorized personnel (i.e. maintain availability). In fact maintaining confidentiality, integrity and availability were the main tenants for managing security. Today because the nature of the organization and scope of information processing has evolved, managing information system security is not just restricted to maintaining confidentiality, integrity and availability. Perhaps issues related to organizational structures, business processes, integrity of people and trustworthiness of people are as important, if not more.

Changing structures, advances in information and communication technologies and the greater reliance of companies on information indeed poses a number of challenges for maintaining good management practices. In recent years clearly organizations have fallen short of developing adequate policies to deal with the information security problems. Various authors have reported increases in incidents of computer crimes because of violation of safeguards by internal employees of organizations (as high as 80% of total computer crimes). There also seems to be a 'policy vacuum' to deal with information security problems. This is evidenced not only by increases in incidents of system penetration (e.g. hacking), but also in inability of authorities to establish adequate basis to deal with such computer crimes. One example is the case of Randal Shwartz where there were difficulties to establish whether illicit use of computers by Shawartz amounted to an occurrence of a computer crime. Advances in information technologies have introduced a yet another kind of a problem for organizations, which many classify as 'input crimes'. In one case a former employee of a wholesaler was convicted under the UK Computer Misuse Act when he obtained for himself a 70% discount when the regular staff of the wholesaler were otherwise engaged. Given the increased dependence of businesses on computers, one would assume that most companies would have well established contingency and disaster recovery plans. Unfortunately research seems to suggest otherwise. Based on survey findings Adam and Haslam [1] suggest that adequate importance is not being placed on disaster recovery planning. Many managers tend to think that disaster recovery planning is an insignificant issue and hence prefer to concentrate on projects that generate revenues.

## THE CHALLENGES

It goes without saying that, incidents of computer crime, information security problems and information technology enabled frauds have been on the increase. And any attempt to deal with the problem demands an adequate understanding of the challenges that exist in the new millennium. Such challenges can be classified into four categories:

- The challenge of establishing good management practices in a geographically dispersed environment and yet being able to control organizational operations.
- The challenge of establishing security policies and procedures that adequately reflect the organizational context and new business processes.
- The challenge of establishing correct structures of responsibility, given the complex structuring of organizations and information processing activities.
- The challenge of establishing appropriate information

technology disaster recovery plans.

Numerous studies have indicated that there is a problem in managing information security especially with respect to regulating the behavior of internal employees. Research has also shown that many a time internal employees subvert existing controls to gain undue advantage essentially because either an opportunity exists to do so or they are disgruntled. The problem gets compounded even further when an organization is geographically dispersed and it becomes difficult to institute the necessary formal controls. This was evidenced in the case of Nick Lesson who brought about the downfall of Barings Bank in Singapore[3]. Barings collapsed because by relying on information technology Leeson was able to successfully conceal the positions and losses from the Barings management, internal and external auditors, and regulatory bodies in Singapore and the Bank of England. Leeson's case is illustrative of breaches of control, trust, confidence, and deviations from conventional accounting methods or expectations.

The management of Barings had confessed in one of the internal memos that clearly their systems and controls were distinctly flaky. However there was nothing new in this confession, since it has long been established that lapses in applying internal and external controls is perhaps the primary reason for breaches in information security. Failure of management to curtail Leeson's sole responsibilities, which empowered him to create an environment conducive to crime, lack of independent monitoring and control of risk, communication breakdown between managers, and the believe that information technology can overcome basic communication problems in organizations were other reason that created an opportunity for Lesson to engage in a criminal act.

There is also the challenge of establishing appropriate security policies and procedures that adequately reflect the organizational context and new

---

[3] Detailed discussion of Barings Bank case can be found in

5. Dhillon, G., *Violation of safeguards by trusted personnel and understanding related information security concerns.* Computers & Security, 2001. **20**(2): p. 165-172.,

10. Willison, R.A., *Opportunities for Computer Abuse: Assessing a Crime Specific Approach in the the Case of Barings Bank.* Unpublished PhD Thesis, 2002, London School of Economics and Political Science, University of London, London.

business processes. Such challenges exist at two levels. First at an internal organizational level where it is increasingly becoming difficult for businesses to develop and implement appropriate security policies. Second at a broad contextual level, where it is becoming difficult to rely on traditional legal policies to regulate behavior. At an internal organizational level, there is a problem with respect to establishing security policies. For one there is a lack of awareness within organizations that such a need exists. Based on a longitudinal study of information security problems within the health services sector and the local government councils, Dhillon [4] contends that there is not only a lack of commitment from top management in the security policy formulation process, but security policies are conceived in a formal-rational manner. This results in an 'acontextual' assessment of the security problems and the responses address the issues in a rather superficial manner.

At a broad contextual level, although a number of *cyberlaws* have been enacted in recent years their nature and scope seems to be at odds with the reality. Clearly there are a number of computer crime situations where it is important to institute punitive social controls in order to curtail criminal activities, and in some cases to recover stolen money or goods. There are perhaps a number of other computer crimes where severe punitive control may not be the best option. In many cases monetary gain is not the prime motive, the intellectual challenge of tearing apart computer systems is. In such cases it would perhaps be counter-productive to institute severe punitive controls.

Another challenge in managing information system security in the new millennium relates to establishing correct structures of responsibility. Information security problems resulting from either the inability to understand the nature and scope of such structures within organizations or to specify new ones are abound. When Japan's Daiwa Bank fell short of understanding the patterns of behavior expected of businesses operating out of the US and allowed Japanese normative structures to dominate, it resulted in a bond trader, Toshihide Iguchi, accruing losses to the tune of $1.1 billion. Besides it also allowed Iguchi to engage in at least 30,000 illicit trades. The drama ended in Iguchi being prosecuted and Daiwa's charter to conduct business in the US being suspended. Situations such as the one represented by Daiwa pose a challenging issue of managing access to information processing facilities. Merely stating 'read only' or 'write only' accesses matching an organization's hierarchical structure are insufficient, especially in light of the changing organizational forms. It can be argued that modern enterprises are in a constant state of 'schizoid incoherence' and there are very short spells of stability in organizational forms. This is especially true for businesses that tend to organize themselves in a 'networked' or 'virtual' manner. The evolving organizational forms seem to question the applicability of formal methods in instituting access control.

It is indeed a challenge when dealing with information technology disaster recovery plans and policies. Many a time disasters occur because of complacency of staff. Recently Northwest Airlines were left to wonder why their backup system was disabled. In fact a sub-contractor laying new lines in Eagan, Minnesota bored through a cluster of cables and ended up cutting 244 fiber optic and copper telecommunications lines. As a consequence airline passengers nationwide were left stranded since the lines linked the Northwest's Minneapolis-St. Paul hub to the rest of the nation. Apparently the redundant system lines ran alongside the ones used for backing up. A 1996 IBM survey on business continuity practices, "A risk too far", reported that the 300 companies surveyed had suffered 293 events in 1995 alone. The loss of system capability was estimated to have threatened some 500,000 manhours of work in the respective locations. The IBM study suggested that 89% of the companies surveyed believed their PCs to be critical. Nearly a quarter of the companies stored 60% of their data on the PCs and 76% were not aware of the cost of back up. Over the years the situation has not changed. Adam and Haslam's [1] study of Irish experiences in disaster recovery planning supports this assertion.

## SEARCHING FOR A SOLUTION

Solutions to the problem of managing information security in the new millennium hark back at shifting emphasis from technology to business and social process. Although many researchers have placed calls for such an orientation, in practice over-formalized, acontextual and ahistorical solutions designed in a reactive manner, still dominate. Such ill-conceived solutions mark the beginning of a disastrous information technology implementation with an inadequate consideration of information security.

Establishing formalized rules is one step that could lead towards a solution for managing information security. Such formalized rules may take the form of security policies that help in facilitating bureaucratic functions in order to resolve ambiguities and misunderstandings within organizations. Both academics and practitioners have made numerous calls for formulating security policies and many of these calls have stopped at just that. Although security policies are essential for laying down rules of conduct, success of security policies is clearly a function of the level of their integration with the strategic vision. If we accept that a secure environment is an enabling condition for the smooth running of an enterprise, then security considerations are a strategic issue and there is a need to configure them for maintaining the consistency and coherence of organizational operations.

In the past security policies have been formulated based on checklists and hence tend to identify specific responses to specific conditions. However if organizations want information security management to be an antecedent to a highly integral business environment, focus needs to shift towards creating a security vision and strategy where adequate consideration is given to the threats and weaknesses of the information technology infrastructure within the broader scope of computerization. Security policies then tend to take on the role of functional strategies. This not only moves the information security agenda to the top management list, but also ensures buy in from the senior management stakeholders. Arguments in support of formulating an information system security vision and strategy stem from the corporate strategy literature where it has been contended that "good managers don't make policy decisions" [11]; p32). By focusing on a security vision instead the danger of being trapped in arbitrating disputes arising from a stated policy are elevated. A detailed discussion focusing on the importance of a security vision appears in Dhillon [4] pg 137-142.

Hitchings [7] has suggested the importance of considering human issues in designing information security and uses a 'virtual methodology' to consider human centered controls in an organization and its environment. Clearly a lack of human centered controls result in increasing the probability of occurrence of adverse events. Such events could either be a consequence of disgruntled employees or merely an opportunity being exploited. Poor quality of management and inadequate management communication has also been considered as precursors of an unethical environment, thus making an organization vulnerable to a crime. Since most organizational workplaces are characterized by such predicaments, the importance of establishing an ethical environment within an organization cannot be overstated.

In proposing solutions to information security problems arising because of inability to appreciate human factors, there are calls for establishing normative controls. Normative controls are a by-product of a dominant security culture, which is the totality of patterns of behavior in an organization that contribute to the protection of information of all kinds. A lack of a security culture results in problems of maintaining integrity of the whole organization and indirectly threatens the protection of technical systems. Most adverse events can be traced back to a lack of security culture and a consequence of breakdown in organizational communications. An issue related to the security culture is that of monitoring employee behavior. Besides personal factors, work situations and opportunities available allow individuals to perform criminal acts. Evidence to this contention appears in the case of Kidder Peabody, where its becomes evident that the prevalent work situation and the opportunity to commit criminal acts affected the primary belief system of perpetrator, thus resulting in a criminal act being performed. The ability to leverage work situations and opportunities to engage in computer crimes suggests that monitoring of employee behavior is an essential step in maintaining the integrity of an organization. Such monitoring does not necessarily have to be formal and rule based. In fact informal monitoring, such as interpreting behavioral changes and identifying personal and group conflicts, can help in establishing adequate checks and balances.

In the previous section the problems with establishing structures or responsibility was mentioned. Clearly adopting adequate structures will go a long way in establishing good management practices and will set the scene for effective computer crime management. The notion of structures of responsibility goes beyond the narrowly focused concerns of specifying an appropriate organizational structure. Although important, exclusive focus on organizational structure issues tends to skew the emphasis towards formal specification. Backhouse and Dhillon [2] introduced the concept of structures of responsibility to the information security management. And suggest that such structures provide a means to understand the manner in which responsible agents are identified within the context of the formal and informal organizational environments. A structures of responsibility focus also facilitate an understanding of the range of conduct open to the responsible agents, the influences they are subjected to, the manner in which they signify the occurrence of events, the communications they enter into. The most important element of interpreting structures of responsibility is the ability to understand the underlying patterns of behavior. The positive connotations of interpreting behavioral attributes in developing and designing secure environments has been well documented.

Besides focusing on formalized rule structures and establishing an adequate understanding of behavioral practices, it is also important to develop and implement adequate technological controls. Adequacy and appropriateness are a key to the design of technical control measures. In the literature there are a number of approaches available. And most of these have been tested for their validity and completeness. The US Department of Defense has been using the Trusted Computer System Evaluation Criteria for years, and clearly they are valid and complete. So are the Bell La Padula and Denning Models for confidentiality of access control. Similarly the validity and completeness of other models such as Rushby's Separation Model and Biba Model for integrity has also been established. However their validity exists not because of the completeness of their internal working and their derivations through axioms, but because the reality they are modeling is well defined, i.e. the military organization. The military, to a large extent, represents a culture of trust among its members and a system of clear roles and responsibilities. Hence the classification of information security within the models does not represent the constructs of the models, but instead reflect the very organization they are modeling. A challenge, however, exist when business organizations are using models based on a different reality. Obviously in the commercial environment the formal models for managing information security fall short of maintaining their completeness and validity.

## PRINCIPLES FOR MANAGING INFORMATION SECURITY

Previous sections in this chapter have focused on identifying problems and challenges in managing information security in various contexts. The focus of this section is to present a synthesized framework for managing information security in the electronic years. It is important to develop such a conceptual understanding since the challenges of managing information security permeate various aspects of our personal and business life. May it be booking flights over the Internet, buying a book or simply browsing to gather information, challenges to protect personal information exist and there are simply no straightforward answers. Similarly for businesses, protection of information is absolutely critical. Obviously no company would like, for example, its competitors to have access to their sales data. Or for that matter, companies would neither appreciate unauthorized use of computers by their employees nor would a violation of safeguards by trusted personnel go down very well. For these reasons it is important that companies consider certain fundamental principles that could be used as pointers for not only establishing an information security vision and strategy, but would also facilitate in mapping out a detailed security policy.

This section sketches out three classes of principles. Following a brief description of the class, each principle is elaborated and suggestions made thereof as to its applicability. The three classes of principles are:

- Principles for managing the pragmatic aspects of an organization.
- Principles for managing the formal rule based aspects of an organization
- Principles for managing the technical systems

## Principles for managing the pragmatic aspects

The various studies into the management of information security suggests the importance of broader social and organizational concerns. Pouloudi [9] argues that a particular context may make fraud a legitimate activity. Therefore it is important to understand the context in which an information technology is being implemented. She further suggests that by carefully interpreting issues and concerns of various stakeholders, it is possible to understand the interaction between technical and social aspects of an information technology implementation, thus facilitating fraud prevention. By evaluating the unethical computer use practices of Jett at Kidder Peabody, it is suggested that it is important to inculcate a culture or trust and responsibility. It becomes apparent therefore that organizations need to develop a focus on the pragmatic aspects in managing information system security. The various principles that need to be adopted are as follows.

**Principle 1: Education, training and awareness, although**

**important, are not sufficient conditions for managing information security. A focus on developing a security culture goes a long way in developing and sustaining a secure environment.** Research has shown that although education, training and awareness are important in managing the security of enterprises, unless or until an effort to inculcate a security culture exists, complete organizational integrity will be a far-fetched idea. Dhillon [4] has suggested that "a mismatch between the needs and goals of the organization could potentially be detrimental to the health of an organization and to the information systems in place.... organizational processes such as communications, decision making, change and power are culturally ingrained and failure to comprehend these could lead to problems in the security of information systems" pg 111. While discussing issues in disaster recovery planning, Adam and Haslam [1] notes in an earlier chapter that although managers are aware of the potential problems related with a disaster, they tend to be rather complacent in taking any proactive steps. Such an attitude could be a consequence of the relative degree of importance placed on revenue generation. As a consequence, while automating business processes and in a quest for optimal solutions, back-up and recovery issues are often over looked.

**Principle 2: Responsibility, integrity, trust and ethicality are the cornerstones for maintaining a secure environment.** Earlier we noted that given that the nature of organizations has evolved from a predominantly hierarchical organization to a more networked form, traditional security models and approaches fall short of developing secure environments. Dhillon and Backhouse [6] have argued that traditional "information security principles of Confidentiality, Integrity and Availability are fine as far as they go, but they are very restricted". In response to the changing organizational contexts they suggest the RITE (responsibility, integrity, trust and ethicality) principles. The RITE principles hark back to an earlier time period when extensive reliance on technology for close supervision and control of dispersed activities was virtually non existent. Beniger [3] terms this as the 'factorage system of distributed control' where the trade between cotton producers in America and British merchants was to a large extent based on trust (pg 132-133). The extensive reliance on information technologies today questions the nature and scope of individual responsibilities and many a times challenges the integrity of individuals. Trust is also broken especially when technology is considered as an alternative supervisor.

## Principles for managing the formal rule based aspects

Research conducted by organizational theorists has suggested that formalized structures are a consequence of increased complexity within organizations. Mintzberg [8] illustrates this assertion by narrating Ms Raku's story of her pottery business and how she organized her work as her business evolved from a basement shop to Ceramics Inc. (pg 1). Computers are subsequently used to automate many of the formal activities in a business. And there is always a challenge in deciding as to which aspects one should computerize and which should be left alone. It is important therefore to understand the nature and scope of formal rule based systems and understand as to how information security could be adequately designed into an organization. The following paragraphs present principles that need to be considered in instituting adequate control measures.

**Principle 3: Establishing a boundary between what can be formalized and what should be norm based is the basis for establishing appropriate control measures.** Clearly security problems arise as a consequence of 'over-formalization' and managerial inability to balance the rule and norm based aspects of work. At a formal level an organization needs structures which support the technical infrastructure. Therefore formal rules and procedures need to be established which support the IT systems. This would prevent the misinterpretation of data and misapplication of rules, thus avoiding potential information security problems. In practice, however, controls have dysfunctional effects. This is primarily because isolated solutions (i.e. controls) are proposed for specific problems. These 'solutions' tend to ignore other existing controls and their contexts.

**Principle 4: Rules for managing information security have little relevance unless they are contextualized.** Following on from the previous principle, exclusive reliance on either the rules or norms falls short of providing adequate protection. Clearly an inability to appreciate the context while applying rules for managing information security is perhaps detrimental to the security of an enterprise. It is therefore important that a through review of technical, formal and pragmatic interventions is conducted. Many a times a security policy is used as a vehicle to create a shared vision to assess how the various controls will be used and how data and information will be protected in an organization. Typically a security policy is formulated based on sound business judgment, value ascribed to the data and related risks associated with the data. Since each organization is different, the choice of various elements in a security policy is case specific and it's hard to draw any generalization.

## Principles for managing the technical systems

With the discussion presented in this and the previous chapters, it would have become apparent that security of the technical edifice is clearly a function of the level of assurance provided by the formal and pragmatic organizational arrangements. This is because organizations are usually viewed as purposeful systems and security has traditionally not been considered part of the 'useful system' designed for the purposeful activities. Rather security has always been considered as a form of guaranty that the useful activities of an organization will continue to be performed and any untoward incidents prevented. Dhillon [4] however, in his previous work, challenges this mindset and calls for developing security visions and strategies, where information security management is considered a key enabler in the smooth running of an enterprise. Two fundamental principles need to be considered for adequately managing the technical systems. These are presented below.

**Principle 5: In managing the security of technical systems a rationally planned grandiose strategy will fall short of achieving the purpose.** There has been an ongoing debate between those who support rationally planned strategies and those who consider strategy formulation and implementation as an emergent phenomenon. There are others who have suggested that a context is the determining factor in ones choice of a rationally planned or an emergent strategy. Within the domain of information technology management, characterized by emergence of new technologies, constant innovation and its unique influence of structure and management processes, context seems to have a profound influence on maintaining organizational integrity. In recent years, the context has become even more important sine newer technologies have constantly been redefining the boundaries of the firm. In an earlier era, when a hierarchy was the dominant organizational structure, a rationally planned approach for information security development and implementation would have sufficed. However with the emergence of networked and virtual enterprises, a rationally planned grandiose strategy would perhaps fall short of achieving the purpose, i.e. managing the security of technical systems.

**Principle 6: Formal models for maintaining the confidentiality, integrity and availability (CIA) of information cannot be applied to commercial organizations on a grand scale. Micro-management for achieving CIA is the way forward.** Any formal model is an abstraction of reality. The preciseness of a model is judged on basis of the extent to which it represents a given subset of the reality. Most information security models were developed for the military domain and to a large extent are successful in mapping that reality. It is possible to do so since the stated security policy is precise and strictly adhered to. In that sense a security model is a representation of the security policy rather than the actual reality. This suffices as far as the organization works according to the stated policy. In recent years however, with the widespread reliance on Internet to conduct business, problems arise at two levels. First, the organizational reality is not the same for all enterprises. This means that the stated security policy for one organization is bound to be different from that of the other. Second, a model developed for information security within a military organization may not necessarily be valid and true for a commercial enterprise. It follows therefore that any attempt to use models based on the military, are bound to be inadequate for the commercial organizations. Rather, their application in a commercial setting is going to generate a false sense of security (This assertion is based on a definition of security that goes beyond simple access control methods). The way forward is to create newer models for particular aspects of the business for which information security needs to be designed. This would mean that micro-strategies be created for unit or functional levels.

## FINAL WORD

This chapter has presented six principles for managing information security in the new millennium. Information system security has always remained an elusive phenomenon and it is rather difficult to come to grips with it. No one approach is adequate in managing the security of an enterprise and clearly a more holistic approach is needed. The information system security principles presented in this chapter include:

- Developing a security culture as being central to maintaining IS security.

- Responsibility, integrity, trust and ethicality as cornerstones for maintaining a secure environment.
- Appropriateness in control identification and selection as being critical to the success of the security program.
- Rules for managing information security as having little relevance unless they are contextualized.
- Managing security of technical systems in a rationally planned manner as falling short of achieving the purpose
- Thrust being placed on micromanagement for maintaining confidentiality, integrity and availability.

## REFERENCES

1. Adam, F. and J.A. Haslam, *A study of the Irish experience with disaster recovery planning: high levels of awareness may not suffice*, in *Information security management: global challenges in the next millennium*, G. Dhillon, Editor. 2001, Idea Group Publishing: Hershey, PA.

2. Backhouse, J. and G. Dhillon, *Structures of responsibility and security of information systems.* European Journal of Information Systems, 1996. **5**(1): p. 2-9.

3. Beniger, J.R., *The control revolution: technological and economic origins of the information society*. 1986, Massachusetts: Harvard University Press.

4. Dhillon, G., *Managing information system security.* 1997, London: Macmillan.

5. Dhillon, G., *Violation of safeguards by trusted personnel and understanding related information security concerns.* Computers & Security, 2001. **20**(2): p. 165-172.

6. Dhillon, G. and J. Backhouse, *Information system security management in the new millennium.* Communications of the ACM, 2000. **43**(7): p. 125-128.

7. Hitchings, J. *The need for a new approach to information security.* in *10th International Conference on Information Security (IFIP*

*Sec '94)*. 1994. 23-27 May, Curacao, NA.

8. Mintzberg, H., *Structures in fives: designing effective organizations*. 1983, Englewood Cliffs, NJ: Prentice-Hall.

9. Pouloudi, A., *Addressing prescription fraud in the British National Health Service: technological and social considerations*, in *Information security management: global challenges in the next millennium*, G. Dhillon, Editor. 2001, Idea Group Publishing: Hershey, PA.

10. Willison, R.A., *Opportunities for Computer Abuse: Assessing a Crime Specific Approach in the the Case of Barings Bank*. Unpublished PhD Thesis, 2002, London School of Economics and Political Science, University of London, London.

11. Wrapp, H.E., *Good managers don't make policy decisions*, in *The strategy process*, H. Mintzberg and J.B. Quinn, Editors. 1991, Prentice-Hall: Englewood Cliffs. p. 32-38.

## DISCUSSION QUESTIONS

1. You are a Chief Privacy Officer for a retail company in the business of selling Fast Moving Consumer Goods. Business has been generally good, but in order to increase relationships with customers, you have been tasked with profiling customers and suggest strategies for developing relationships. What are the critical issues that you will consider such that security of data is not compromised in any way?
2. Confidentiality, Integrity and Availability of information have been considered as the panacea of information system security. Comment.
3. Consider the following scenario. You have taken over as Director for IT systems for a large hospital. The Health environment in general is confounded with the issue of instituting controls given the federally mandated legislative requirements. The hospital does not have a security policy at the moment. While all the administrators want such a policy and have all the right controls, the clinicians on the other hand do not like any controls. Nurses are confused as to what should be the right set of controls. In this situation how would you go about developing consensus and identifying the right set of security policy guidelines? What aspects of the organization should you consider in terms of a well conceived security program?

4. We have in this chapter argued that establishing structures of responsibility is an important aspect of the overall security program for a company. How would you go about establishing responsibility structures? What is the relationship between roles that individuals might occupy and responsibility? How would issues of dual access (access by two people to one resource) be handled? In addressing these questions think of a hypothetical organization.

# 11. SOCIAL RESPONSIBILITY IN THE INFORMATION AGE

Over 80% of Thailand's population still lives in rural areas, yet less than 40% of telephone lines in the country are in non-urban areas.

There are 14 million phone lines in all of Africa – fewer than in Manhattan or Tokyo.

In the US Hispanic households are still roughly as likely to own a computer as White households in the US and nearly 2.5 times less likely to use the Internet.

**Social Responsibility in Action**

During the 1970's the Department of Justice of the United States of America pursued various avenues to standardize management information systems. The goal of this search was to assist law enforcement offices across the country in the recordkeeping and tracking of criminal cases. To this end, the Law Enforcement Assistance Administration (LEAA) funded the development of the Prosecutors Management Information System or PROMIS. The design of the software was initially undertaken on a nonprofit basis by INSLAW, a corporation funded almost entirely through Government grants and contracts. During the Carter administration LEAA was terminated. Subsequently INSLAW became a for-profit corporation commercially marketing PROMIS. The new corporation made several significant improvements to the original PROMIS software which later became known as Enhanced PROMIS.

In March 1982, the DOJ awarded INSLAW with a ten million dollar three year contract to supply and implement the original public domain version of PROMIS at 94 U.S attorney's offices. The contract quickly became embroiled in bitterness over the ownership of the privately funded Enhanced PROMIS software. The DOJ claimed they had unlimited rights to the software even after a contractual modification in 1983. All attempts by INSLAW to resolve the matter were met with hostility by the DOJ. Eventually the DOJ canceled part of the contract and withheld at least $1.6 million in payments to INSLAW. As a result the company was on the brink of insolvency and was threatened by dissolution. The DOJ claimed that the case was a contractual disagreement that had been blown out of proportion, while the owners of INSLAW persisted with there belief that there was a high level conspiracy by the DOJ to steal the PROMIS software.

The allegations made by the proprietors of INSLAW centered on their belief that the contractual disagreement was intentionally concocted by the DOJ to force the company into bankruptcy. The investigation discovered high level officials including Edwin Meese and Attorney General Lowell Jensen were involved with these decisions. The insolvency of INSLAW would have forced the sale of all its assets, including Enhanced PROMIS to a rival computer company called *Hadron Inc*. The owner of Hadron Inc. was a Dr E. Brown who had previously worked with Attorney General Meese in the cabinet of the Governor of California Ronald Reagan. The ultimate goal of the conspiracy was to position Hadron and other companies owned by Dr. Brown to utilize the $3 millions worth of automated data processing upgrade contracts planned by the DOJ.

Several worn affidavits were obtained by the owner of INSLAW attesting to the fact that the Enhanced PROMIS software was criminally acquired by Dr. Brain for modification of the program for use in covert intelligence. Two of the sources for these affidavits came from Ari Ben-Menashe a former Mossad officer and Micheal Riconosciuto who has links with covert intelligence agencies and allegedly programmed the Trojan Horse subroutine (Colin Brown, "Spies, Lies and Inslawgate", and "CIA Computer Consultant Alleges Massive Conspiracy", TC Technical Consultant, August-September 1192, pp.6, 10, 11, and 13). The software was modified to incorporate a Trojan Horse subroutine that could be used by U.S intelligence agencies to open a backdoor into the systems when required. Subsequently the software was distributed to several federal agencies, including the FBI, CIA and the DEA. Later the software was sold internationally to 88 different countries, according to Riconosciuto these countries included Iraq and Libya.

In 1986, INSLAW filed a law suit against the DOJ. A year later, the Bankruptcy Court ruled that the DOJ had stolen the Enhanced PROMIS software through "trickery, fraud and deceit" (INSLAW, Inc, vs United States, 83 B.R 89, Bankruptcy District Court 1988 at 158, Findings 399) and further attempted to cause the liquidation of INSLAW. In 1989, Senior U.S District Judge W. Bryant upheld the $8 million judgment, made by Bankruptcy Court, against the DOJ. He ruled that even the uncontested evidence virtually compelled the findings of the Bankruptcy Court "under any standard review". He added:

> *The Government accuses the bankruptcy court of looking beyond the bankruptcy proceedings to find culpability by the Government. What is strikingly apparent from the testimony and depositions of key witnesses and may documents is that INSLAW performed its contract in a hostile environment that extended from the higher echelons of the Justice Department to the officials who had the day-to-day responsibility for supervising its work.*

However, these rulings were overturned on narrow jurisdictional grounds in the Court of Appeals in 1991. The Court did not disturb any of the 399 findings of fact about the DOJ's malfeasance against INSLAW. In 1992, the U.S Supreme Court of Appeals declined INSLAW a hearing on the decisions made by the U.S Court of Appeals.

On September 10, 1992, the Committee on the Judiciary of the House of Representatives concluded a three year investigation into allegations of a high level government conspiracy to pervert the course of justice. The findings of the committee corroborated the rulings of the two lower federal courts. It believed that the INSLAW software was stolen by the DOJ and that the plans to harm INSLAW had began no later than the first month of the three year contract. According to evidence uncovered by the committee these plans were masterminded by the highest-ranking officials of the Justice Department. Further evidence was found that corroborated the testimony of the former covert intelligence agents. The private sector associates of the leadership of the DOJ illegally sold PROMIS software domestically and internationally. The software was sold to intelligence agencies around the world for financial gain and to further the intelligence and foreign policy objectives of the United States. The committee concluded that the conduct of the DOJ "clearly raises the specter that the Departments actions taken against INSLAW in this matter represents an abuse of power of shameful proportions".

The committee also probed allegations by newspaper journalist that the suicide of an investigative reporter, Mr. D. Casolaro was connected to the INSLAW affair. The lifeless body of Mr. Casolaro was found in a hotel. He lay in a bathtub with each of his wrists slashed seven times. He had just completed a manuscript of the INSLAW affair and had told his family that he would be traveling to Martinsburg to obtain the final crucial piece of evidence for his book. Mr. Casolaro met his death in Martinsburg and the manuscript of his book had vanished. The case was judged as suicide. After much campaigning by Mr. Casolaro's brother the case was reopened, but the second verdict remained suicide. The committee believes that there is a link between Casolaro's death and the INSLAW affair.

Throughout the whole investigation the DOJ were either reluctant to pass information over to the Committee or blatantly ignored requests. Consequently, there were no charges brought against Mr. Meese, Dr. Brian or any of the other high ranking officials accused of conspiring to cause the bankruptcy of INSLAW. However, there is no dispute that the DOJ acted in bad faith and with hidden agendas.

---

There is no doubt that information technology has permeated all aspects of our lives – from booking flights to buying insurance and getting a home mortgage. Not only can most tasks be carried out without speaking to a single person, they are based on highly automated electronic systems. The way in which information technology has permeated our lives also questions our values, morals and responsibilities. Would we indeed like computers to take control of our lives? Would we like to let go of our personal private space? Can we really trust the electronic systems for their reliability and quality of information they produce? What about an array of freedom of speech, property right and ownership issues? All these questions are important ones to consider and are discussed in this chapter.

## ACCESSIBILITY TO TECHNOLOGY

Accessibility to technology is a growing concern, for different societies. Not only there are disparities between the economically advantaged and disadvantaged countries, there are also significant inequalities within individual countries. Such inequalities might arise as a consequence of gender, race or simply the economic status of some societies. Clearly there are some groups that are more disadvantages than others – low-income persons living in rural areas, young and single parent families. In his book *The new barbarian manifesto*, Ian Angell [1] has argued that advances in information and communication technologies are in fact fostering divisions in society and as a consequence are widening the gap between those who "have" and those who "have not". Such disparities can be observed not only within countries, but also at a global scale.

Researchers tend to present differing viewpoints as to the consequences of varying levels of access to technology. There are a group of researchers who seem to feel that advances in information and communication technologies, and Internet in particular, are going to decrease the divide between those who have access to technology and those who do not. The first argument, as maintained by Ian Angell, [2] is that technological divide will give rise to a 'new barbarian' and there is bound to be a lot of turmoil in the information age. Reich [3] and Ohmae [4] resonate somewhat with this view in their claim that in years to come we will see an emergence of the 'symbolic-analyst', who could be construed as 'information rich' and the others who would be 'information poor'. Ohmae [4] makes an economic argument to propose that *inter linked economies* are the organizing logic of the future as opposed to nation states. To a large extent this is abetted by the convergence of information and communication technologies. In many ways this dispiriting future is here. Dhillon et al [5] illustrate this phenomena by presenting a review of networked firms operating in an *inter linked economy* and the challenges that a developing country faces.

There is some merit is postulating the negative consequences of information technology advent and increased divide between groups of people. For instance, in the wealthiest nations, there are 31,046 Internet hosts per million inhabitants while for the poorest nations there are only 9 per million inhabitants. International Telecommunication Union [6] has reported that more than 90% households in high-income countries have a telephone line and in some cases have more than one, but in comparison only 2% of households in low-income countries have the service. It is also estimated that out of 950 million households in the world, 65% of the total do not have a telephone. Access to telephone service is not only a good indicator of a country's telecommunications infrastructure, but also a suitable gauge of the level of access to information. This suggests that there is clearly a significant level of disparity between those who have access to information and those who do not, which perhaps could have negative consequences for the society at large.

The second argument, as contended by Burn and Loch, [7] is that the Internet will help in closing the divide between the have and have-nots. Burn and Loch [7] give the example of Egypt where a model of technology diffusion was developed that includes education and training, infrastructure, and IT. The applications developed in Egypt were both culturally and socially appropriate so as to gain widespread acceptance. Although education and training have been argued as cornerstones of realizing a technological diffusion, the benefits derived could be marginal since a majority of the populace may not have access to even basic education. Clearly as with any technological innovation majority of the benefits reside in the related changes.

## PROPERTY RIGHTS AND OWNERSHIP ISSUES

Intellectual property and ownership are crucial issues in the information age. Software piracy remains one of the foremost intellectual property right issues, and yet a complex one. Although monetary losses because of software piracy in the US have been significant ($13 billion for 1996) the software piracy rates when compared with rest of the world are rather modest. The Software and Information Industry Alliance (SIIA) has however reported a decline in software piracy in 1999 to $11 billion. The 1994 figures from Business Software Alliance estimate US software piracy rate at 35%. Although Europe has the highest overall piracy rate, piracy in Asia costs the software industry highest in monetary terms. The Hong Kong piracy rate is almost double that of the US (with an average of 72%). Hong Kong and China perhaps pose a very serious threat to the software industry. It has been estimated that there are some 26 'factories' in China that produce some 75 million pirated compact discs each year. The local market absorbs less than 1% of the total production. These copies are often smuggled to Latin American and European countries.

Numerous studies have been conducted to explain reasons behind software piracy. These have ranged from ease of theft and people's sense of proportional value to cost, censure and availability as the main drivers [8]. The SIIA has vehemently argued that since software piracy is an illegal act, the associated activities of buying and selling are also illegal and hence makes calls for increased legislation and enforcement. Although SIIA explains the decline in software piracy between 1994 and 1998 simply in terms of cost, cost *per se* does not seem to figure in SIIA's drive in managing piracy. This suggests that perhaps software developers are charging more than necessary for the software. One reason could be the near monopolistic environment in which most companies operate.

There are also researchers who argue (e.g. Weckert, [9]) that unauthorized copying is not morally wrong, except when its morally wrong to act illegally. Weckert poses three scenarios to make his point. First, where an individual may copy software just for evaluation, with the intent of buying it if it proves to be satisfactory. Second, where an individual copies a game, but would never buy it because he thinks it's not worth doing so. Third, where an individual copies software for commercial gain and if the software was not available for copying, the individual would buy it. According to Weckert, clearly the owner of the software is harmed in the third case. Based on these assertions Weckert contends that copying is certainly not immoral and that a case against copying ought to be firmly established before restrictions are put in place.

There are various other viewpoints on software piracy and intellectual property rights. Swinyard, et al. [10], for example, argue that the notion of copyright is a Western concept and that for the Asians becoming skilled means to copy the master. Therefore the authors contend that high piracy rates in Asia are a cultural issue with individuals viewing software piracy relative to potential benefits to self, family and community. Conner and Rumelt [11] argue that existence of pirated software is actually beneficial to software developers since it draws people into the software market and also is a means to distribute 'free' copies to potential customers, who otherwise might not be aware.

## FREEDOM OF SPEECH ISSUES

Aspects of freedom of speech have always been of concern to a broad cross section of the populace. Even today freedom of speech issues are hotly contested. Only recently there were a lot of feelings expressed with the destruction of Buddha's statues in Afghanistan. Such occurrences have always been the musings of scholars and theologians alike. However with the recent advent of technology and the Internet, freedom of speech issues seem to have become of interest to the public.

In the United States the First Amendment to the Constitution (Freedom of Speech) has always acted as a shield between citizen and the government. Individual States have tried to enact legislation to 'criminalize' the intentional transmission of 'obscene and indecent' messages but it has been rather difficult to define what constitutes 'obscene' or 'indecent'. Some headway was made in the 1996 Communication Decency Act where 'obscene' and 'indecent' are defined as the transmission of information which depicts or describes 'sexual or excretory activities or organs' in a manner deemed 'offensive' by community standards. However understanding and regulating 'community standards' in the cyberspace is not only difficult, but also subjected to standards of the most restrictive communities in the nation. The act was challenged (and lost) on grounds that it violated the First Amendment insofar as that it caused 'blanket restriction' of free speech. The act also failed to define 'indecent' adequately. Although this was an attempt by the moral leaders to manage content on the Internet, at the same time it was a victory for those who supported free speech over the Internet.

Sex sites are not the only sites that are under fire. Hate speeches, online stalking and 'recipe books' for terrorist groups are also of concern. As Warren and Hutchinson [12] suggests, today a number of terrorist groups are using the Internet to further their cause. Prominent among these are the Zapatista Movement web site detailing their struggle against the Mexican authorities and TamilNet, the voice of the Tamil Tigers. Many terrorists groups not only use the Internet to raise funds, disseminate information, they are also using information and communication technologies to engage in denial of service and even direct attacks. For instance the Portuguese hacker group, PHAIT (Portuguese Hackers Against Indonesian Tyranny) rewrote a number of Indonesian government and commercial web sites to protest about East Trimor (as quoted in Warren and Hutchinson [12]).

There are two viewpoints regarding such 'bad speech' on the Internet. First, and the most obvious, is to strictly regulate the traffic. Such an action, however, comes under attack from the proponents of freedom of speech. Second, that the pursuit of truth is best served by allowing all kinds of views to be presented in the 'market of ideas'. The inherent contention is that only by free discussion of ideas and arguments will the real truth emerge (Elgesem [13]).

## QUALITY AND RELIABILITY OF INFORMATION AND RELATED SYSTEMS

Issues of quality and reliability of information and the related systems have perhaps received the most attention. Earlier work on quality of information was essentially carried out by software engineers [14]; [15]. The software engineers tried to describe quality of software by identifying series of attributes. Attributes in turn would have more attributes. Identifications and description of such attributes helped in formulating a set of quality characteristics that could help in defining system specification and help in simplifying the quality assurance process. This earlier work went a long way in developing quality practices and in laying down the foundation for present day software metrics. In recent years a number of additional best practices and codes have been developed. Adherence to such codes helps in enhancing system reliability. The IEEE/ACM ethical codes are presented in the appendix.

Quality attributes were also pivotal in defining good and bad, ethical and unethical software engineering practices. For instance the software development practices followed in commissioning Therac-25 machines in mid 1980s was criticized because basic software quality attributes had not been considered. Therac-25 was a computerized radiation therapy machine, where software from the earlier Therac-6 and Therac-20 had been reused. Following the death of six patients between 1985 and 1987, a number of social responsibility issues were raised. In the Therac-25 case the specialist machine operator upon whom the patients (and the public at large) were relying, did not hone up to their responsibilities. Patients were subjected to repeated radiation doses in spite of the operators knowing that the machines were malfunctioning. The manufacturer was clearly negligent in relation to this treatment equipment, from the original design stage through the much overdue safety renovations. The developers mistakenly believed that taking pieces from various proven machines would create a likewise successful new machine. This was a serious flaw in system design. More importantly, though, the priorities in system quality were poorly arranged with simplicity of use threatening safety. There is a level of social responsibility (even greater in a industry such as medicine) that companies are entrusted with as we proceed into an era of all consuming technology. The developers would have been far better off to meet those responsibilities proactively rather than reactively.

In recent years the social responsibility issues related to quality and reliability of information and the related systems have been repeatedly questioned. When the London Ambulance computer aided dispatch system failed in 1992; who was to blame? London Ambulance, presumably the largest in the world covering over 600 square miles and a resident population of nearly seven million, carries over 5000 patients and receives between 2000 and 2500 calls per day. But numerous problems related to contractor selection, planning, project management and implementation resulted in complete failure of the computer-based system. The inquiries that ensued found that the system did not meet functionality or performance criteria and much of the design had fatal flaws that would, and did, cumulatively lead to all of the symptoms of system failure. This resulted in lengthy response times, numerous callbacks, and a large wait time to speak with a dispatcher.

When systems as critical as Therac-25 and London Ambulance fail, there are obviously social responsibility concerns. Clearly lack of quality in systems analysis, design and management results are the root causes. Ultimately, as observed by Bowen [16], "it is unethical to develop software for safety-related systems without following the best practice available". As a matter of fact it is unethical to develop software for any kind of a system, may it be safety-critical or not. By following unethical information systems project management best practices, the baggage handling systems of the Chek Lap Kok airport in Hong Kong and Denver airport in the US resulted in disasters. The Nevada, California and Oregon Department of Motor Vehicle systems had a similar fate because corners were cut and basic guidelines for software development and project management were not followed.

## ASPECTS OF A VIABLE SOCIAL RESPONSIBILITY PROGRAM

The previous sections have identified and addressed a broad range of social responsibility issues, which if ignored are going to result in some ethical strain. In the paragraphs below, based on an understanding of potential ethical strains, key elements of a viable social responsibility program are identified and described.

## Socially responsible individual practice

As has been noted elsewhere, even law and regulatory frameworks call upon individuals to engage in some sort of 'self regulation'. However, prior to expecting individuals to self regulate, it is not only important to make them aware of the various issues, but also train, and motivate them to consider various social responsibility issues.

In a recent paper, Dhillon [17], while discussing violations of safeguards by trusted personnel notes that had individuals within Barings Bank been aware and well trained to be socially responsible, the demise of the 223 year old merchant bank could have been prevented. Since various groups of individuals within the bank lacked the ability to recognize patterns related to abuse of position and circumvention of organizational and technological controls, they failed to recognize any mis-dealings on part of Nicholas Leeson, the accused.

In a similar vein, if an average user of technology is not made aware of the manner in which various Internet businesses infringe the right to individual privacy, they would not be able to even recognize if any transgression has taken place. Such an issue is more important today than ever before, since concrete laws either do not exist or are still in the process of being defined.

## Ethical systems development

Given that majority of IT implementations within organizations result in failure or inappropriate use, there is a need to consider the ethical aspects of the systems development process. Consider the recent Nevada Department of Motor Vehicle's (DMV) systems development fiasco. The goal was to implement one stop shopping for drivers' licenses and registration, Internet and telephone transactions, registration at smog check stations, and of course, the reduction of abnormally long waiting times. This was to be achieved using a $35 million computer system that was, unfortunately, not implemented skillfully; full of bugs and slower than expected; it certainly did not help the backlog that DMV was struggling with initially. In months subsequent to the implementation failure, the bugs were removed and the system improved, albeit at a cost. However low employee morale and high turnover besides a bothered public are some of the legacies left behind. Yet the new system at the branch level is not much easier, and not any quicker, than the old.

At the heart of the DMV's problem with the computer system, is not so much a technological issue, but a shear lack of ethical standards and inadequate social responsibility. Clearly a lack of good management - poor planning and design undermined the good intentions. The political (and contractual) constraints on time and staffing, as well as other problems that come with being a state agency, set the stage for a "mission impossible". Still, the legislature believed two consultants were up to the task, and for enough money they took it on. These are ethical and social responsibility IT project management issues that clearly need to be adequately understood.

There are several issues that contributed to the poor implementation, untimely completion, and unsatisfactory result of the DMV computer system. Among these is poor project management, the confusing role of two consultants, non-replaced downtime of existing employees for training and other human resource matters. As has been argued elsewhere (e.g. see Wood-Harper, et al [18]; Rahanu, et al [19]) such issues could have been rectified by focusing on project management and systems development ethics. Clearly the system analysts had a social responsibility to elicit the right requirements, systems developers the responsibility to design a system to fit the needs of the current environment and project managers the responsibility to meet stakeholder expectations.

## Establishing responsibilities

The call to establish responsibility structures can best be described by considering the context of the Therac-25, a computerized radiation therapy machine briefly mentioned in the previous section. This machine had been built after the Therac-6 and the Therac-20 models, originally developed in the early 1970's. The Therac-25 was considered more compact, more versatile and possibly more user friendly then the previous two models. The Therac-25 had some software that was reused from the Therac-6 and Therac-20 but it eliminated the use of some of the hardware previously used. Because the Therac-25 took advantage of the computer's abilities to control and monitor the hardware, it was decided not to duplicate all the safety mechanisms and interlocks that the previous models used. The manufacturer, perhaps to cut the expenses, removed the hardware interlocks and backups thus putting more faith on software. There were eleven Therac-25's installed in the US and Canada in 1985. Between 1985 and 1987, six accidents involving massive overdoses to patients occurred. In

1987 the Therac-25 was recalled so that not only the software could be corrected but also the machines could be redesigned to include hardware safeguards against software errors. During this recall, it was discovered that related problems existed in the Therac-20 software.

This case calls forth numerous questions about responsibility and liability related to modern technology. More specifically, given the medical use of the technology in this case, questions of professional standards and ethical codes are raised. It seems all too often, as with this case, consumers (or patients) find themselves nowadays in a state of "buyer beware". But as the patient or the consumer, is this really your responsibility? It is completely unreasonable to expect that individuals in need of radiation therapy would have in depth knowledge (or bear the time and cost to obtain it) regarding all the medication and equipment that will be inflicted upon them. Clearly in the Therac case the specialist upon which the patients (and the public at large) were relying, did not hone up to their responsibilities. The manufacturer was clearly negligent in relation to this treatment equipment, from the original design stage through the much overdue safety renovations. The manufacturer mistakenly believed that taking pieces from various proven machines would create a likewise successful new machine. This was a serious flaw in system design. More importantly, though, the priorities in system quality were poorly arranged with simplicity of use threatening safety. There is a level of social responsibility that companies are entrusted with as we proceed into an era of all consuming technology. The manufacturer would have been far better off to meet those responsibilities proactively rather than reactively. As a manufacturer, however, the company is not held to any professional ethics like doctors themselves.

Another question that arises is to ask where the governmental agencies should step in? Although it is true the Therac-25 was saving many lives in the same period in which it took some, and irreparably damaged others. The manufacturer, however, being previously negligent in their responsibilities should not have been instructed (and entrusted) to notify the users. The FDA should have taken the notification actions itself. While the two exchanged meaningless correspondence about what the users should be told, more patients were harmed. The FDA's likewise reactive approach also leaves a lot to be desired. The agency should be far more proactive in regulating the initial release of equipment, than ambulance chasing later to find enough faults for recall or required renovations.

In this case the middlemen, the technicians, are not without some responsibility. Taking a carefree and resigned approach as they did to using machinery of this magnitude was erroneous on their part. Machines should never have been told to proceed as many as 5 times after malfunctioning, or patients segregated from the technician in such a manner that they could not be seen or heard. The continued use through the day of malfunctioning equipment is troubling at best.

It is therefore important to understand and establish adequate responsibility structures. It may be prudent to delineate the roles when say a new technology is introduced or a change is made in the functionality. Not only is it important to identify high level stakeholders, so as to influence current and future policy initiatives, but also to establish stakeholders at an operational level so as to have identifiable incumbents where the buck would stop. Such individuals would obviously have to be empowered. In the Therac case, had the technicians been empowered to take a decision not to use the machines, a number of tragedies could have been prevented. Another important issue related to empowerment is that of training, which would enable individuals to recognize that a problem exists in the first place.

## Instituting training programs

Besides a lack of planning, inadequate training is perhaps an important reason for failure of IT implementations [20]. Any organization is socially obliged and is responsible for training end users to manage technology. As is evident from a number of case studies, lack of training has a knock on effect on customer service, employee morale and increased incidents of crime and fraud.

In the Nevada DMV case discussed above, besides other reasons, inability of the organization to institute well thought through training programs resulted in an organization failing to capitalize on the technology. Since a DMV system services the needs of a large proportion of the population, one could argue that the organizations failed to uphold its social responsibility. Similar instances of lack of training and inability of the employees and end users to understand and appreciate corporate change initiatives can be found in IT implementations at the Oregon DMV, Californian DMV, the 1992 London Ambulance IT implementation fiasco, to name a few.

What can easily be taken from the above studies and conclusions is that organizations need to take the time to really get to know their employees. Rapid technological change is going to continue into the next decade and unprepared reactive response to that change is not going to be good enough. Organizations need to begin to prepare themselves now by restructuring the human resources and training and development departments of their business. The goal behind this restructuring should be to create a highly skilled, motivated, and self-assured and socially responsible groups of individuals who will be prepared for change when it comes about. Organizations will need to begin to address and improve the issue of low self-efficacy through on-going training courses tailored to the knowledge and confidence level of these associates. These courses should be designed to address the individual areas of concern and increase their self-efficacy prior to the need for new technology training by slowly introducing computer functions at an individual pace. Training should not solely be focused on technological aspects, but psychological issues of low self-efficacy should be concentrated on as well. Therefore, motivational training should be a large portion of this undertaking. As Smith-Jentsch, et al [21] note "pre-training motivation is expected to prepare trainees to learn by heightening their attention and increasing their receptivity to new ideas."

Corporations can no longer afford to let their own employees hinder them from continued growth. Therefore, organizations that can recognize now the need to escort their associates into the future by preparing them ahead of time for inevitable technological changes will be the ones that would be more successful, more ethical and responsible.

## End-users need a lesson in ethics

Clearly end-users need a lesson in ethics. This is because business corporations and governments alike have increasingly become dependent on IT. However, we are constantly reminded of spectacular intrusions into supposedly secure computer installations for a variety of illicit purposes, including theft, fraud and sabotage. Such is the concern that international bodies such as the Organizations for Economic Co-operation & Development, the International Chamber of Commerce and the Council of Europe, among others, have focused on the question. In UK the Department of Trade and Industry has also launched several initiatives to address the issue.

While it is clear that business organizations and society at large are directly affected because of their dependence on computers, it is difficult to find reliable figures for monetary loss, and assess the extent of impact. The 1994 UK Audit Commission survey revealed that in the previous three years the total value of cases reported went up by 183%. Figures coming from the US suggest anything up to yearly damages of $2bn could be involved, although something in the region of $145m-$730m seems more realistic.

What may be trivial in its self-evidence but profound in its truth is that prevention of computer related abuse is more effective than treatment. At a societal level, the diffusion of ideas about ethical use of computers as part of the cultural infrastructure could reduce the burden placed on the shoulders of IT managers. Many large organizations are engaging in awareness campaigns that seek to increase understanding of and sensitivity towards misuse/abuse of computers among the broad base of their employees, rather than merely concentrate on those with responsibility for computer systems. There are initiatives being developed seeking to educate youngsters in ethical use of technology as they learn about computers.

Ultimately the need is to have both a higher level of awareness among the workforce generally about the costs and benefits of good ethical practices, and a framework of computer law and enforcement to provide necessary support where the more informal system of checks and balances fails.

## CONCLUSION

Clearly there is a need to understand various aspects of ethical strains and potential social responsibility concerns. Such issues gain significance when the task at hand is of either managing a new technology or introducing innovative technologies into business settings. Mars [22] for instance notes, "there is only a blurred line between enterpreneuriality and flair on the one hand and sharp practice and fraud on the other". This is indeed an outcome of an ambitious attitude of the society towards many fiddles. Mills [23] portrayed business as operating in a 'subculture of structural immoralities'. Moreover Croall [24] feels that the 'blurred line' gives ample scope for the offenders to argue that their activities fall on the right side of the line.

Today, management fears computer fraud more than any other kind of fraud. Evidence coming from across the globe indicates that computer related crime afflicts practically all nations, even those we might consider unlikely. For the organisations, the pressing question is how to control this new affliction. One of the cornerstones of control and management of computer crime is a social responsibility framework and ethical principles to adequately protect and manage diverse systems. However control can be implemented at two levels. At a macro level by enacting relevant laws and at a micro level by adopting better management practices. Associated with fears of security and crime are also the issues of reliability and quality, and managers involved in dealing with each of the concerns should give due consideration to the social responsibility challenges. It is our hope that issues identified in this chapter set the tone for setting an agenda that will hone in on social responsibility concerns in the information age.

## REFERENCES

1. Angell, I.O., *The new barbarian manifesto: how to survive the information age?* 2000, London: Kogan Page.

2. Angell, I.O., *Economic crime: beyond good and evil.* Journal of Financial Regulation and Compliance, 1996. **4**(1).

3. Reich, R.B., *The work of nations*. 1992, New York: Vintage Books.

4. Ohmae, K., *The end of the nation state*. 1995, New York: The Free Press.

5. Dhillon, G., T. Moores, and R. Hackney, *The emergence of networked organizations in India: a misalignment of interests?* Journal of Global Information Management, 2001. **9**(1): p. 25-30.

6. International Telecommunication Union, *World Telecommunication Development Report 1998*. 1998, ITU: Geneva, Switzerland.

7. Burn, J.M. and K.D. Loch, *The societal impact of the World Wide Web - key challenges for the 21st century.* Information Resources

Management Journal, 2001. **14**(4).

8. Moores, T. and G. Dhillon, *Software piracy: a view from Hong Kong*. Communications of the ACM, 2000. **43**(12): p. 88-93.

9. Weckert, J. *Intellectual property rights and computer software*. in *3rd International conference on values and social responsibilities of computer science (ETHICOMP96)*. 1996. Madrid, Spain, November: Universidad Complutense de Madrid.

10. Swinyard, W., H. Rinne, and A. Kau, *The morality of software piracy: a cross cultural analysis*. Journal of Business Ethics, 1990. **9**(655-664).

11. Conner, K.R. and R.P. Rumelt, *Software piracy: an analysis of protection strategies*. Management Science, 1991. **37**(2): p. 125-139.

12. Warren, M. and W. Hutchinson, *Cyber terrorism and the contemporary corporation*, in *Information security management: global challenges in the new millennium*, G. Dhillon, Editor. 2001, Idea Group Publishing: Hershey. p. 53-64.

13. Elgesem, D. *Freedom of expression and the regulation of Internet access in academia*. in *3rd International conference on values and social responsibilities of computer science (ETHICOMP96)*. 1996. Madrid, Spain, November: Universidad Complutense de Madrid.

14. Boehm, B.W., *et al.*, *Characteristics of software quality*. 1978, Amsterdam: North Holland.

15. McCall, J.A., *An introduction to software quality metrics*, in *Software quality management*, J.B. Coper and M.J. Fisher, Editors. 1979, PBI: New York.

16. Bowen, J., *The ethics of safety-critical systems*. Communications of the ACM, 2000. **43**(4): p. 91-97.

17. Dhillon, G., *Violation of safeguards by trusted personnel and understanding related information security concerns*. Computers & Security, 2001. **20**(2): p. 165-172.

18. Wood-Harper, A.T., *et al.*, *How we profess: the ethical systems analyst*. Communications of the ACM, 1996. **39**(3): p. 69-77.

19. Rahanu, H., J. Davies, and S. Rogerson. *Ethical analysis of software failure cases*. in *3rd International conference on values and*

*social responsibilities of computer science (ETHICOMP96)*. 1996. Madrid, Spain, November: Universidad Complutense de Madrid.

20. Martocchio, J.J., *Microcomputer usage as an opportunity: the influence of context in employee training*. Personnel Psychology, 1992. **45**: p. 529.

21. Smith-Jentsch, K.A., *et al.*, *Can pretraining experience explain individual differences in learning?* Journal of Applied Psychology, 1996. **81**(1).

22. Mars, G., *Cheats at work. An anthropology of workplace crime*. 1982, London: George Allen & Unwin.

23. Mills, C.W., *The power elite*. 1956, Oxford: Oxford University Press.

24. Croall, H., *White collar crime*. 1992, Milton Keynes, UK: Open University Press.

## DISCUSSION QUESTIONS

1. The globalization of work supported by information and telecommunications technology and the advent of 'networked' organizations has produced a potential dilemma in how to balance the interests of the new global company and the long-term national interests of the country supplying the workforce. A networked organization is one that is decentralized and has regional offices that deal with part of the business operation. For instance, an IT center in one location and a Sales office in another. Global decentralization is motivated primarily in order to exploit cheap, skilled labor where so ever it is found in the world. In true Dickens style, however, the emergence of such organizations has the potential to produce the best of times and the worst of times. On the one hand, the investment made in the economy by contracting the local workforce can produce regional micro-economies that become an engine of prosperity by reshaping global markets - *the best of times*. On the other hand, by failing to capitalize and promote further the competence that is attracting companies to the region in the first place, major infrastructure issues are being ignored by central planners - *the worst of times*. Discuss.

2. No one single factor can be held responsible for the current and projected crisis in Information Systems Ethics. For instance, the massive proliferation of inexpensive computing power has actually created an environment without which some crimes and unethical acts would never have been possible. The software piracy epidemic has only been possible because of the huge growth in the number of microcomputers in use. Because this tremendous growth in computing power has been coupled with a similar decline in costs, many more people today have ready access to enormous quantities of information and the inexpensive means to manipulate it. Comment on the relationship between relatively inexpensive technology and the potential to abuse it. How can the business context be made more ethical?
3. With corporate America going global like never before more and more technology is leaving the US at an increasing rate and the American business culture is changing as well. Many American companies are no longer controlled by people who were born and raised in the United States. The US has become a home for many new immigrants from all over the world. They are integrating themselves with corporate America. Identify the range of social responsibility issues that are critical for any society to be safe and secure. Do you think that the government needs to take a careful look at its export laws and control policies to find better ways to protect information that is critical to its national security?

## APPENDIX

### IEEE/ACM Code of Ethics and Professional Practice for Software Engineers (version 5.2)

Computers have a central and growing role in commerce, industry, government, medicine, education, entertainment and society at large. Software engineers are those who contribute by direct participation or by teaching, to the analysis, specification, design, development, certification, maintenance and testing of software systems. Because of their roles in developing software systems, software engineers have significant opportunities to do good or cause harm, to enable others to do good or cause harm, or to influence others to do good or cause harm. To ensure, as much as possible, that their efforts will be used for good, software engineers must commit themselves to making software engineering a beneficial and respected profession. In accordance with that commitment, software engineers shall adhere to the following Code of Ethics and Professional Practice.

The Code contains eight Principles related to the behavior of and decisions made by professional software engineers, including practitioners, educators, managers, supervisors and policy makers, as well as trainees and students of the profession. The Principles identify the ethically responsible relationships in which individuals, groups, and organizations participate and the primary obligations within these relationships. The Clauses of each Principle are illustrations of some of the obligations included in these relationships. These obligations are founded in the software engineer's humanity, in special care owed to people affected by the work of software engineers, and the unique elements of the practice of software engineering. The Code prescribes these as obligations of anyone claiming to be or aspiring to be a software engineer.

It is not intended that the individual parts of the Code be used in isolation to justify errors of omission or commission. The list of Principles and Clauses is not exhaustive. The Clauses should not be read as separating the acceptable from the unacceptable in professional conduct in all practical situations. The Code is not a simple ethical algorithm that generates ethical decisions. In some situations standards may be in tension with each other or with standards from other sources. These situations require the software engineer to use ethical judgment to act in a manner which is most consistent with the spirit of the Code of Ethics and Professional Practice, given the circumstances.

Ethical tensions can best be addressed by thoughtful consideration of fundamental principles, rather than blind reliance on detailed regulations. These Principles should influence software engineers to consider broadly who is affected by their work; to examine if they and their colleagues are treating other human beings with due respect; to consider how the public, if reasonably well informed, would view their decisions; to analyze how the least empowered will be affected by their decisions; and to consider whether their acts would be judged worthy of the ideal professional working as a software engineer. In all these judgments concern for the health, safety and welfare of the public is primary; that is, the "Public Interest" is central to this Code.

The dynamic and demanding context of software engineering requires a code that is adaptable and relevant to new situations as they occur. However, even in this generality, the Code provides support for software engineers and managers of software engineers who need to take positive action in a specific case by documenting the ethical stance of the profession. The Code provides an ethical foundation to which individuals within teams and the team as a whole can appeal. The Code helps to define those actions that are ethically improper to request of a software engineer or teams of software engineers.

The Code is not simply for adjudicating the nature of questionable acts; it also has an important educational function. As this Code expresses the consensus of the profession on ethical issues, it is a means to educate both the public and aspiring professionals about the ethical obligations of all software engineers.

**Principles**

Principle 1: PUBLIC

Software engineers shall act consistently with the public interest. In particular, software engineers shall, as appropriate:

1.01. Accept full responsibility for their own work.

1.02. Moderate the interests of the software engineer, the employer, the client and the users with the public good.

1.03. Approve software only if they have a well-founded belief that it is safe, meets specifications, passes appropriate tests, and does not diminish quality of life, diminish privacy or harm the environment. The ultimate effect of the work should be to the public good.

1.04. Disclose to appropriate persons or authorities any actual or potential danger to the user, the public, or the environment, that they reasonably believe to be associated with software or related documents.

1.05. Cooperate in efforts to address matters of grave public concern caused by software, its installation, maintenance, support or documentation.

1.06. Be fair and avoid deception in all statements, particularly public ones, concerning software or related documents, methods and tools.

1.07. Consider issues of physical disabilities, allocation of resources, economic disadvantage and other factors that can diminish access to the benefits of software.

1.08. Be encouraged to volunteer professional skills to good causes and contribute to public education concerning the discipline.

Principle 2: CLIENT AND EMPLOYER

Software engineers shall act in a manner that is in the best interests of their client and employer, consistent with the public interest. In particular, software engineers shall, as appropriate:

2.01. Provide service in their areas of competence, being honest and forthright about any limitations of their experience and education.

2.02. Not knowingly use software that is obtained or retained either illegally or unethically.

2.03. Use the property of a client or employer only in ways properly authorized, and with the client's or employer's knowledge and consent.

2.04. Ensure that any document upon which they rely has been approved, when required, by someone authorized to approve it.

2.05. Keep private any confidential information gained in their professional work, where such confidentiality is consistent with the public interest and consistent with the law.

2.06. Identify, document, collect evidence and report to the client or the employer promptly if, in their opinion, a project is likely to fail, to prove too expensive, to violate intellectual property law, or otherwise to be problematic.

2.07. Identify, document, and report significant issues of social concern, of which they are aware, in software or related documents, to the employer or the client.

2.08. Accept no outside work detrimental to the work they perform for their primary employer.

2.09. Promote no interest adverse to their employer or client, unless a higher ethical concern is being compromised; in that case, inform the employer or another appropriate authority of the ethical concern.

Principle 3: PRODUCT

Software engineers shall ensure that their products and related modifications meet the highest professional standards possible. In particular, software engineers shall, as appropriate:

3.01. Strive for high quality, acceptable cost and a reasonable schedule, ensuring significant tradeoffs are clear to and accepted by the employer and the client, and are available for consideration by the user and the public.

3.02. Ensure proper and achievable goals and objectives for any project on which they work or propose.

3.03. Identify, define and address ethical, economic, cultural, legal and environmental issues related to work projects.

3.04. Ensure that they are qualified for any project on which they work or propose to work by an appropriate combination of education and training, and experience.

3.05. Ensure an appropriate method is used for any project on which they work or propose to work.

3.06. Work to follow professional standards, when available, that are most appropriate for the task at hand, departing from these only when ethically or technically justified.

3.07. Strive to fully understand the specifications for software on which they work.

3.08. Ensure that specifications for software on which they work have been well documented, satisfy the users' requirements and have the appropriate approvals.

3.09. Ensure realistic quantitative estimates of cost, scheduling, personnel, quality and outcomes on any project on which they work or propose to work and provide an uncertainty assessment of these estimates.

3.10. Ensure adequate testing, debugging, and review of software and related documents on which they work.

3.11. Ensure adequate documentation, including significant problems discovered and solutions adopted, for any project on which they work.

3.12. Work to develop software and related documents that respect the privacy of those who will be affected by that software.

3.13. Be careful to use only accurate data derived by ethical and lawful means, and use it only in ways properly authorized.

3.14. Maintain the integrity of data, being sensitive to outdated or flawed occurrences.

3.15. Treat all forms of software maintenance with the same professionalism as new development.

Principle 4: JUDGMENT

Software engineers shall maintain integrity and independence in their professional judgment. In particular, software engineers shall, as appropriate:

4.01. Temper all technical judgments by the need to support and maintain human values.

4.02. Only endorse documents either prepared under their supervision or within their areas of competence and with which they are in agreement.

4.03. Maintain professional objectivity with respect to any software or related documents they are asked to evaluate.

4.04. Not engage in deceptive financial practices such as bribery, double billing, or other improper financial practices.

4.05. Disclose to all concerned parties those conflicts of interest that cannot reasonably be avoided or escaped.

4.06. Refuse to participate, as members or advisors, in a private, governmental or professional body concerned with software related issues, in which they, their employers or their clients have undisclosed potential conflicts of interest.

Principle 5: MANAGEMENT

Software engineering managers and leaders shall subscribe to and promote an ethical approach to the management of software development and maintenance . In particular, those managing or leading software engineers shall, as appropriate:

5.01. Ensure good management for any project on which they work, including effective procedures for promotion of quality and reduction of risk.

5.02. Ensure that software engineers are informed of standards before being held to them.

5.03. Ensure that software engineers know the employer's policies and procedures for protecting passwords, files and information that is confidential to the employer or confidential to others.

5.04. Assign work only after taking into account appropriate contributions of education and experience tempered with a desire to further that education and experience.

5.05. Ensure realistic quantitative estimates of cost, scheduling, personnel, quality and outcomes on any project on which they work or propose to work, and provide an uncertainty assessment of these estimates.

5.06. Attract potential software engineers only by full and accurate description of the conditions of employment.

5.07. Offer fair and just remuneration.

5.08. Not unjustly prevent someone from taking a position for which that person is suitably qualified.

5.09. Ensure that there is a fair agreement concerning ownership of any software, processes, research, writing, or other intellectual property to which a software engineer has contributed.

5.10. Provide for due process in hearing charges of violation of an employer's policy or of this Code.

5.11. Not ask a software engineer to do anything inconsistent with this Code.

5.12. Not punish anyone for expressing ethical concerns about a project.

Principle 6: PROFESSION

Software engineers shall advance the integrity and reputation of the profession consistent with the public interest. In particular, software engineers shall, as appropriate:

6.01. Help develop an organizational environment favorable to acting ethically.

6.02. Promote public knowledge of software engineering.

6.03. Extend software engineering knowledge by appropriate participation in professional organizations, meetings and publications.

6.04. Support, as members of a profession, other software engineers striving to follow this Code.

6.05. Not promote their own interest at the expense of the profession, client or employer.

6.06. Obey all laws governing their work, unless, in exceptional circumstances, such compliance is inconsistent with the public interest.

6.07. Be accurate in stating the characteristics of software on which they work, avoiding not only false claims but also claims that might reasonably be supposed to be speculative, vacuous, deceptive, misleading, or doubtful.

6.08. Take responsibility for detecting, correcting, and reporting errors in software and associated documents on which they work.

6.09. Ensure that clients, employers, and supervisors know of the software engineer's commitment to this Code of ethics, and the subsequent ramifications of such commitment.

6.10. Avoid associations with businesses and organizations which are in conflict with this code.

6.11. Recognize that violations of this Code are inconsistent with being a professional software engineer.

6.12. Express concerns to the people involved when significant violations of this Code are detected unless this is impossible, counter-productive, or dangerous.

6.13. Report significant violations of this Code to appropriate authorities when it is clear that consultation with people involved in these significant violations is impossible, counter-productive or dangerous.

Principle 7: COLLEAGUES

Software engineers shall be fair to and supportive of their colleagues. In particular, software engineers shall, as appropriate:

7.01. Encourage colleagues to adhere to this Code.

7.02. Assist colleagues in professional development.

7.03. Credit fully the work of others and refrain from taking undue credit.

7.04. Review the work of others in an objective, candid, and properly-documented way.

7.05. Give a fair hearing to the opinions, concerns, or complaints of a colleague.

7.06. Assist colleagues in being fully aware of current standard work practices including policies and procedures for protecting passwords, files and other confidential information, and security measures in general.

7.07. Not unfairly intervene in the career of any colleague; however, concern for the employer, the client or public interest may compel software engineers, in good faith, to question the competence of a colleague.

7.08. In situations outside of their own areas of competence, call upon the opinions of other professionals who have competence in that area.

Principle 8: SELF

Software engineers shall participate in lifelong learning regarding the practice of their profession and shall promote an ethical approach to the practice of the profession. In particular, software engineers shall continually endeavor to:

8.01. Further their knowledge of developments in the analysis, specification, design, development, maintenance and testing of software and related documents, together with the management of the development process.

8.02. Improve their ability to create safe, reliable, and useful quality software at reasonable cost and within a reasonable time.

8.03. Improve their ability to produce accurate, informative, and well-written documentation.

8.04. Improve their understanding of the software and related documents on which they work and of the environment in which they will be used.

8.05. Improve their knowledge of relevant standards and the law governing the software and related documents on which they work.

8.06. Improve their knowledge of this Code, its interpretation, and its application to their work.

8.07. Not give unfair treatment to anyone because of any irrelevant prejudices.

8.08. Not influence others to undertake any action that involves a breach of this Code.

8.09. Recognize that personal violations of this Code are inconsistent with being a professional software engineer.

# CASES

# CASE 1: IS PLANNING AT SUNRISE COUNTY

The Department of Family and Youth Services (DFYS) is a unique and complex social service agency for Sunrise County. DFYS is ultimately responsible for providing two primary services: juvenile justice and child protection services. The Department is made up of seven divisions. Child Haven and Child Protective Services perform investigative and intervention services for cases involving child abuse and/or neglect. The Detention, Probation and the Sunny Spring Youth Camp divisions all serve cases involving juvenile delinquency and youth crime incidents. The remaining two divisions perform support functions for the entire department.

Like all Sunrise County government agencies, DFYS faces tremendous pressures due to the rapid growth in population. DFYS investigated the growing demand for their services and found:

- A 265% increase in Juvenile violent crime charges in the last 10 years
- A 55% increase in child abuse and neglect investigations in the last 10 years
- A more than 53% likelihood that victims of child abuse or neglect will be arrested before the age of 18
- The fact that more than 70% of the parents of abused and neglected children served have serious alcohol, drug or mental health issues

With this rapid increase in both youth crime and child abuse, the DFYS had two options: (1) simply expand their resources (add more caseworkers and officers, build more facilities) to cover the growing need or (2) take pro-active measures to help alleviate child abuse and delinquency.

Instead of just increasing their existing resources and facilities, the Department decided to also make a pro-active strategic plan to aid in the prevention of child abuse and youth delinquency in the long run. The Department realized that the last two threats in the above list could actually provide them with opportunities. The fact that juvenile delinquency was so closely tied to abused children meant that they could target abused children (labeled "at risk" children) for prevention programs to help lower the risk of them committing crimes in the future. The fourth point in the above list illustrated that in order to face the increasing youth problems, more attention must be focused on assessing the child's family environment.

## THE VISION

The hiring of Mr. Kirby Burgess four years ago set the stage for change. He amended the original mission statement of DFYS to express his goals in what was titled "Our Vision":

> ***The Mission of Sunrise County Family and Youth Services:***
>
> *The Family and Youth Services Department assists abused, neglected, out-of-control, and delinquent children to become law-abiding, independent, productive citizens by providing prevention, guidance, care, and control services to them and their families.*
>
> ***Our Vision:***
>
> *The department of Family and Youth Services is a bold and dynamic organization, nationally known as a leader in integrating the protection of children and the community, making significant and measurable contributions to the quality of life in Sunrise County.*

In order to make this new Vision a reality, the strategic planning for GenerationX was spearheaded three years ago. At the heart of this plan was a new networked IT system (later titled FamilyTRACS). This system would greatly improve the accuracy and efficiency of the data used by the Department. However, to successfully make significant contributions to the quality of life in Sunrise County requires more than just expanding resources and increasing the efficiency of the Department. In order to accomplish the goals of the Vision, significant changes would have to be made in the way DFYS performed their business. GenerationX set out to change the current processes of DFYS and develop a new more expansive "family-focused" approach to providing services to abused/neglected and delinquent children.

## THE "NEW LOGICAL MODEL"

In February, the first steps of GenerationX were initiated. Management teams were formed which included one representative from each of the seven divisions of DFYS. These representatives were to remain with the project for one year. The project team set out to discover what was needed to successfully accomplish the goals of the new Vision. To make a comprehensive impact on the Department, they would need to completely redesign the way the Department functions through an effort they called "business process re-engineering" (BPR). This process encompassed an analysis of the existing Departmental core processes, identification of new core processes and a radical re-engineering of the processes based on customer priority needs and best practice surveys through benchmarking.

First, the team set out to thoroughly analyze the current processes of every aspect of DFYS's operations. This proved to be one of the most difficult tasks. Employees often do routine procedures instinctively, and it's difficult to step back and recognize every little procedure. Harvey Huncovsky (who later became the director of GenerationX) commented that this was one of the most important tasks to the success of the project. "Many of the little problems we encountered later [in the implementation phase] happened because we failed to recognize the process in the initial internal analysis", said Huncovsky.

After analyzing the current processes, the management team set out to identify new processes that could not only improve the performance and efficiency of the Department, but also achieve the Vision of reducing the incidents of child abuse and delinquency in the long run by becoming more family-focused. The product of this effort was titled the "New Logical Model" (NLM). This model acted as a "blueprint" throughout the entire project. It provides detailed descriptions of the proposed changes and illustrates how the future DFYS will function. Much like a national constitution, this model provided the foundation of the plan and was constantly referred to throughout the various phases of GenerationX. In particular, the Project team stressed that the new design (GenerationX Website):

- Support a Family Focus rather than a child/youth incident focused approach
- Be driven by cross-organizational processes
- Extensively utilize Team Work
- Focus on results

## DEFINING THE NEW LOGICAL MODEL

To define and analyze DFYS's main business processes, the NLM was divided into 5 distinct modules (outlined in Figure 1). The first three modules (RECEIVE, ASSESS, and DELIVER) encompass the primary business processes of DFYS. The remaining two modules (EDUCATE and CENTRAL SUPPORT) are concerned more with the development and support of these functions. While the modules were not implemented in a strict chronological manner, they are progressive in both complexity and functionality. In other words, the success of later modules depends upon the success of the previous ones.

The first two modules, RECEIVE and ASSESS, are the key operations to DFYS. These modules represent the processes and documentation involved with recording an incident (of abuse or delinquency) from the first step through to the last step. The RECEIVE module encompasses the first steps taken, such as recording a public inquiry about a child and routing the report to the proper division for further investigation if necessary. The ASSESS module focuses on the documentation of the actual caseworker's investigation and their assessment of the situation. The ASSESS module also includes the client's dealings with the court system. These documents provide background information of a child and his/her family. Not only are these documents used within DFYS and the family court system, but many of them must be provided to other agencies, such as the District Attorney. The information must be accurate and up to date (indeed, inaccurate information could actually be harmful).

*Table 1 - Five Modules of the "New Logical Model"*

| | |
|---|---|
| RECEIVE | Recording public inquiries<br>Recording and routing reports and allegations<br>Recording and routing referrals<br>Generation of forms and documents. |
| ASSESS | Recording investigations and assessments<br>Court Management<br>Generation forms and documents |
| DELIVER | Development of a family view of a case<br>Automate assessment tools used by SMYC, Child Haven and Detention<br>Incorporate issuance of court orders and court directives into the case plan<br>Improve the families' transition from DFYS support to self-reliance in the community |
| EDUCATE | Change Management<br>Develop new ways of using information<br>Get DFYS management and staff to understand and change the processes required to fully utilize the FamilyTRACS sys. |
| CENTRAL SUPPORT | Provide technical support<br>Provide change management support |

Many improvements would have to be made in these two modules. First, the accuracy and efficiency of the data and the processes of recording and transferring the data would have to be improved and automated. Additionally, in order to accomplish the goal of family assessment (rather than assessing clients incident by incident) more data would have to be recorded on each family. The current information system was struggling to keep up with the current data requirements. It was often quite slow, even to the extent of requiring that an investigating social worker drive to the courthouse and look up documents on microfilm. Also, the data was not always accurate. Updating the information was difficult and time-lapse problems were frequent. Much time was spent on analyzing and restructuring the processes in these two modules. The adage "Garbage-In-Garbage-Out" is quite appropriate here, and the success of the next module (DELIVER) would be highly dependent on the quantity and quality of information provided by the processes outlined in these first two modules.

The strategic element of GenerationX lies in the DELIVER and

EDUCATE modules. The DELIVER module focuses on finding ways to utilize the information provided by the first two modules and revolutionize the way caseworkers do their jobs. Major business processes would have to be drastically changed and redefined to incorporate the desired "family-focused" view. Assessment tools would be designed to aid the employees in efficiently using the increased amount of data that the family approach requires. The EDUCATE module encompasses the change management plans required to implement the DELIVER module. Upon successful completion of these modules, caseworkers will have the ability to use vast amounts of information on a child and close family members to assess whether a child's needs can be met in his/her current situation.

The CENTRAL SUPPORT module refers to support functions. Primarily, it concentrates on creating a sufficient amount of support for the new DFYS once GenerationX is complete.

## IT REQUIREMENTS OF THE NEW LOGICAL MODEL

In order to support the New Logical Model, a new IT system would be required. The current automated records system (called JUVI[4]) was not only inefficient but, more importantly, also quite limited in scope. The new system would provide improved processes of collecting, recording and accessing information such as case histories of clients and their families. This will enable the Department to handle the rapidly increasing number of cases without needing to dramatically increase resources (such as staff and buildings). The new automated system, called FamilyTRACS (Family Tracking, Reporting and Automated Case Support), would have several advantages. In regards to the RECEIVE and ASSESS modules, it would (recent Annual Report ):

- Rigorously manage the receipt, generation, and dispersal of information
- Reduce redundancy in tasks involved in data entry
- Update case information can be done remotely at any time even for workers out on the field (via laptop computers)

[4] JUVI is a mainframe system, which provides "dumb terminals" to only a few records employees.

- Provide information in a usable, logical format to all divisions in the agency

The DELIVER module of the NLM required the IT system to provide the technology for employers to take a different approach to providing services to families. In order for the caseworker to get a broad view of a client and their family's situation, they must be able to access and process as much information on them as possible. Sharing and properly utilizing information such as incident reports, investigation documents, and police/judicial records throughout the Department allows them to see instances of abuse/neglect or delinquency not as isolated incidents, but as pieces of a comprehensive story. In order to support this effort, the IT system must create open channels of information and communication between all of the departments of DFYS as well as access to relevant data from other agencies. It was quickly decided that the current records tracking system (JUVI) was incapable of providing this comprehensive information to such an array of people. The new IT system would have to be much more flexible and provide a networking system between the divisions of the Department as well as other outside agencies.

Once the system has effectively been implemented within the Department, GenerationX envisions using the case management system to form communication channels between DFYS and other agencies that provide family-based community services. Even before the initiation of GenerationX, caseworkers would often refer families to outside agencies for aid (such as Boys' Town or Shade Tree). However, communication with the agencies was quite limited. The new system could provide very useful information to both the community service agency as well as DFYS. For instance, a caseworker could contact an agency to inquire whether or not they could provide services for a child. That agency could access some of the information from FamilyTRACS via the Internet to get an idea of whether or not they can treat them and how to approach treating the particular client. In addition, the agency could enter the progress of the family into the system, and give the caseworker a better idea of how the family is progressing (or if they are even attending).

## IMPLEMENTING GENERATIONX

During the development of the New Logical Model the project team investigated the departments of family and youth services in other states. Part of this effort was to give them insight on the kind of IT system that would be needed to support the NLM. One challenge during this investigation was that very few agencies are structured like the DFYS. Most county and state systems have separate divisions for child welfare and detention/delinquency services. Given this fact, it would be impossible for Sunrise County to use a "turnkey" system; it would have to be designed. However, it was decided that the Statewide Automated Child Welfare Information System (SACWIS) in Oklahoma could provide a sufficient starting point in the development of their own system. Because of their involvement with the design and implementation of the Oklahoma SACWIS system, the GenerationX team chose D & T Consulting to help them with the technical design, change management issues and the overall implementation of GenerationX.

The Project was to be implemented in four phases. At the time of writing this case study, it was in its third phase. Each phase is marked by a new contractual agreement between DFYS and D & T Consulting. In the spring, the first contract between the Department of Family and Youth Services and D & T Consulting Group was drafted. The purpose of this phase was to create a comprehensive plan for GenerationX. This phase, named "Phase 1A", consisted of three main activities: Refining the New Logical Model and its requirements, identifying design alternatives, and presenting the costs and risks of each alternative.

The first activity to be accomplished in Phase 1A was to meet with D & T and describe the work that the GenerationX Team had done thus far. The detailed definition of the five modules of the New Logical Model proved to be very useful in this early planning phase. D & T was given a GenerationX Requirements Document, which outlined the requirements of the NLM. The goal was to refine the Model and outline the rest of the project. Realizing that D & T was very experienced in projects like this, they encouraged D & T to critically analyze the plan. In the attachment to the Phase 1A contract, they listed several questions for D & T to consider:

1. Is the model complete and functionally correct?

2. Is the Model consistent with DFYS program vision and goals?
3. Are there suggestions that would enhance the model?
4. Is the model cost effective?
5. What risks are associated with the implementation of the model?
6. What constraints may impact the implementation of the model?

After the NLM was refined and agreed upon, D & T was asked to submit one or more design alternatives. In particular, the proposed design was to be very specific about the technology that would be used. For instance, D & T was to investigate the application architecture alternatives, identify the requirements of the database environment, and specifically define the topology and architecture of the client/server system.

The final activity to be accomplished in Phase 1A was for D & T to perform a cost and risk analysis. The cost analysis was to include all of the one-time costs associated with the creation of hardware, operating system software, communication software, application software and the organizational costs (i.e. staff, training and change management costs). The risk analysis was to include technological, business and financial risks. While it may seem that DFYS would have a better grasp of the risks in its own environment, D & T's experience with implementing this type of system (such as the ones in other states ) would give added insight to the inevitable troubles that GenerationX would face. Finally, D & T was to evaluate the best way to implement the project with regard to the number of phases and the scope of each phase.

The next contract (Phase 1B) was primarily involved with the technical design and implementation of the IT system called FamilyTRACS. This phase was limited to the functions defined in the RECEIVE and ASSESS modules of the NLM. Primarily, the focus was on the automation of records handling. Some future planning for the design of the change management program was created in this phase, but implementation of changes were primarily focused on training users on the FamilyTRACS system. Significant resources of both DFYS and D & T went towards training the employees on a pilot system for a week or

FamilyTRACS went live two years ago. Like any IT implementation, the implementation of this system was not without its problems. Most of the problems were due to errors in the data that was converted from the old JUVI system to the new FamilyTRACS database. Problems such as misplaced or missing data were common. However, since the JUVI system was kept running (and, in fact, still is running) it was not difficult to compare the documents from each system and find out what data would need to be edited. While this process was quite frustrating and time consuming, the efforts paid off. The data in FamilyTRACS is now very accurate.[5]

Phase 2 continued the efforts of the previous phase and began to make plans for the next phase. Since Phase 2 started only a few months after FamilyTRACS went live, many of the resources during this phase dealt with fixing technical "bugs" and maintaining the FamilyTRACS system. Additional attention was also given to training users on how to use the new computer system. Partial design and implementation plans of the DELIVER functions also occurred during this phase and some initial work was done on the change management concepts of the EDUCATE module.

Phase 3, which began a year ago, focused on three main aspects. First, they continued the design and implementation of the DELIVER functions that had begun in the previous phase. In addition, they focused on integrating the FamilyTRACS system with two other major systems: the Sunrise County Clerk's System (BLACKSTONE) and the Nevada Department of Human Resources system known as UNITY. The integration with the UNITY system has proved to be quite frustrating, because that system was only recently implemented and was experiencing major problems and delays. The last aspect of this phase involves making plans so that DFYS will be self-sufficient by the end of the Phase 4 (sometime in the next two years). Primarily this involved incorporating Sunrise County's Center for Enterprise Information Technology (CEIT). This agency provides IT services to Sunrise County Departments and other government entities. The eventual objective is to have CEIT perform all of the technical support for FamilyTRACS by the end of the GenerationX.

---

[5] Data Errors of 750 documents on FamilyTRACS as of April 2000 was 1%, compared to an average of 6% to 8% in comparable SACWIS systems.

## DFYS CRITICAL SUCCESS FACTORS

1. *The decision for DFYS to capitalize on its current structure to face growing number of incidents.* It was mentioned that DFYS was structured unlike most state/county systems, where there are two separate departments, one for child abuse and one for delinquent children. Past experience led DFYS to recognize that abused children often become delinquent. In fact, it is a vicious cycle: a child is abused/neglected, becomes a juvenile delinquent, and may even have children of their own whom they abuse. Most government systems treat this child as three different people, rather than recognizing that it is one child going down the wrong life track.

GenerationX was designed and treated as a strategic system to take full advantage of the current organizational structure of the department. Since both abuse and delinquency services fell under the same department in Sunrise County, it offered the DFYS a "competitive advantage" (so to speak) in proactive rehabilitation of families. The department did not require drastic organizational restructuring from the ground up. What it required was significant changes in the processes within each division to help coordinate and unify the department as a whole to use a more "family oriented" approach. The FamilyTRACS system complemented the DFYS structure and successfully opened up the required information/ communication channels between the divisions.

2. *Thorough internal analysis and careful planning of the new DFYS.* DFYS spent over a year on its internal analysis alone. By including people from each division of the department, the team was able to get proficient insight on how each division functioned. Processes that were often done by "instinct" had to be spelled out in this phase of the planning. For instance, when a document on a child abuse incident was signed by a particular person, everyone within the abuse/neglect divisions simply knew what particular division the document came from. They knew this intuitively because they knew the name of the person. But for the new system to properly integrate all divisions and even the community, this intuitive process would have to be more formalized. By investigating the processes that each division did on a day-to-day basis, the members of the team were able to get an understanding of the department as a whole.

Another critical success factor for DFYS was the meticulous planning and documentation that went into creating the New Logical Model. This model offered an extensive blueprint for nearly every aspect of the project, both technical and organizational. In a project of this magnitude, several years often pass during the implementation phases. Consequently, the project team members often change and the project can lose direction. While the GenerationX team did incur several changes in its human resources, the well thought-out and thoroughly documented NLM has allowed the project to keep its focus thus far. The success of this planning effort is apparent in the fact that the New Logical Model has not been significantly altered over the last 5 years since it was created.

3. *Effective contract agreements with D & T Consulting.* Short-term contracts have proved successful for GenerationX. Many medium-to-large scale IT outsourcing contracts are long term, often five to ten years. After this amount of time, the agreement between the two parties drifts towards a partner-like relationship. As history has shown, partnerships are very difficult to maintain because each party begins to see the project differently. The resulting lack of coordination between the two parties often leads to disastrous results. By using multiple short-term contracts, DFYS was able to avoid this pitfall. Since each contract only covered approximately one year, there was minimal "drifting" of focus by either party. In addition, good faith of both parties was inherently promoted by using a series of contracts. D & T Consulting was given incentive to do a good job so that they could obtain the next contract. In addition, it was in DFYS's best interest to continue hiring D & T because they received more and more knowledge about GenerationX as it progressed. So, the end result of the series of short-term contracts was a long-term relationship sustained by yearly incentives to continue the relationship.

Since the time frame of these contracts was short, uncertainty in the future was reduced. This allowed DFYS to be quite specific about exactly what it expected of D & T during that particular contract (phase). With the use of the different modules described in the New Logical Model, each of the contracts could be very specific about which processes would be focused on. The NLM kept the projects focused in the long term, even through several different contract agreements. In between the contracted phases, DFYS was able to assess the strengths and the weaknesses that resulted from the previous phase. When D & T would be brought back in for the next phase, they could be filled in as to the progress of the project and work from there. A nice advantage of this is that the relationship between them did not get "old". Each time D & T would come back to the project, it would provide a boost of energy and enthusiasm to the Project directors. At the same time, DFYS did not have to spend time explaining the project to a new party for each phase. In sum, the contractual structure between DFYS and D & T permitted detailed, specific terms inherent in short-term contracts, while still allowing them to create an established relationship often found only in long-term agreements.

## POTENTIAL THREATS

GenerationX has been very successful in creating and implementing the FamilyTRACS system. This system provides an enormous amount of information to employees of DFYS as well as other governmental agencies. It has tremendously improved the accuracy of the data by allowing data to be entered and accessed almost instantly by all DFYS employees on the local area network. It has even begun successful integration of parts of the system to the Internet, so that caseworkers in the field can access and even change information in the database. These accomplishments have greatly increased the speed and accuracy of data available to DFYS. In addition, Phase 3 has begun to allow other large Nevada and Sunrise County agencies to use this information. These facts alone warrant GenerationX as a success.

However, there are still many objectives that remain unaccomplished. The problems lie primarily in the area of change management. It is not to say that change has not occurred at all. On the contrary, painstaking efforts by both the Project team as well as all of the DFYS employees has been made in learning how to navigate, access and enter data into FamilyTRACS. However, FamilyTRACS currently has many capabilities beyond merely automating data. There is doubt, however, to whether this powerful function is currently being utilized by end users.

Assessing the needs of a child is not an exact science. Different caseworkers may assess an investigation quite differently. Consider the situation at the Child Abuse Hotline. A call is received from a teacher at a school district that a young child has shown up with bruises on his arms for three consecutive weeks. Does this case require a formal investigation? It depends upon the details received from the caller, the family history and, to some extent, the attitude of the social worker. One social worker may think it a very serious situation and route the case to an investigator. However, another may think that there is not enough evidence that the child is being abused. These types of judgmental assessments occur throughout the incident investigation. To whom should the child be referred? Should the child remain with the family? Should the child be taken away and put into foster care?

While many decisions such as these could never be (and should never be) automated, the DELIVER module was designed to provide many workload functionality improvements. Currently the system has several automated assessment tools. These tools allow the system to guide the caseworker in properly assessing incidents and investigations. This is important because now the caseworker is faced with an incredible amount of information to assess. If used properly, FamilyTRACS has the ability to speed the assessment process. But it has been indicated that employees still do much of the assessment "in their heads". Rather than enter the information as they get it, they wait until the end of the process to enter it. Where the FamilyTRACS is meant to guide them through a certain process, they end up actually guiding the system to follow their own mental assessment of the case. This counteracts many of the efficiency improvements of the system, and limits the accuracy of the assessment.

Initially, GenerationX spent a reasonable amount of time planning for change management, but it seems that it has not fully been implemented successfully. To make matters worse, the Project currently seems to be more focused on increasing the functionality of the IT system and less on changing employee processes to fully utilize the system. The original strategic goal of GenerationX was to change DFYS's services to a "family-focused" approach to proactively reduce child abuse/neglect and delinquency incidents in the long-term.

A recent announcement may make this whole situation worse. In April, it was announced that the FamilyTRACS system must make plans to provide functional services of the state's child welfare agency, Nevada Division of Child and Family Services. This agency is somewhat similar to DYFS but also includes adoption/foster care services and interstate placement of children. The State agency has been designing and implementing a similar SACWIS-based IT system. However, the implementation has been less than successful. Like other agencies requesting services from the FamilyTRACS system, the state sees this system as the answer to their problems. The details of exactly what FamilyTRACS is supposed to provide the state are currently unclear, but any integration of services that DFYS does not currently provide (such as adoption) will require a significant change in the focus of GenerationX.

FamilyTRACS was meant to be a tool to support services that had a "family-focused" approach to proactively reduce child abuse/neglect and delinquency incidents in the long-term. However, it is quickly becoming the primary focal point of the Project. What went wrong? Was it to do with external pressures to increase the scope of FamilyTRACS beyond the NLM? Or was something wrong with the liaison roles between the DFYS divisions and the GenerationX directors?

# CASE 2: AUTOMATED DISPENSING TECHNOLOGY AT HORIZON HOSPITAL

In October 2009 installation of the RobotRx system was completed at Horizon Hospital and Medical Center. The promise of the system meant the conversion from a labor-intensive, error-prone process to a highly accurate and efficient automated one. Horizon was the first hospital in the HCA Healthcare company to implement the system, and Horizon would be used as a proving ground for the value of the system. The return on investment (ROI) had to be achieved at Horizon before many other facilities would have their RobotRx agreements approved. The system would cost $2.2 million over five years, but promised savings of $2.7 million.

One year later the facility decision-makers are evaluating performance of the system and reflecting back on the decision to implement the system, and its impact on the operation of the pharmacy. The system was operating at a level below initial projections. Staffing to operate the system far exceeded initial estimates. Inventory was lost and unaccounted for. Data system interface errors had resulted in the loss of $250,000 in potential revenue. Errors in medication picking by the robot had occurred. And the estimated return on investment and savings was in doubt. Reliability of the system was being questioned as the department had experienced four downtimes of extended duration that affected drug distribution. In what areas were expectations met and where were they not met? What have the decision-makers learned from this experience and what direction should the facility take from here?

## SYSTEM DESCRIPTION

RobotRx is a robotic drug distribution system that utilizes barcode technology to identify patient records and medications. It is a centralized system that automates the storage, dispensing, return, restocking and crediting of unit dose, inpatient medications. A robotic arm propelled by compressed air moves along horizontal and vertical rails to retrieve medications from storage rods and deposit them in patient-identified bins or envelopes. The system uses bar codes to verify; retrieve and track the movement and location of medications throughout the supply chain from drug wholesaler to the patient.

The robot software, Connect-Rx, receives patient-specific medication and location information transmitted from the hospital information system. //Operation of the robot required minimum of six computers interconnected via a Windows NT local area network. Each computer had a specific function, a central database server, two support workstation PCs to operate the robot, robot motion controller PC to direct the movement of the robotic arm, an interface PC to process data transferred from the hospital system, and a packager PC to control packager operation and track offline inventory.

Information was transferred to the robot using a series of interfaces. Information transferred from the hospital information system consisted of patient admission, discharge and transfer data, and new medication order data, batch filling data, and billing data. The format of the data crossing the interfaces needed to be customized to the hospital specific record definition, as industry standard does not exist.

RobotRx requires uniform packaging and bar coding of medications. Information provided in the packaging included generic/brand drug name, strength, size, and expiration date and lot number. McKesson would also provide this package service based on an up-charge per dose packaged agreement.

Although the robotic technology did offer significant benefit, it had limitations that needed to be considered. The robot did not have refrigeration capabilities, so refrigerated medications needed to be handled through a manual system. Also, the robot did not have the security to store and dispense controlled substances.

RobotRx is existing technology present in approximately 150 hospitals nationwide. This technology is primarily present in larger facilities (> 200 beds), but it is increasing being justified in smaller hospitals with limited staff and services.

System quality was considered to be excellent. RobotRx was considered to be state of the art technology. At the time of the feasibility evaluation no other commercially available hospital-based systems existed. The purported benefits of the system included reducing manual tasks, reducing labor and inventory costs, eliminating medication dispensing errors, improving inventory management, increasing medication charge/cost capture.

## FIRM DESCRIPTION

At the time of the initial evaluation for the robot, third quarter, Horizon Hospital and Medical Center had 688 beds with an average annual patient census of 532. The Department of Pharmacy Services provided medications for all areas in the hospital and dispensed approximately 8000 medication doses daily for inpatients. The department consisted of 77 full-time equivalents, including 26.5 FTE staff pharmacists and 30 FTE technicians. Unit dose distribution was a manual process whereby medication orders entered into the hospital computer system generated labels for new orders or a batch fill list for existing orders to be filled for the next 24 hours. Medications were then pulled from storage bins by pharmacy technicians, labeled, and then checked by a pharmacist prior to delivery.

Medication control and distribution is an important aspect of care at the hospital. The robotic dispensing technology offered the ability to create a more accurate and efficient cart fill and first-dose process. Safety of the medication use process is a priority for the organization; RobotRx had record of no picking errors, and based on the technology, a theoretical error rate of less than one in a million picks. The existing manual cart fill system had picking error rate of approximately 0.5 to 1%, based on internal quality assurance measurements. This would improve an important operational task critical the organization's objectives. Further, RobotRx provided the foundation to build upon with other technologies to improve safety in the medication use process.

### Project Timeline

May 2008 McKessonHBOC Automated Healthcare (MAH) is awarded a sole source provider agreement with HCA Healthcare (HCA) for pharmacy automation. The duration of the agreement is five years.

June 2008 MAH presents RobotRx to Horizon Pharmacy administration.

July 2008 MAH and Horizon personnel collect data on-site to determine the feasibility of RobotRx at Horizon.

Aug. 2008 Feasibility study is completed and an estimated return-on-investment is determined.

Sept. 2008 MAH presents the first contract proposal to Horizon administration.

Oct. 2008-

Feb. 2009 Contract negotiations between HCA and MAH occur.

Mar. 2009 HCA and MAH agree to a RobotRx contract. It will be a model contract for all HCA hospitals.

May 2009 Horizon signs the RobotRx contract. The duration of the agreement is five years.

July 2009-

Aug. 2009 Central Pharmacy is renovated to accommodate RobotRx.

Aug. 2009 RobotRx hardware is installed.

Sep. 2009 Medication utilization database is created and interface development begins.

Oct. 2009 Interface is tested and reconfigured.

Nov. 2009 RobotRx commences operation of 24-hour cart fill on selected nursing units.

Dec. 2009 RobotRx 24-hour cart fill is expanded to all nursing units.

Feb. 2010 Cartless Delivery System enhancement installed.

July 2010 RobotRx commences first dose distribution during limited daily hours.

Aug. 2010 ROI guarantee measurement performed.

Oct. 2010 RobotRx first dose distribution is expanded to 24-hour coverage.

## OPERATIONAL/STRATEGIC CONSIDERATIONS

Being part of the hospital industry, Horizon offered standardized services like many other hospitals. The quality of care is a constant taken for granted by payors and patients. And because hospital care is largely a prepaid expense through insurance premiums, prices are set contractually by private insurers or government entities and similar among local hospitals. Thus, competition among hospitals is based on non-direct patients care types of services, those considered value-added. Value-added services in hospitals are customer service oriented include valet parking, food services, transport services, aesthetics of the facility, and courtesy and helpfulness of the staff. These services help make hospital stays more pleasant and can make the difference in the hospital a patient or employer chooses, but they are easily duplicated. With fixed reimbursements and duplicable value-added services, the success of hospitals is mostly dependent on the ability of institutions to control costs. RobotRx offered a return on investment (net savings as % of costs) of 125%. RobotRx also had the potential to address a current political and regulatory issue, medication errors.

Errors in the prescribing, dispensing, and administration of medications was a major issue facing health care, one that growing in prominence due to media coverage and regulatory focus. McKesson claimed more than 45 million doses dispensed by its robotic systems with zero errors. Although dispensing was not a major stage at which errors occurred, accounting for 8% of all errors, the bar-coding of medications required by the robot set the stage for use of technology to reduce errors at other stages in the medication use process.

Although Horizon was not as advanced in the use of automated systems, the implementation of RobotRx would be the first of its kind in the state. The public relations and image of Horizon as a technologically advanced facility with a focus on safety could help differentiate the facility from others. All other local hospitals were using manual systems to perform 24-hour cart fill. The manual cart-fill and first-dose processes at Horizon were labor intensive processes, requiring 8.25 and 2.8 technician full-time equivalents (FTEs), respectively, one-third of total technician staff. Further, pharmacist time to double-check technician unit dose picks accounted for approximately 3.0 FTEs. Through negotiation with the vendor, Horizon agreed to eliminate 12 FTEs, ten technician and two pharmacist positions. These positions were eliminated through attrition and transfer of personnel to McKesson for RobotRx operation. McKesson indicated it would take approximately 3.3 FTEs to operate the robot and another 1.4 FTEs for packaging support.

The facility had a history of being slow to adopt new technologies, unsure of their value and hesitant to radically change processes as a result of IT. Part of this reluctance was also due to poor management and acceptance of the assimilation of new IT into its operations. History of failed and underutilized implementations had made decision-makers reluctant to embrace new IT. But Pharmacy Services is one department comfortable managing, using, and experimenting with IT. The department had volunteered to be a beta site for several new software updates and knew automated systems, some of which worked and others that did not.

RobotRx would be the largest IT project, in terms of scope and dollars,

Pharmacy Services had ever undertaken. Because of its cost and potential operational impact, it would require executive approval at the corporate level of the company. Pharmacy management dedicated significant resources on developing a justification and educating hospital executives on the benefits of the system. RobotRx was seen as an opportunity to promote change and reengineer the way medications were processed in the facility. The first of a three-part implementation of technology to automate the medication use process.

Pharmacy management was committed to the success of the project. It was viewed as an opportunity to further automate the drug distribution process and provide better service to patients. RobotRx improve efficiency and accuracy, and provide cost savings. The system would introduce the use of barcode technology into the medication use process. Bar coding of medications would enable the use of other technologies to improve safety and accountability in the medication use system. Pharmacy management supported the use of technology that could reduce manual technical tasks, allowing reallocation of additional pharmacist time to direct patient care activities. Although RobotRx and other enhancing technologies primarily replaced technician labor, this technician labor could be retrained and re-skilled to displace other pharmacist-performed tasks that did not require professional judgement. Expansion of the patient care role of pharmacists had multiple potential benefits. The medical literature had several examples of improvement in patient outcomes (e.g., reduction in preventable adverse drug events, reduction in medication errors, improved therapeutic results) and cost savings when pharmacists are focused on clinical activities. Further, pilot projects at Horizon had demonstrated positive outcomes and cost reductions when pharmacists were dedicated full-time on patient units focused on preventing medication-related problems. A secondary benefit was improved job satisfaction and retention with this practice environment. Through direct feedback, needs assessment, and satisfaction surveys the pharmacist staff had indicated this practice environment was more professionally rewarding, and resulted in enhanced inter-professional relationships.

There existed some reluctance by the end-user staff (pharmacy technicians) to utilize the RobotRx; thus, their commitment to the success of the project was uncertain. There were concerns about the robot replacing jobs and the adequacy of training and needed skills for those involved in its operation. Further, there were concerns about the split in staff that would occur as a result of the outsourcing agreement. This required reassurance of the staff involved that the MAH employees would be important part of the department and included in all hospital and departmental activities (e.g. staff meetings, celebrations).

The goal of automating this process was aligned with the business goals of the organization. Use of this technology would help address two operational objectives. The institution had struggled, like many others, with providing adequate professional staffing. There is a nationwide shortage of nurses and pharmacists, and an opportunity to reduce their time involved in the medication use process, a significant portion of their daily work, could prove particularly valuable. RobotRx was projected to save some pharmacist labor, but primarily would replace manual labor performed by pharmacy technicians. Nursing labor savings could be achieved by add-on technologies enabled by RobotRx. It would be the job of the pharmacy managers to champion this project and clearly elucidate the costs and benefits of the system to the facility.

Pharmacy management saw strategic value, not in RobotRx itself, but in the ability to use RobotRx as a foundation to add other technologies and ultimately address issues that required immediate attention, namely patient safety and staffing shortages. Dispensing errors accounted for only 8% of the total errors. Most errors occurred at the prescribing/transcription and administration stages of the process. Implementation of hand-held barcode reading devices would address many of the errors at the administration stage. McKesson offered software that worked on PDA devices equipped with barcode readers that would allow scanning of patient bar-coded wrist bands, scanning of bar-coded nurse's badge, and scanning of the bar-coded medication. This sequence of steps provided the information to assess the five rights of medication administration (right drug, right dose, right route, right time, and right patient). RobotRx can also transmit information unidirectional manner to unit-based dispensing cabinets (AcuDose).

Availability of many medications on the nursing units in automated dispensing cabinets in combination with scanning technology at bedside has the potential to improve to critical issues in the process. Medication availability at the time needed for administration provided a significant advantage over the current system where most medication required dispensing from a central or satellite pharmacy. Medication turn-around-time (time from ordering to administration) could be significantly reduced with unit-based cabinets, but this increased access to medications needed to be complimented with bedside scanning, because experience had demonstrated increased access through automated dispensing devices without commensurate control did not reduce administration errors.

High buyer power and intense competition form rivals characterize the hospital industry. There was price competition, forcing prices downward or to remain unchanged. High quality and service orientation was demanded and expected. Customer loyalty was important to continued growth. IT projects were needed to differentiate services and improve price performance. Increasing the switching cost of buyers, such as large insurers and employers, would important to customer retention.

## RETURN ON INVESTMENT

The RobotRx agreement guaranteed an ROI of at least 25%, meaning for every dollar invested in RobotRx a minimum $1.25 in savings was expected, and the projection for Horizon was even higher at 30%. The savings consisted primarily of labor reduction (73% of the total) with minor savings in supply costs, training costs, overtime reduction, expired medications and inventory reduction. On the investment side the costs included RobotRx labor fees (3.3 FTEs), equipment and software fees, one time installation fees, barcode packaging and labels. The 3.3 FTEs for RobotRx operation were to be offset by an equivalent reduction in technician labor from Horizon. If the minimum ROI was not achieved, the contract indicated the monthly RobotRx fees would be adjusted downward until savings were 125% of total costs.

To achieve the needed savings, Horizon needed to eliminate 12 FTEs, two pharmacist and 10 technician positions. There were no job losses anticipated as a result of RobotRx implementation, as many unfilled positions existed within the department. Most of the position reductions were achieved through attrition with the remainder being hired by MAH to operate the robot.

## Outsourcing Issues

Initial proposals for the robot involved purchase or leasing of the system. As negotiations progressed, the need for an operational and/or capital lease became the preferred method. To comply with the Medicare financing guidelines and to meet financial goals of the company, a service structure was created which involved not only leasing the equipment, but also required McKesson to provide personnel to operate the system. HCA facilities considering RobotRx would have to agree to outsource their unit dose distribution process. This arrangement would allow the costs of the robot to be treated as an operational lease, rather than a capital expense. Horizon would be the first HCA facility to enter into such an arrangement.

McKesson had not previously been involved in such arrangements and had only leased or sold the equipment. The automated division of McKesson had no experience with outsourcing services and similarly, Horizon's pharmacy management team had had limited experience with outsourcing. With this new agreement many details needed to be considered and implemented.

The contract only dictated that McKesson would provide personnel to operate the robot, but did not address specific tasks. Because unit dose distribution was such an integral part of the pharmacy operation, it would be difficult to segregate those activities from the rest of the drug distribution processes.

MAH provided necessary expertise in robotic technology that was not available internally, but the RobotRx onsite staff did not have this experience as most of them were former Horizon employees and none had past robotic experience. All robot personnel required introductory training on the system, but would have to learn by doing to gain full functional competence.

From a facility management view point drug distribution was not a core competency, and considered an ancillary service. And the pharmacy management viewpoint it was an important and essential function, but one that was operational rather than strategic, enabling focus on strategic services. From an HCA corporate perspective, as an operational expense, it meant cost savings that could be realized in less than six months and an increased return on equity. The contract was a risk-sharing type of agreement that encouraged both parties to work together to achieve the target savings. This was the most appropriate type of agreement as uncertainty existed in the benefits of the technology, and a loose degree of contractual definition was present.

## Outcomes

Although MAH recommended a total implementation time line of six months, pharmacy management pressured MAH to try to get the system installed and functional within three months. A major quality accrediting organization would be evaluating the hospital in November 2009 and RobotRx would be an ideal technology to display to this group. Installation of the RobotRx took three days. Development of the interface between the RobotRx software and the hospital system took over three weeks. Horizon was the first facility within HCA to install RobotRx so there was no existing operational interface with the HCA hospital system.

The system installation was completed within the financial budget allocated for system setup. The pharmacy required renovation, which involved installation of data lines, an uninterrupted power supply, and compressed air. Installation of robot hardware took three days. The software interface between the robot software and the hospital system took an additional three weeks to be completed. The robot transmitted information in HL7 compatible format, an emerging healthcare industry standard. Data crossing the interface would be bi-directional and included patient location, admission, transfer, and discharge status, billing, and medication information (type, dose, and quantity). Even with the robot using a standard format to transmit and receive information, the interface required significant revision to ensure accurate data transmission.

RobotRx had experienced data interface errors that affected quantities dispensed and amounts billed to patients. In December 2009 it was discovered that an alteration in the data transmission and software function of the robot had resulted in the erroneous crediting of over $300,000 in valid charges for medications. This crediting had gone on for 10 days before it was discovered. Some of this activity was rechargeable, but much was not and the hospital lost approximately $250,000 in potential revenue. Periodic robot software updates had resulted in dispensing excessive quantities and missing some orders altogether. The facility notified MAH that any future updates would require prior approval and pre- and post-installation monitoring.

In October 2010 RobotRx efficiency was averaging 86%, meaning 86% of unit dose medications were processed through the robot and the remaining 14% were manually picked. Efficiency was expected to be at least 90%. RobotRx efficiency is an important issue as it directly effected the labor involved in the unit dose process. Lower robot efficiency meant additional technician time to manually process orders and additional pharmacist time to check those doses. October 2010 was the start of full processing of all medication doses entered into the hospital system. Up to that point the robot only processed orders during certain hours of the day.

The agreement required an evaluation of the ROI at six months after implementation. This process was delayed and did not occur until ten months after go-live. Once the guarantee measurement was presented to hospital administration it was discovered that it was requiring 7.9 FTEs of labor to operate the robot instead of the 3.3 FTEs originally projected in the contract. Further, the facility was unaware of the labor component because MAH had not invoiced the facility for labor during the first 10 months of operation. All other aspects of the estimated savings had met or exceeded projections. Because of the much larger robot labor needs the guaranteed 25% ROI was not being met, pharmacy management was asked by MAH to eliminate another 0.5 FTEs of pharmacist labor to achieve the needed savings. Investigation of the labor discrepancy revealed two primary causes. The facility's patient volume had increased 9% since the original feasibility study, and MAH had not taken into account all the needed aspects of staffing for the robot (e.g., coverage for nonproductive time, administrative responsibilities).

Because in many ways Horizon was the initial site for RobotRx in HCA, there were not other firms to consult on the unresolved issues. HCA used a proprietary system, vendor-modified from commercial system, for its hospitals, so interface requirements were unique. Furthermore, its effect on other technology that interfaced with the hospital system was not known, and would be site specific. MAH had not previously had a service agreement that required segregation of the robot staffing and thus, did not have accurate volume-based estimates of robot labor required.

RobotRx had four extended downtimes during the first 12 months of operation. Each resulted in the implementation of a downtime contingency plan, a process of manual filling and verification. Each of these downtime occurrences was related to either mechanical or system issues (e.g., server, software, hardware). Several procedures were put in place to address outstanding issues. Information system policies and procedures and restriction of access and user functionality were implemented to address interface and software issues that were encountered. Industrial engineers were brought in to evaluate the work processes and make recommendations for improvement. This team discovered redundancies and inefficiencies, including the continuation of some manual tasks from the pre-robot distribution processes. The group also recommended changes to the physical work environment to facilitate efficient tasks. Poor performance in packaging and other areas were also identified, resulting in the redefinition of work performance criteria and changing of roles. Cooperation issues between Horizon and MAH staff were also addressed to promote improved working relationships.

## Recommendations

The facility learned many lessons from the RobotRx implementation. Project management was the weakest aspect of the initial planning process and was a factor in initial problems with implementation of the system. Better initial planning and closer monitoring of software manipulations will be essential elements of future technology projects. A realistic timeline and methodical implementation would have made for a smoother transition. Extensive monitoring of data transfer across the interface should have occurred. Software updates need to be pre-approved by the facility, tested before implementation, and monitored for performance. Contracting should be more explicit to prevent conflicts when outsourcing an inseparable element of a service. Clearly defined roles and goals in the contracting process can prevent ambiguities and misperceptions. With these caveats the facility management team is exploring future technology enhancements.

## Enhancements

Several enhancing technologies are planned for the future. Implementation of a high-speed bulk packager that packages at a rate three times faster than the current one, and uses much less packaging is planned. This new packager can improve efficiency of the packaging process, and, because less packaging is used, the storage capacity of the robot will increase.

Development is underway by two pneumatic tube system manufacturers and MAH to develop a system interface between the two technologies. This would allow the two systems to work together so RobotRx could dispense by patient or location directly into a tube carrier device, and this device would delivery the robot dispensed medications directly to nursing units. This would reduce much of the manual delivery of medications with the potential to increase delivery accuracy and decrease medication turn-around-time.

MAH also produces unit-based medication dispensing cabinets (AcuDose). These cabinets are located on the nursing units within the hospital and operate similar to ATM machines. The cabinets are stocked with commonly used medications with par levels set based on volume history. Nurses are given PIN numbers for identification and enter this information along with a request for the needed medications. Software that interfaces with the hospital system and RobotRx software operate the cabinet. The medication is dispensed from the cabinet with an electronic record generated of the medication, the patient, and the nurse involved. RobotRx monitors inventory in each cabinet and, rather than filling by patient, it fills needed medications by location on a regular schedule. This system has the potential to increase access to medications, provides better tracking of medication use, and decreases medication turn-around-time.

Another technology, which is being evaluated, is the AcuScan system. Bar coding of medications with RobotRx allows the use of personal digital assistants equipped with barcode readers running from a radio frequency network to document medication administration. This process involves barcode identification of the medication, patient, and nurse. Before a medication is administered the nurse scans the patient armband, his/her employee badge, and the medication. This process activates several safety checks, including right drug, dose, route and time, creates an administration record, and transmits billing information.

# ABOUT THE AUTHOR

**Dr. Gurpreet Dhillon** is Professor of Information Systems in the School of Business, Virginia Commonwealth University, Richmond, USA. He holds a Ph.D. from the London School of Economics and Political Science, UK. His research interests include management of information security, ethical and legal implications of information technology. His research has been published in several journals including *Journal of Management Information Systems, Information Systems Research, Decision Support Systems, European Journal of Information Systems, Information Systems Journal Information & Management, Communications of the ACM, Computers & Security, and International Journal of Information Management* among others. Gurpreet has authored eight books including *Principles of Information Systems Security: text and cases* (John Wiley, 2007). He is also the Editor-in-Chief of the *Journal of Information System Security*. Gurpreet's research has been featured in various academic and commercial publications and his expert comments have appeared in the *Knowledge@Wharton, New York Times, USA Today, Business Week, NBC News*, among others. In 2013 Gurpreet also published his first poetry book – *The Inner Truth.*